The Urban Section

The design of streets, and the connections between streets of different character, is the most important task for architects and urbanists working in an urban context. Considered at two distinct spatial scales – that of the individual street – the Street Section – and the complex of city streets – the City Transect – *The Urban Section* identifies a range of generic street types and their success or otherwise in responding to climatic, cultural, traditional, morphological, social and economic well being.

Using comparative studies a profile of best practice in street and city design is identified, showing methodologies in both the analysis of, and design for, successful streets and public places – place-making.

In uniquely dealing with both the historic and contemporary description and analysis of urban 'streets' around the world, the work is of both academic and professional interest to architects, urban planners and designers, highway engineers, landscape and urban design advisers in both the public and private sectors; students, amenity and civic societies, city authorities and government agencies.

Robert Mantho is an architect, teacher, and researcher. He has worked in N.Y.C., London, Portland, and Vermont, working on a wide range of building projects, community projects and competitions. Robert is the Stage 5 Leader at the Mackintosh School of Architecture at the Glasgow School of Art. Robert's research is focused on urban spatial configuration, digital processes in the generation of space and collaborative design.

Alan Jackson Simpson is an architect, urbanist, teacher and writer.

The Urban Section

An Analytical Tool for Cities and Streets

Robert Mantho

with contributions from Alan Jackson Simpson

Routledge
Taylor & Francis Group

LONDON AND NEW YORK

First published 2015
by Routledge
2 Park Square, Milton Park, Abingdon, Oxon OX14 4RN

and by Routledge
711 Third Avenue, New York, NY 10017

Routledge is an imprint of the Taylor & Francis Group, an informa business

10 0724 150 X

British Library Cataloguing in Publication Data
A catalogue record for this book is available from the British Library

Library of Congress Cataloging in Publication Data
Mantho, Robert.
 The urban section : an analytical tool for cities and streets / by Robert Mantho
; with contributions from Alan Jackson Simpson.
     pages cm
 Includes bibliographical references and index.
 1. Streets. 2. City planning. I. Title.
 NA9053.S7M36 2014
 711'.41--dc23
                              2014007256

ISBN: 978-0-415-64258-3 (hbk)
ISBN: 978-0-415-64259-0 (pbk)
ISBN: 978-0-203-07990-4 (ebk)

Typeset in Univers LT Pro
by Fakenham Prepress Solutions, Fakenham, Norfolk NR21 8NN

Printed and bound in Great Britain by Bell & Bain Ltd, Glasgow

This book is dedicated to all my students, with whom I have learned so much.

Contents

List of Figures   ix

Foreword   xvii

Acknowledgements   xxi

Introduction   xxiii

1 Urban Design – An Additional Tool   1

2 The City Section   25

3 The Street   44

4 Cities and Streets: The Data Set   98

5 Analysing Streets: The Methodology   232

6 Conclusion   274

Index   280

List of Figures

2.1 Genoa City Section

2.2 Fès City Section

2.3 Glasgow City Section

2.4 Paris City Section

2.5 Chicago City Section

3.1 Polk St., San Francisco

3.2 South State St., Chicago

3.3 Rue Talaa Kebria, Fès

3.4 Bath St., Glasgow

3.5 Sidewalk Zones

3.6 Poor Spatial Definition

3.7 Intermittent Street Wall

4.1A Amsterdam City Plan

4.1B Amsterdam City Section

4.1C Amsterdam Street Plan

4.1D Amsterdam Street Section

4.1E Amsterdam Photo

4.2A Bangkok City Plan

4.2B Bangkok City Section

List of Figures

4.2C	Bangkok Street Plan
4.2D	Bangkok Street Section
4.2E	Bangkok Photo
4.3A	Beijing City Plan
4.3B	Beijing City Section
4.3C	Beijing Street Plan
4.3D	Beijing Street Section
4.3E	Beijing Photo
4.4A	Boston City Plan
4.4B	Boston City Section
4.4C	Boston Street Plan
4.4D	Boston Street Section
4.4E	Boston Photo
4.5A	Buenos Aires City Plan
4.5B	Buenos Aires City Section
4.5C	Buenos Aires Street Plan
4.5D	Buenos Aires Street Section
4.5E	Buenos Aires Photo
4.6A	Cape Town City Plan
4.6B	Cape Town City Section
4.6C	Cape Town Street Plan
4.6D	Cape Town Street Section
4.6E	Cape Town Photo
4.7A	Chicago City Plan
4.7B	Chicago City Section
4.7C	Chicago Street Plan
4.7D	Chicago Street Section
4.7E	Chicago Photo
4.8A	Copenhagen City Plan
4.8B	Copenhagen City Section
4.8C	Copenhagen Street Plan

4.8D Copenhagen Street Section

4.8E Copenhagen Photo

4.9A Fès City Plan

4.9B Fès City Section

4.9C Fès Street Plan

4.9D Fès Street Section

4.9E Fès Illustration

4.10A Genoa City Plan

4.10B Genoa City Section

4.10C Genoa Street Plan

4.10D Genoa Street Section

4.10E Genoa Photo

4.11A Glasgow City Plan

4.11B Glasgow City Section

4.11C Glasgow Street Plan

4.11D Glasgow Street Section

4.11E Glasgow Photo

4.12A Lagos City Plan

4.12B Lagos City Section

4.12C Lagos Street Plan

4.12D Lagos Street Section

4.12E Lagos Photo

4.13A London City Plan

4.13B London City Section

4.13C London Street Plan

4.13D London Street Section

4.13E London Photo

4.14A Mexico City City Plan

4.14B Mexico City City Section

4.14C Mexico City Street Plan

4.14D Mexico City Street Section

List of Figures

4.14 E   Mexico City Photo
4.15 A   Montevideo City Plan
4.15 B   Montevideo City Section
4.15 C   Montevideo Street Plan
4.15 D   Montevideo Street Section
4.15 E   Montevideo Photo
4.16 A   Montreal City Plan
4.16 B   Montreal City Section
4.16 C   Montreal Street Plan
4.16 D   Montreal Street Section
4.16 E   Montreal Photo
4.17 A   Mumbai City Plan
4.17 B   Mumbai City Section
4.17 C   Mumbai Street Plan
4.17 D   Mumbai Street Section
4.17 E   Mumbai Photo
4.18 A   Newcastle upon Tyne City Plan
4.18 B   Newcastle upon Tyne City Section
4.18 C   Newcastle upon Tyne Street Plan
4.18 D   Newcastle upon Tyne Street Section
4.18 E   Newcastle upon Tyne Photo
4.19 A   New York City Plan
4.19 B   New York City Section
4.19 C   New York Street Plan
4.19 D   New York Street Section
4.19 E   New York Photo
4.20 A   Paris City Plan
4.20 B   Paris City Section
4.20 C   Paris Street Plan
4.20 D   Paris Street Section
4.20 E   Paris Photo

4.21A Pittsburgh City Plan
4.21B Pittsburgh City Section
4.21C Pittsburgh Street Plan
4.21D Pittsburgh Street Section
4.21E Pittsburgh Photo
4.22A Rio de Janeiro City Plan
4.22B Rio de Janeiro City Section
4.22C Rio de Janeiro Street Plan
4.22D Rio de Janeiro Street Section
4.22E Rio de Janeiro Photo
4.23A Rome City Plan
4.23B Rome City Section
4.23C Rome Street Plan
4.23D Rome Street Section
4.23E Rome Photo
4.24A San Francisco City Plan
4.24B San Francisco City Section
4.24C San Francisco Street Plan
4.24D San Francisco Street Section
4.24E San Francisco Photo
4.25A San Miguel de Allende City Plan
4.25B San Miguel de Allende City Section
4.25C San Miguel de Allende Street Plan
4.25D San Miguel de Allende Street Section
4.25E San Miguel de Allende Photo
4.26A St. Petersburg City Plan
4.26B St. Petersburg City Section
4.26C St. Petersburg Street Plan
4.26D St. Petersburg Street Section
4.26E St. Petersburg Photo
4.27A Shanghai City Plan

4.27B   Shanghai City Section

4.27C   Shanghai Street Plan

4.27D   Shanghai Street Section

4.27E   Shanghai Photo

4.28A   Singapore City Plan

4.28B   Singapore City Section

4.28C   Singapore Street Plan

4.28D   Singapore Street Section

4.28E   Singapore Photo

4.29A   Tokyo City Plan

4.29B   Tokyo City Section

4.29C   Tokyo Street Plan

4.29D   Tokyo Street Section

4.29E   Tokyo Photo

4.30A   Vancouver City Plan

4.30B   Vancouver City Section

4.30C   Vancouver Street Plan

4.30D   Vancouver Street Section

4.30E   Vancouver Photo

5.1   Orientation

5.2   Proportion / Height to Width Ratio

5.3   Scale

5.4   Scale of Parts

5.5   Horizontal Layers

5.6   Vertical Layers

5.7   Public / Private Character

5.8   Spatial Definition – Simple

5.9   Spatial Definition – Layered

5.10   Poor Spatial Definition

5.11   Enclosure and Exposure

5.12   Base of Street Wall – Soft

5.13   Base of Street Wall – Hard

5.14   Facade Articulation

5.15   Transparency and Opacity

5.16   Volumetric Interaction

5.17   Orientation – East Third Street

5.18   Proportion / Height to Width Ratio – East Third Street

5.19   Scale – East Third Street

5.20   Scale of Parts – East Third Street

5.21   Horizontal Layers – East Third Street

5.22   Vertical Layers – East Third Street

5.23   Public / Private Character – East Third Street

5.24   Spatial Definition Layered – East Third Street

5.25   Enclosure and Exposure – East Third Street

5.26   Base of the Street Wall – Soft or Hard – East Third Street

5.27   Facade Articulation – East Third Street

5.28   Transparency and Opacity – East Third Street

5.29   Volumetric Interaction – East Third Street

5.30   Orientation – South Bridge Road

5.31   Proportion / Height to Width Ratio – South Bridge Road

5.32   Scale – South Bridge Road

5.33   Scale of Parts – South Bridge Road

5.34   Horizontal Layers – South Bridge Road

5.35   Vertical Layers – South Bridge Road

5.36   Public / Private Character – South Bridge Road

5.37   Spatial Definition Open Layered – South Bridge Road

5.38   Enclosure and Exposure – South Bridge Road

5.39   Base of the Street Wall – Soft or Hard – South Bridge Road

5.40   Facade Articulation – South Bridge Road

5.41   Transparency and Opacity – South Bridge Road

5.42   Volumetric Interaction – South Bridge Road

Foreword

The idea for this book began on a street in Amsterdam, when I was trying to explain something to students. I was trying to describe the street and its physical characteristics, most importantly how the street and the interior spaces lining the street were connected; how the relationships between the various elements came together to form the space and the specific place of the street and how they influenced fundamental urban relationships. What I was trying to explain was a method for thinking about and understanding a place. As I was describing the street in words, I could see a perplexed look on the faces of the students. I realized that I was falling into the age-old trap of the experienced professional involved in teaching: expecting tacit knowledge to be understood, while neglecting to make this knowledge explicit.

This led me to think carefully about what I was doing as I built an understanding of the street and how I could make this technique apparent to the students. First I stopped and traced the procedure I used to understand the street. I noticed that I started by building a mental section of the street, drawing in my mind a cross-sectional cut through the street and placing the various elements of the space in relation to each other with this analytic tool. I then realized that I used the results of this analysis to frame an understanding of the urban qualities of the street.

To demonstrate this thought process to the students, I began, at first with my finger in space and then with a pencil in my sketch book, to draw the section of the street and to diagram the physical, spatial and urban consequences for them. I explained the value of sectional analysis and using sketches of the street in plan and section, demonstrated how these analytic tools could reveal a series of fundamental features, which when taken together resulted in much more nuanced understanding of the place and its context.

As is typical in this type of moment, another common technique I used without conscious acknowledgement occurred to me, comparative analysis. I realized that while I sketched my mental section and plan, I was also comparing the results to streets that I knew, streets that were similar and streets that were different. I asked the students to think of a street they knew well and to sketch a section and plan of that street and to compare the sections and plans to see the differences and similarities. The conversation progressed to a discussion about the strengths of the street we were in and how it related to the streets around it and to Amsterdam.

Asking students to look at streets and to analyse what they were seeing raised the issue of the significance of the street and the various roles they play. Like numerous other aspects of architecture and urbanism, the street is a piece of everyday experience that is taken for granted, but which has great significance for architects and for cities. Many urban thinkers consider the street to be the basic building block of cities, most obviously because it provides for the movement of people, vehicles and goods, but also importantly, because the street establishes the relationship between individual buildings to form the coherent urban whole. Streets are the most basic form of the public realm, where the unremarkable forms of public life occur and streets form the context for the cities they make up. While squares and parks provide the accents in the public realm, streets are the network in which these special moments are contained and through which they are connected. It is through the street and the specific physical conventions they set up that the urban character of a city is defined. Understanding the streets of a particular city is fundamental to building a useful understanding of the context for architecture and urban design.

Contemplating the importance of understanding streets, I realized that this means of analysing streets and places was common practice among experienced architects and urban designers, but that it was reflexive and possibly "hidden" as a result. As I thought about this later and during numerous conversations with other students and colleagues, I realized that embedded in this practice was a useful methodology, and as a teacher it seemed essential to make this available to students. I began to examine more carefully how I analysed and compared streets and two things became clear: first that it would be very useful to have a set of drawings of streets from a wide range of cities to use for comparative analysis and second that the informal set of mental diagrams for studying relationships needed to be developed into a workable method. This resulted in a period of questioning, drawing, discussions and discovery and a realization that there was a great deal about streets and cities that I took for granted.

I began a period of research into urbanism: urban design history, urban analysis and urban design theory. It became clear that the field of urban design has a wide spectrum of concerns in an expanding body of knowledge. A great deal of important and compelling work has been done over the last 30 years to build a comprehensive understanding of cities, how they are formed, how they are used and how they change. This book is part of what Carmona et al.[1] refer to as the visual dimension, or what I would call the physical tradition. This tradition focuses on the study of physical information and attempts to derive valuable knowledge from the study of that information.

The limitations of this set of physical information and any knowledge derived from it are accepted and this book is not an argument against other approaches to understanding urban issues. However, the book does argue that the physical configuration of cities has a significant impact on the quality of urban experience. The methodology and the understanding that results from its use can be extended through the integration of other approaches; for example, understanding the arrangement of elements and spaces on a street, coupled with knowledge of the social context, results in a much deeper reading. As two streets might have very similar physical qualities but vastly different socio-economic circumstances, leading to very distinct urban characters. Physical properties are not the sole definers of urban experience, but they are one of the primary contributors to it.

Note

1. Matthew Carmona, Steve Tiesdell, Tim Heath and Taner Oc. eds. (2010). *Public Places-Urban Spaces.* London: Architectural Press.

Acknowledgements

I would like to thank a long list of people for their help over the period during which this book was researched and written.

First I would like to thank Professor David Porter, who encouraged me to pursue my initial thoughts and supported the first stages of the research which led to the book. Professor Chris Platt continued this support, providing assistance and funding while I was writing the book. On two separate occasions the Glasgow School of Art's Research Development Fund supplied funds for the production of research drawings which formed the basis of the final drawings in this book. Without this financial help the book would not have been completed. I am very grateful to the professors and the institution for this support. I would also like to thank Alan Simpson for all the valuable discussions which have contributed to the book.

I would like to thank my research assistants Sabeya Ali, Paul Hawkes and Rob Harvey for their hard work in helping to produce the research and base drawings for the final illustrations included in the book. Sabeya's research and drawings for the individual street plans and sections were the foundation for a major component of the book. Paul's work on the large-scale city section and plan drawings was another critical part of the research central to the book. Rob's help in formatting the drawings and diagrams was essential to the production of clear final illustrations.

Acknowledgements

I would also like to thank all the students who participated in workshops and produced various versions of sections and plans, of both cities and streets, over the last 4 years as I was developing the book. Exploring the techniques and thinking the book is founded on with them has been very helpful, allowing me to clarify and expand the early concepts into a more refined and complete body of thought. Those students include: Maroof Ansari, Afeef Choorapulakkal, Chithan Kadir Mani Chandrabose, Nicole Davidson, Michael Godden, Kshitij Kumar, Helen McCormack, Kanakkumari Mishra, Naomi Ronan, Vikrant Singh, Kartik Vaid, Sydney Wallace, Chih-Chieh Yang and I-chen Yeh.

Another group of people who made an important contribution were those who helped to secure information and materials regarding individual cities. I would like to thank the following people for their help: Maroof Ansari, Anela Anwar, Michael Archer, Azeem Arshad, Christina Batman, Dolores Battro, Natalie Bennett, Vivian Carvalho, Hugo Corbett, Henrietta Dax, Luciana Frigerio, Ashley Gersuk, Gregory Gersuk, Mary Gersuk, Jack Hughes, Aura Moreno Lagunes, Agnes Lanfranco, Craig Laurie, Toyin Lawal, James Maxwell, Adam McGlennon, Kenneth McGuire, Pablo Jimenez Moreno, Natsuka Muto, Ruairi O'Connell, Jane Ray, Galen Richardson, Andreá Sales, Sue Schlabach, Ditte Marie Resen Steenstrup, Charles Stone, Arak Thripsuwan and Jontahan Bruno Vazquez.

A very big thank you is required for all of my colleagues whose discussions and comments were vital during the process of writing the book. First and foremost was Johnny Rodger, who read portions of the text and supplied essential feedback throughout. Always willing and insightful, I cannot thank Johnny enough for his help and support. Joanna Crotch, Stuart Dickson, Julia Radcliffe and Florian Urban also listened and commented at key moments, and I appreciate their contributions. Claire McDiarmid gave me great advice and supplied important perspective, for which I am very grateful. I also want to thank Philip Woodrow and Carmen Mias for loaning me a quiet place to write.

Finally and most importantly, I would like to thank my wife Sara Pinto, who suggested I write the book in the first place and whose constant encouragement, support and endless help were critical; from research to writing, her patience and willingness to listen were fundamental to the success of the project.

Introduction

In this book the goal is to provide a practical tool for the investigation of cities, through the collection of information from around the world and the synthesis of an analytic method. The drawings in the book provide a way of examining a range of cities at both the macro scale and the more detailed scale of the street. These are analytical drawings, very consciously leaving out information so that specific relationships can be studied. The drawings provide a rigorous framework for investigation, being accurate and to the same scale. The methodology uses a set of clear diagrams as a means of investigating, creating a systematic process and making explicit information and relationships and uses comparative analysis to expand understanding about specific cities and streets, building a more general knowledge of urban conditions. The data set and the methodology contribute to the growing body of knowledge in the field of urban design and analysis, adding to the array of tools available for understanding the complexity of cities.

The first chapter begins with a short history of urban design, particularly that branch of urban thinking which focuses on the physical aspects of cities in the effort to improve how they function. The development of the physical approach to urban design is explained, with the major contributors to this tradition identified to establish the context for the proposed methodology. The chapter also includes a discussion of the emergence of a concern for place making in urban thought and the role that space plays in defining places and the importance of understanding the physical elements which form urban spaces. The importance of the plan as a tool for examining urban conditions and its use for communicating design proposals is briefly discussed, with reference to some important historical examples. The chapter concludes by arguing that the inclusion of sectional information and the systematic analytical methods proposed will provide a variety of benefits to those engaged in examining and creating urban places.

Chapter two examines the idea of the section at the macro scale, and the increased understanding of urban form that results. Beginning with the place of the large-scale diagrammatic section, or the transect, in understanding cities and their formation by Patrick Geddes at the turn of the 20th century and New Urbanism more recently, the significance of vertical relationships to city form is outlined. A set of city types are proposed based on classification practices common in the field, to provide a framework for discussing the range of vertical relationships in cities around the world. Each city type is briefly explored using a large-scale city section and descriptive analysis to reveal the vertical qualities of the various urban forms. The chapter finishes with a discussion of the value of understanding the vertical urban grain and the expansion of the knowledge of spatial relationships achieved when plan and section analysis are used to study a city.

In Chapter three the fundamental position of the book is detailed, with the proposition that the street is the basic building block of cities and that understanding streets is essential to the analysis and design of cities. This view is widely held in contemporary urbanism, with numerous publications dedicated to good design or best practice in street design developing this argument. A range of these resources are reviewed to establish the contemporary approach to street design. The book extends this position by also arguing that the ground-floor spaces adjacent to the street are part of the space of the street and that it is essential that ground floors engage the street to create active urban spaces. The primary characteristics of streets are examined using street sections to build a vocabulary for discussion. The chapter concludes that sectional analysis shows the space of the street and when combined with plan analysis, important relationships and properties are revealed, both for understanding streets and for the designing of streets; helping designers understand the components of working streets and the means of designing an urban dialogue between the interiors and exteriors that form streets.

Chapter four contains drawings of thirty cities from across the world. For every city there is a set of drawings, which include a city section and large-scale plan, a cross section and plan of a specific street and a photograph. The drawings are accompanied by a short description of the city form, some fundamental observations about the spatial arrangement at the macro scale and a description of the manner in which the street illustrated is configured and its spatial features are identified. Each set of drawings are drawn at the same scale, such that they can be used for comparative analysis. The cities and streets come from Africa, Asia, Europe and both North and South America. The goal is to provide a wide variety of urban forms that respond to a range of conditions, allowing users to examine urban models that both match circumstances familiar to them and some less well-known situations. This will make the book useful to users from around the world and expand the set of urban references available for analysis. The cities and streets are selected for the broader reasons stated above, but they were also selected to allow the examination of cities and streets that are not "special". All cities are "special", with unique qualities and characteristics, but the point is not to pick the "superior", but examples that are everyday working urban organisms. This selection is aimed at identifying how common streets are constructed, to identify the spatial and physical relationships of cities of all types, not just those cities, such as Rome or Paris, that are deemed beautiful. This is to some degree a response to the frequent use of exemplars and a desire to illustrate that examples from places not typically considered have valuable lessons as well. The specific streets in each city are selected for their representative character, while also attempting to select a range of streets, such that the complete set of thirty could provide a group of generic types, which can be used in the analysis of a wide spectrum of urban situations.

The specific analytic method for investigating the characteristics of streets is explained in Chapter five, along with brief discussions of how this methodology and the thinking outlined in Chapter 2 regarding the large-scale study of cities, can be used to address various urban design and planning practices. To demonstrate the methodology at the core of the book, two examples from the collection of streets in Chapter four are examined using a set of analytic diagrams at the scale of the individual street, with the results of these individual examinations being compared to reveal other layers of information about each individual case, but also information that allows more general concepts to be derived. Each diagram contributes a piece of information to a collection of interrelated observations, showing the basic physical facts through which more complex relationships are constructed. The chapter goes on to present ways in which this methodology can be applied to specific areas of concern within the broader field of urban design. The chapter provides a brief summary of how the thinking, at both the macro and micro level, can be used to enhance understanding of the issues surrounding urban regeneration, urban conservation and urban design. Each of these circumstances requires a wide range of analysis and knowledge, and information specific to their central focus and the proposed methodology contributes to each practice in general terms as well as in particular ways. The chapter discusses how the information about a city can be used to construct a comparative analysis to investigate an individual instance of urban conservation for example, or how more general concerns can be studied by comparing the information for multiple streets included in the book. Chapter five demonstrates how the methodology and the drawings can be useful practical tools for people confronted with the demanding tasks in the various fields of urban design.

The book concludes with a discussion of the central premises and their value to urban designers and to the current debates surrounding cities. It takes the position that the structure of cities and the spaces within cities can be understood on many levels and through numerous analytical perspectives, with the physical facts being critical to a fully formed picture and that these facts are enhanced through the rigorous systematic analysis of plans and sections. Importantly, an argument is made that the examination of the vertical grain of various cities and the close analysis of individual streets supports the contention that the interaction between the space of the street and the ground-floor spaces adjacent to it is fundamental to a healthy urban form. Vibrant streets are essential for cities and a basic goal for urban designers. Frequently, designers propose closed ground floors, which offer little to the street, generating listless streets and poor urbanism. How the interior life of buildings becomes part of the street is one of the primary problems for architects and urban designers; this is true in cities across the globe and understanding the various ways this is achieved is important knowledge for anyone involved in urbanism.

This book started with a desire to explain a personal method for understanding a street and through the street a place and a city. The recognition that combining horizontal and vertical information to build a spatial image, allowing a complex set of urban relationships to be examined, led to an extensive period of research and multiple discussions with colleagues and students. This research has resulted in the development of a methodology and the collection of data for thirty cities. The methodology has been used in workshops and tested through a series of studies in preparation for writing this book, the results of both point to the value of the methodology. The presentation of the drawings and concepts in this book is based on the belief that this methodology can contribute to expanding the set of tools available for the study of urban conditions.

Architects and Urban Designers are required to look carefully at what is usually taken for granted, to see and understand the actual material facts which frame and to some extent shape experience; this is always the first step in the process of understanding a set of conditions. The goal of this book is to use a straightforward and clear analytic method to examine this basic physical information to provide just such a starting point for those confronted with urban complexity, offering a methodology that is both rigorous and transparent, allowing a transferable means of disciplined investigation that is based on objective information. Beginning with a teaching moment and developing into an examination of urban analysis and urban design finally led to a useful and accessible means for investigating the intricacy of cities and streets; adding another valuable tool for urbanists and producing a greater understanding of urban environments that meaningfully support human activity.

Chapter One
Urban Design – An Additional Tool

From the beginning of the investigation which led to the development of the ideas in this book, the practical problems faced by designers have been the predominant concern. When thinking about how streets work and how the relationships set up by the physical characteristics of a particular street influence the spatial and experiential qualities of a street, it has been from the perspective of the designer, and in consideration of how this knowledge could assist in improving the design of buildings, streets and cities. Consequently, it is from the position of the designer that this approach to analysing and comparing proposes to contribute to the field of urban design, to add another means of collecting information and constructing knowledge. A major task in establishing how this approach makes a contribution, is defining its position within the context of urban design, and this is accomplished with a brief history of urban design and theory. This is not meant to be a comprehensive or detailed description of urban design thinking, but a summary to describe the broad relationships the ideas in this book have to the major strands of thought within urban design and to appropriately situate the knowledge derived.

The physical tradition

While undoubtedly urban design has taken place in some form in cultures across the globe and in antiquity, the history of modern urban design begins with the re-emergence of classical ideas in the 15th century throughout Europe and most specifically in the Italian renaissance. The earliest examples of modern city planning with a focus on design, or what is now called urban design, were in both the theory and the practice of renaissance Italian architects. Alberti's *On the Art of Building*[1] and the building programme of Sixtus V in Rome[2] are some of the best known cases of the renaissance concern for city making. These early examples, like most of the city design which followed, focused on the physical aspects of the urban environment. How buildings and the reconfiguration of material elements improved the use of the city or improved the aesthetic experience has been the major concern of those architects and thinkers engaged in city design until recently. This focus on the material aspects of the city, which I will term the physical tradition, distinguishes it from more recent areas of interest surrounding the developing discipline of Urban Design.

This focus on how the concrete facts of the built environment could impact on those using cities remained the overt rationale of city design until the critiques of modernist city planning that began in the middle of the 20th century. While the projection of political agendas and public images strongly influenced baroque city planning and continued to play a role well into the essentially late baroque planning activity at the end of the 19th century and beginning of the 20th century, these non-physical considerations were predicated on the impacts of the manipulation of material components. The ultimate consequence of the design discussions still centred on how physical environments could be formed to improve cities, with the art of city design still seen in late baroque terms, with the aesthetic configuration of form to create monumental urban backdrops considered the essential purpose of city making.

The concern with physical elements was at the core of the progressive critiques of the 19th-century city, such as Howard[3] and especially Sitte,[4] with both arguing that the physical configuration of cities was having a negative impact on society and that only by altering the physical fabric of the city could these problems be resolved. This belief that changing the physical environment was the answer to urban problems continued in the development of modernist town planning ideas, which proposed a model that placed the demands of modern transportation and economic activity at the heart of city design. Radical physical changes, the removal of the street through the separation of modes of transportation, individual buildings surrounded by public space and the basic organisation of the city, were presented as the corrective to the overcrowding and sanitation problems of the 19th-century city. The notion of "fixing" the historical city with efficient functionalist answers and modernist aesthetics placed the re-alignment of the physical components at the core of the vision of re-configuring society itself. This culminated in Le Corbusier's famous call for change "Architecture or Revolution".[5]

After World War 2 many cities around the world were re-designed, with urban expressways, single-use zoning and architectural models based on modernist thinking, leading to urban renewal schemes that dramatically altered the traditional urban fabric of cities. Overcrowded and unsanitary conditions were eradicated, but the social cohesion in many communities was irreparably damaged. The efficient movement of vehicular traffic was facilitated, but numerous neighbourhoods were destroyed. The criticisms by Jane Jacobs[6] and others that were levelled at modernist town planning and the impacts that it had on the quality of life for those living in the city led to a crisis in confidence for many in the planning profession. This lack of confidence in the design ideology of modern town planning caused a retreat from the large programmes of physical redevelopment and a new focus on other aspects of planning. Planners began to utilise a broader spectrum of theoretical ideas. A range of disciplines from sociology to economics began to play a part in discussions about how cities could be understood and reconfigured.

The development of town planning in the 1960's and 1970's through the application of the techniques and ideas of sociology, perception, anthropology, and economics radically re-conceived urban thinking. The field saw a massive increase in scholarly activity, an expansion of the territory of the discipline and ultimately the establishment of a new discipline: Urban Design. Urban Design operates at the overlap between architecture, planning, economics and politics, requiring the consideration of all these at numerous levels to successfully operate. The very wide set of issues and range of expertise demanded, has led to the growth of the body of knowledge encompassed by the discipline of urban design. This also accounts for the recent recognition of two distinct branches of urban design thinking, the traditional focus on physical issues and the emergence of a concern with the social issues of urban design. In *Public Places-Urban Spaces*, Carmona, et al.[7] argue that these two approaches form traditions of thought, the visual-artistic tradition and the social usage tradition and that a recent third tradition has emerged: the place-making tradition.[8] In this context, this book is an addition to the physical tradition, providing a means of gathering information about the physical circumstances of the city.

The development of the physical tradition is really the history of what we understand as urban design. The design and analysis of cities has been dominated by a concern with the physical fabric of cities. The renaissance altering of Florence and Rome, along with the cities conceived as idealised expressions of geometry that start the modern tradition of urban thinking, have at their core the belief that physical conditions shape experience and consequently require the application of consideration and the critical thought of design.

From the renaissance until the beginning of modernist town planning, geometry and idealised manipulation of space formed the basis for city planning. Creating order and visual harmony, directing view and shaping dramatic civic places to generate grandeur was considered the ultimate goal of the art of designing cities.[9] The early experiments in Florence and Rome of clearing straight streets through tangled medieval fabric led quickly to the more monumental goals of baroque city design. Although consideration of other factors obviously played a part in decisions, it was the imposition or creation of ordered relationships that dominated baroque urban thinking. The construction of new settlements, such as Versailles, attempts to re-organise existing ones, such as Paris at the Place de la Concorde, or new additions to expanding cities like Regent's Park and Park Crescent; all use geometric order to achieve a conception of beauty.[10] The alignment between the aesthetic qualities of baroque design and the political agendas of centralised forms of government, while not overtly discussed by writers and designers, clearly contributed to the prevalence of baroque design principles for four hundred years of city design. The majority of city making, alterations and additions until the 18th and 19th century, were carried out by autocratic powers of one form or another at various scales. It is not surprising that a physical and visual agenda that focused on displays of power and centralised organisation was considered the correct way to build cities.[11] These baroque ideas found their most popular expression in Haussmann's boulevards, but are also present in the City Beautiful movement in turn of the century America. Central to all these forms of late baroque city planning was the belief that the configuration of the material city shaped the lives of those who lived in it.

The next stage in the development of the physical tradition was the progressive thinking that developed in the latter half of the 19th century in reaction to the problems of the industrialised city. This ultimately led to a transition from late baroque city design ideas to the radical ideas of modernist town planning. The deprivations and dangers caused by the dramatic rise in density, and the inclusion of industrial activities within cities, generated a wave of new thinking focused on improving health and the quality of life for those living in cities, especially the urban poor. Paralleling romantic ideals present much earlier in literature and art, urban thinkers began to assert the importance of nature as a means of mitigating the negative impacts of city life. Parks, greenery, and natural forms were seen as essential to relieving the stress of the chaotic city. With Olmstead's plans for Boston's "green necklace" to the more fundamental re-organisation of Howard's garden city, the basic tenants of baroque urban thinking were displaced with a concern for the well being of individual city residents.[12] Camillo Sitte introduced another set of romantic considerations, arguing that economic rationalisation and the aesthetics of visual order resulted in bland cities.[13] Sitte believed that to excite poetic sensation and delightful experience cities should be re-configured using strategies derived from the study of medieval urban form and spaces. These ideas were also influenced by the late Victorian valorisation of medieval ideals, e.g. Carlyle, Morris and Ruskin, and evidenced in Howard's spatial distribution of greenery for productive and leisure purposes, or in Sitte's use of historical cities and irregular plazas in his arguments for a more artful city.[14] All of these ideas again asserted that the concrete properties of the city, whether chaotic, loud and dirty, orderly and interspersed with nature, or artistically shaped, affected those who used cities and that the focus of city making was the proper arrangement of the physical environment.

The progressive ideals present in so much of late 19th-century and early modern thought raised debates which resulted in a questioning of the basic assumptions of how cities worked, were organised and indeed the purpose of settlement. It was out of these discussions and attempts to address the problems of the industrialised city that the initiatives of modernist town planning emerged. There was a sense that the modern conditions of the early 20th century were so dramatically different than preceding culture that new solutions were required. It was assumed that these new solutions would be a break from the past, with its artistic and historic concerns and instead be based on rational principles and solutions meant to address circumstances never before encountered. The new forms of locomotion, communication and production were seen as providing the needs and opportunity to re-make the physical environment.

Modern town planning sought to improve living conditions and address the needs of industrial economic production through mechanical organisation. This attempt at objective and factual based planning was accompanied by a different aesthetic agenda, but still considered the aesthetic arrangement of the environment as essential to the act of city building. Modernist city design principles were based on a mechanistic world view, stating that efficient operation and the rational relationship between various activities of the city should be the basis for design decisions. Zoning for single use, provision for transportation networks, isolating industrial processes away from the population, creating clear visual order, were all principles conceived to allow cities to function smoothly and to prevent unhealthy living conditions and negative impacts. Scientific processes for evaluating problems and establishing standards, coupled with mass production techniques, were seen as the solution to the range of problems faced by cities and those who lived in them. Public health research identified poor ventilation, poor light, lack of access to clean water, unsanitary conditions and overcrowding as major contributors to ill health and high mortality rates. These conditions were seen as to be the result of unregulated and unconsidered growth. This thinking was also conditioned by the idea that historical thinking and models were corrupt and dishonest, which led to the invention of new forms and visual languages. It was an article of faith that re-shaping cities using modernist principles could resolve social problems such as poverty and crime.[15]

The deployment of modernist town planning strategies to re-build and re-shape post-war cities radically affected urban experience. Slum clearance programmes and urban renewal plans re-located populations and industries and inserted vehicular infrastructure into the urban fabric. These changes transformed cities; reducing density in an attempt to relieve overcrowding and raising sanitation and health standards, while also allowing the provision for automobiles to increasingly dominate organisational strategies. The impacts on public space were dramatic; beginning in the early 1960's these ideas were criticised as destructive to urban life. Jane Jacobs believed that these design ideas led to urban environments devoid of substantial social contact and denuded of vibrant human activity essential to enjoying the city.[16] These and other criticisms led to a crisis in confidence in the discipline of town planning and the eventual abandonment of the belief that physical alteration of the environment was an effective way of dealing with urban problems. Other disciplines such as sociology and economics became the basis for urban planning, with planners relying on quantitative data to analyse cities and provide the basis for policy.[17]

For those designers who remained focused on the physical concerns of urban design, the historic city became a major source of inspiration, leading to forty years of examination and debate. The primary model of historic analysis was the European city, from Aldo Rossi's *The Architecture of the City*[18] to Leon Krier's article "The City Within the City".[19] The argument was made that social interaction and cultural vitality were best supported by urban models which favoured the creation of identifiable public spaces and these could be most readily found in the historic European city. The densely occupied urban core was praised for its visual and spatial vitality and these dense cities were seen as the medium of social exchange and culture; the physical manifestation of civilised society. Urban design was seen as the shaping of the space between buildings to promote social interaction and the defined spaces of the enclosed street and the readable figure of an urban square became the exemplars of urban design.

One vibrant contemporary urban design agenda, New Urbanism, folds this concern for historical models together with other major strands of the physical tradition into a coherent body of thought. This has resulted in a revitalisation of the physical tradition, generating analytic tools, diagrammatic models and design methodologies. New Urbanism bases its critique of urban conditions on clearly articulated principles for the arrangement of the physical environment, calling for the careful composition of elements at the various scales of the city. New Urbanism advocates the alteration of planning policy to support higher density in pursuit of social and environmental goals; mixed pedestrian and vehicular networks, physical definition in public spaces and environments which reflect the regional culture. These principles are presented as the solution to the problems of sprawl: lack of social cohesion and the purported "ugliness" of many urban environments. Again, the belief that the answer to urban and social problems is to be found in physical solutions is being asserted.

Also developing out of the critique of post-war town planning was a critique based on ecological concerns. Beginning with Ian McHarg in the 1960's,[20] ecological thinking was used to analyse urban impacts, leading to propositions that argued for altering everything from development patterns to living units. In the last ten years this approach to urban design has gained momentum, leading to an urbanism that considers a spectrum of sustainability issues, aimed at minimising energy consumption and negative environmental impacts, while increasing social benefits and individual quality of life. Richard Rogers' advocacy for revised planning policy in London, Norman Foster and Partners zero carbon city, Masdar in Abu Dhabi, or Newington, Australia, attempt a sustainable urbanism.[21] This model of sustainable urban design has the potential to contribute to the resolution of the approaching problems of climate change, resource depletion and the increasing urbanisation of the world population.

The most recent addition to the physical tradition of urban design is the emerging approach of parametric urbanism, which attempts to address urban issues using the strategies and processes of computation.[22] Parametricism is seen as a means of generating a responsive urban environment, capable of maximising resources and arriving at design solutions that are aligned with the complex criteria of urban situations. Seeking to apply the power of digital tools to model numerous versions of physical reality and to test the impacts, parametric urbanism proposes that the city is mutable and can be shaped to be optimised for any number of desired results. Like so many of the urbanisms of the past, the focus on the physical disposition of elements and the urban results places this approach in the physical tradition and illustrates the persistence of this conception of urban design.

Within the physical tradition, three dimensional considerations have always been part of the discussion in the design of cities; however, it is also clear that the plan has been central to the design and communication of urban proposals and theory. The plan is the primary tool used to examine existing conditions and to communicate proposed changes; and in the discussion of ideas the diagrammatic plan is the predominant means of illustrating concepts. Plans have always been used to organise and regulate, with the simplification of two dimensions providing a method of managing the complexity of large-scale problems and the coordination of important relationships.

The plan

Perspective and the spatial thinking it inspired played an important role in renaissance city design, evident in the quantity of paintings of ideal cities portrayed in dramatic perspective. However, the plan was seen as the device for examining solutions and expressing the totality of a city proposal. Numerous ideal plans, from Filarete's (Antonio Averlino) design for Sforzinda to Da Vinci's plan for Imola,[23] proposed that the city should be formed using ordered mathematical systems to subdivide a geometric figure. The use of proportional grids, symmetry, harmony and ordered relationships depended on plan views to achieve these design goals.

The role of the plan as a method for a designer to explore the design of cities continued through the baroque period, with the most famous examples of baroque city planning relying on the plan to express their geometrical ordering. Baroque city design is characterised by the elaborate plan figures of roadways radiating out from rond-points and squares of various geometric figures. The network of streets built in Rome by Sixtus VI relied on planimetric knowledge and techniques to establish relationships between important pilgrimage churches and monuments.[24] This information was used to reorganise the city with straight roads drawn through the messy organic medieval fabric in plan. The clearest example of the plan's dominant place in baroque spatial thinking is the layout of Versailles, the road network centred on the palace and the gardens, which use the plan to create complex geometric patterns to pursue the aesthetic agenda of a centralised ordering of space and infinite vistas.[25] It is perhaps due to the baroque emphasis on the plan and its effects which led to the establishment of the plan as the most important tool for the city planner.

As late baroque aesthetic ideals dominated urban thinking until the late 19th century, so the plan maintained its position as the primary tool of the city designer. It was through the plan that the strategies of Beaux Arts city planning were investigated and deployed, as exemplified by the plans of Paris or Barcelona.[26] Although Haussmann's alterations of Paris utilised the section, particularly in the design of streets and the organisation of services, the plan still took precedence, especially in the realms of aesthetics. The avenues and boulevards were examined in section to confirm their mechanical function, but the assessment and communication of their artistic impacts was carried out in plan. The City Beautiful movement in the United States linked baroque design ideals with progressive notions of alleviating problems caused by overcrowding and poor sanitation. Again the organisation of urban space used plan strategies to structure relationships between monumental buildings fronting public spaces and grand tree-lined boulevards linking important civic districts to recreational provisions. While these grand projects were often illustrated with sophisticated perspective renderings, they were essentially baroque plan ideas in the service of progressive democratic social ideas.[27]

The dominance of the plan continued with the development of other progressive urban ideas as well. Ebenezer Howard proposed the reorganisation of cities based on plan diagrams that examined the qualities and relationships of rural and urban habitation. It is Howard's blending of the characteristics of both of these in plan which leads to his alternate approach to town design. His famous illustration from *Garden Cities of Tomorrow* of 1902, "Group of Slumless, Smokeless Cities", demonstrates the significance of the plan to Howard's thinking.[28] The concentric forms of the individual cities, the rings of transportation and the careful location of industrial, agricultural and social resources into specific zones and the overall radial figure are plan conceptions, depending on two dimensional qualities to achieve the visual appeal of the diagram.

Although early modernist theorising about the reconfiguration of the city utilised compelling perspective drawings of newly ordered environments, ultimately it was planimetric strategies that were its foundations. From the Cité Industrialle of Tony Garnier to Le Corbusier's Ville Contemporaine, the plan was used to rationalise and organise the components of the industrial city, utilising the plan as a mechanical device for efficiently ordering urban entities.[29] With city planning being reconceived as a scientific practice, the objective nature of the plan lent itself to the perceived need for disciplined examination and communication. Again this can be read in the insistence on the strict zoning of uses into industrial, commercial and residential districts or into the geometric purity of Le Corbusier's urban plans.[30] For modernism the plan is both an instrument and an ideological icon.[31]

The history of city design and analysis is punctuated by instances of iconic plans. Many of the foundational documents of the discipline are plans – the ideal cities of the renaissance, the Noli plan of Rome, the Pierre L'Enfant plan of Washington D.C.,[32] Le Corbusier's Cité Radieuse,[33] the plans in Colin Rowe's book *Collage City*[34] and the New Urbanist plan of Seaside Florida.[35] The plan is so dominant in the tradition of city design that the discipline and professional practice of designing for cities was actually called town *planning* until the fundamental reconsideration of the field in the mid 20th century. While this reappraisal and the critique of determinism and rigidity of post-war town planning led to the inclusion of an array of new tools and revived the practice of city making, the plan was still the primary tool of investigation and communication. Even today, with the extensive use of perspective sketches, digital models and section diagrams, the plan is still a fundamental tool for urban design and analysis, forming the starting point of most urban design conversations.

The city section

One tool that has been developed to extend urban design thinking beyond plan focused approaches is the transect. The concept of the transect has been an important idea in thinking about urban problems for some time, but in recent years this idea has been increasingly used. The concept originates in biology, where a particular phenomenon is documented along a set line through a defined territory. The goal of the method is to plot the relationship of incidence to location in the mapping of spatial distribution. The relevance of the transect for urbanism derives from the use of the concept by urban thinkers attempting to understand the relationship between humans and the built environments they live in.

The use of the transect in considering urban issues dates back to Patrick Geddes and his efforts to develop ideas about regions and human settlements within them. Geddes borrowed the idea from biology to conceptualise the relationship between human activities, natural environments and ultimately human settlement. For Geddes the application of this biological model explained how the environmental conditions of a specific location developed a corresponding natural human economy.[36] Geddes' attempts to understand the relationships that shaped cities, and the insistence on the importance of understanding the existing conditions of a place, led him to collect, organise and analyse information in a disciplined fashion. It is this discipline which underlies the use of the transect as a device, while it is most frequently remembered as a diagram to communicate a set of regional relationships, at the core is a means for exploring the interaction of habitat and settlement as well as the inter-relationships between these factors across a region. The transect is also a tool for understanding sociological and cultural development in relation to environmental factors and the spatial consequences of these events.

This range of uses illustrates the value of the transect concept, as developed by Geddes, and underlines the significance of spatial factors for ordering knowledge, particularly knowledge related to the built environment.

Ian McHarg also used the transect concept in his book, *Design With Nature*.[37] McHarg's efforts to develop an approach to design which was compatible with nature was predicated on a belief that design which ignored nature was ultimately destructive. To that end McHarg advocated for a detailed knowledge of the environment and ecology prior to formulating project goals or a design strategy. McHarg proposed a systematic analysis of the natural habitat to establish where to locate human interventions to minimise potential damage to the environment. McHarg proposed the use of the transect in this context, aimed at understanding the ecological conditions across a range of distinct habitats to build a clear picture of the system new development would engage with. McHarg was not using the transect to establish the relationship between human activity and the environment, but as an analytical tool to better understand biological facts and systems across a network of habitats. The transect allows information to be grouped and spatially ordered, while facilitating the understanding of the relationships between the groups of information. The use of the transect to both analyse environmental information and to visualise the spatial relationships between distinct habitats highlights the value of the transect as a tool and points to the use for the analysis of urban systems.[38]

In the mid 1990's Andreas Duany began working with the concept of the transect as a means of understanding how different types of urban form interacted to generate a coherent gradation from densely urban to uninhabited nature. The Congress of New Urbanism has subsequently developed the transect as a way to rethink zoning and design guidelines in an effort to address the perceived problem of urban sprawl. The New Urbanist use of the transect to establish a model for the appropriate relationship between the gradation of density in the built environment and the natural habitat suggests a means of examining the vertical spatial component of urban form.[39] The value of this model is the recognition that an accurate picture of urban conditions must include an examination of the spatial facts and that this is achieved by combining both the horizontal and the vertical dimensions. Although there have been numerous issues raised regarding the New Urbanist use of the transect, the concept of using sectional information to understand urban form has undeniable value. By bringing the transect and its consideration of vertical information to the discussion of urban analysis and design, New Urbanism has opened a significant field of interest and provided an important tool for the analysis of cities. Using the section at the scale of the region and the city expands the range of information and allows a more nuanced spatial understanding. It seems obvious that the spatial reading of urban form would be improved through the use of this analytical tool, but it is only since Duany's development of the transect concept that the possibilities of using this type of information more thoroughly have begun to be explored.

Large-scale sections through urban fabric can reveal spatial relationships and consequences that cannot be read in plan alone. While photography or perspective can illustrate space, the section provides a disciplined method of analysis, with accurate relational information. The city section can be used to examine the structure of spatial relationships across a city and within a regional context. This macro scale information is important to forming a comprehensive body of knowledge about both specific cities and cities in general. Using the large-scale city section as an analytical tool for this purpose provides another foundational layer of information and should be a basic tool of analysis for urban designers.

The street

While the transect is concerned with the macro scale of the city, the primary element of the city is the street. As with most aspects of urban design, the history of the street as a concern for designers dates to the renaissance, with the earliest examples of city design being the clearing of medieval buildings to form uncluttered straight streets, such as in Florence and Genoa in the 16th century.[40] It was the renaissance conception of the street as an orderly and harmonised visual entity that led to the urban improvements mandated by the government of Florence.[41] While there were obvious benefits to circulation and commercial activity, there can be no doubt that an expression of civic pride also played a part in the use of aesthetic agendas in streets such as Genoa's Strada Maggiore.[42] The recognition that the public realm is fundamentally defined by the street and the space it makes for public life begins with this period.

The street and its variations were also at the heart of baroque planning, from the great radial road patterns of Rome, to the allées of Versailles. It was through the street pattern that the geometric order of baroque city planning was implemented and through the regular ordered facade that contained the space of the street that views were organised to establish vistas of unlimited space. These monumental streets that connected the significant monuments, places and public buildings are what created the aesthetic effects of baroque city design.[43] The arrangement of the linear spaces of streets, with a uniform architectural language for the facades, was considered a demonstration of a rational and civilised outlook, expressing the values of society.[44] Most importantly, the clarity and organisation that homogenised architecture along straight streets created, communicated the power and authority of the absolutist political governments of the baroque period.[45] The baroque street and its characteristics hold both practical benefits as well as philosophical and political meaning.

In the 19th century the late baroque street was the instrument of city building and seen as the means of curing social and economic problems. Haussmann's engineered streets with the mandated facades and organisation of services were designed to provide both more efficient movement for civil and military traffic and to open up the labyrinthine medieval core. The destruction of this core allowed the government to displace the urban poor, removing a source of rebellious opposition and providing new opportunities for conformist economic activity.[46] Haussmann's streets were also designed as modern infrastructure, using the most advanced road building techniques; housing water, sewage and gas lines and lined with trees and gas lamps.[47] The Paris street became the model for city planners around the world, with the characteristics of the wide tree-lined street of uniform facades and engineered service being the definition of the modern street.[48]

Another major discussion in late 19th-century city planning, in opposition to the monumental agendas of the late baroque, was raised by Camillo Sitte in his 1889 book *City Planning According to Artistic Principles*.[49] Sitte argued that the street and the space of the street had a profound impact on the experience of the city. He stated that the straight wide streets of the 19th-century city lacked the aesthetic pleasure of the medieval street. The surprise and visual vitality of the sinuous street was more humane and artistically pleasing in Sitte's view. While these ideas were over emphasised due to a poor first translation, it was this version of Sitte's arguments which had the most impact in urban design debates.[50] Sitte criticised the rationalised streets of contemporary city planning, believing they lacked the variation and stimulation necessary for aesthetic experience, which Sitte felt was essential for urban life. Sitte's ideas influenced city designers of the period and were still influencing the debate in the 1920's. Le Corbusier famously ridiculed his ideas as the "Pack Donkey Way" in his argument for the design of cities based on rational principles.[51] Ironically it was Sitte's theories that provided rhetorical and intellectual ammunition for some of the criticism by postmodern urban theorists of the modernist planning ideas advocated by Le Corbusier.[52]

In his book *Der Stadbau*,[53] Joseph Stubben used the comparative analysis of streets across Europe to establish a rationalised system for street configuration in the industrialised city. Stubben was seeking a method for providing streets that could accommodate all the various needs of the modern city; pedestrians, private vehicles, buses and trams, dimensioning minimum requirements for the various elements and illustrating multiple arrangements. By comparing examples from various cities, Stubben tries to provide general principles that can be used to solve specific problems confronted by city designers. Stubben's book covers other aspects of city planning, but his systematic approach and efforts to establish data-based criteria for streets using comparative analysis are unique.

While also using systematic approaches and pursuing rational solutions, the street was viewed from a very different perspective by modernism. Modernism's efforts to do away with the traditional street, with its perceived drawbacks of restricted light, confusion of mixed transport modes and overcrowded visual field, led to the rhetoric of streets in the air, visions of efficient movement, visual elegance and the romance of gravity-defying technology. The modernist urban space was not defined, with clear visual boundaries, but one which flowed around individual objects, with separate layers of efficiently moving traffic and the traditional street form of the enclosed corridor of movement and commercial interaction was viewed as obsolete. The mechanistic model used to rationalise human activity was seen as inherently good, but also expressive of the contemporary world with its rapid movement and dynamic nature. The modernist public realm, with its rational and efficient organisation, was designed to serve the scientifically determined needs of the city, not the exalted position and pomp of the rich and powerful. The city would be egalitarian and objective, a civic place for everyone; unencumbered by the aesthetic ideologies of oppression and privilege. Modernist architecture and city planning were conceived as an answer to the evils of overcrowding, unsanitary conditions and the dangerous mess of the 19th-century slums and a recognition that everyone in society deserved a minimum standard of accommodation. The newly conceived street, its use and its space have practical, social, aesthetic and ideological significance within this design agenda.

The critique of these modernist urban ideas began with Jane Jacobs' defence of the traditional street and all of its messy variety. Jacobs argued that the central role of the street was to provide the public space for everyday social interaction and that the street required the mix of uses and the comings and goings of multiple entrances contained in the pre-modern street. Jacobs stated that modern architecture's homogeneity and visual restraint, coupled with its consolidation of multiple small plots into large-scale blocks, diminished both the visual stimulus and physical activity of the street, resulting in depopulated streets which held little interest for city dwellers. This left streets that were empty and dangerous, creating physical, social and economic isolation. She felt that traditional streets with their mix of economic activity, social interaction and constant flow of people provided a sense of community even in neighbourhoods with socio-economic problems.[54] Jacobs makes her case against modernist architecture and planning based on an analysis that places the street's social function above its role as a conduit of vehicular traffic, arguing that the mechanical view of the street is limited and destructive to the urban environment.

Throughout the 1960's, '70's and '80's a variety of people began examining the street and how it worked in an attempt to understand how cities worked, with the ultimate recognition that as the life of the street goes, so goes the life of the city.[55] From Appleyard's assessment of the impact of vehicular traffic on social connectivity[56] to Rudofsky's attempts to point out that streets that were enjoyable for people were essential to vibrant urban experience.[57] Allan B. Jacobs' book *Great Streets*[58] of 1993 looks at streets from around the world in an effort to determine what are the characteristics of great streets and what can be learned from them. Much like the methodology that follows in this book, Jacobs uses the section and the plan to examine the space of the street. While his analysis is predominantly verbal and qualitative, the inclusion of sections allows spatial characteristics to be factored into his evaluations. This interest in the street and the role it plays in urban life has continued, with a large expansion of research and materials for street design, from New Urbanist books like *The New Civic Art*[59] to government design guidelines, such as the Chicago Department of Transportation's *Complete Streets Chicago*[60] or the U.K. Dept. for Transport's *Manual for Streets*[61] of 2007.

The analysis of streets and the components of which they are comprised is fundamental to urban design. Understanding streets cannot be achieved through a simple record of the physical elements, as the complex social and economic influences on them cannot be captured by this limited set of information. However, the street can be better understood through the careful analysis of its physical properties. Physical analysis cannot reveal why streets are used as they are, but it can be used to discover the framework for this activity and to help illustrate how activity is allowed and supported. If the street is the basic building block of the city, a detailed knowledge of the material characteristics of the streets is critical to building an operational knowledge for urban design. While extracting general principles from specific analysis has limitations, analysing streets offers the opportunity to collect valuable and useful information for wider urban understanding and for the use in resolving particular design problems.

An additional tool

The section as a tool for understanding spatial problems developed with the discipline of architecture. The use of street sections dates to at least 19th-century Paris, as designers working on the new industrialised streets used sections to study the components of these and the relationships between them. The use of the section to examine urban constructs has a more limited history, with the most obvious example being the transect diagrams of New Urbanism discussed above, where a model of vertical organisation is proposed. The section at the scale of the street continues to be used by designers today, with diagrams and scale drawings used to communicate and test the configuration of streets. The methodology proposed in this book adds to this practice in simple and straightforward ways.

The first principle of the proposed method is the application of rigour to the sectional study of cities and streets. There are numerous examples of descriptive and observational discussions of streets and the urban fabric which they form. This method asserts that a disciplined investigation can provide useful information not revealed otherwise. The method uses a defined process to examine a given situation at two scales, the macro of the city in its totality and the micro scale of specific streets.

The next core principle of the methodology is comparative analysis. The comparison of consistent information collected from two situations reveals differences and similarities, more generalised concepts and most importantly the unique characteristics of each case. Comparative analysis also allows a disciplined exposition of assumed understandings and requires a careful consideration of implicit judgements which can go unexamined when observations are limited to individual cases.

The comparative analysis is supported at the macro scale through the use of a set of plans and sections of cities from around the world. The approach also calls for those using the method to construct a plan and a section of the city they are examining and to compare these to a plan and section selected from the set provided. The exercise of constructing these drawings has the obvious benefit of consolidating and extending the knowledge of the subject of study. By comparing these with another city, spatial patterns in both the horizontal and vertical dimensions can be observed. Comparing two cities of a similar pattern can reveal the specificity of both and highlight the unique spatial structure of each city. Comparing cities with different basic patterns clarifies the distinct nature of each urban form, illustrates both the basic character of the type and the similarities that can arise in apparently divergent urban fabric.

At the micro scale the analysis takes the form of comparing individual streets. Starting with the construction of a scale section and plan of the street to be examined, followed by a defined process of analysis to gather a specific set of information. This information is collected through the use of a standardised set of tools, with each tool highlighting a specific aspect of the street's physical characteristics. The careful examination of each particular aspect provides the fundamental information regarding the street. When each piece of information is combined a complex understanding of the street is formed. The specific elements of each street and the relationship between them are made clear, revealing the formal properties and the spatial character of the street formed by them.

The examination continues with a comparative analysis based on the systematic study of the drawings of the selected street and drawings for a street provided in the book. Each street is investigated layer by layer and the layers from each street are compared to discover correspondences and distinctions. As with the comparative analysis at the scale of the city, comparing the individual streets demonstrates the shared elements of streets, those things which allow a street to operate at the most basic level. How such elements are disposed in each street shows the organisation and structure of these streets. Differences found when comparing the streets also illustrate the fundamental properties of each street, making clear why each street has its particular identity. By confronting knowledge derived from one street with information from another, the knowledge from each is reconsidered and challenged, opening up new opportunities to expand and deepen the knowledge.

The methodology has a range of uses, from the individual designer exploring a particularity, to those interested in exploring urban conditions in general. The designer facing a design task in an urban setting can use this method to build a detailed understanding of the context for the design problem. At the macro scale the method can be used to read the street conditions of the surrounding fabric, helping to determine the response and the impact it will have on its neighbours. Also at the macro scale analysis can be used to examine the spatial structure of a district, helping determine scale and the possible relationships to significant aspects of the urban form.

At the other extreme the methodology could be used to examine cities in the broader sense. Large-scale urban analysis can be supported by examining a set of city plans and sections to study how different cities are organised to explore a general understanding of urban form. Comparing the vertical grain of two cities can expand an understanding of the influence of climate. Cities can be investigated in the abstract as well as the specific, using the collected city sections and plans for either type of analysis.

Those analysing urban form can deploy the street analysis to enhance the spatial reading, informing a wider assessment of urban conditions to include the vertical make up of streets and how the vertical components of the street impact perception. Existing streets from across the world can be studied to find solutions to problems shared by all streets or to discover how particular qualities are generated by a specific street.

The examples above demonstrate the potential range of uses for the methodology, with a variety of other possible uses for designers and those involved with urban problems. The goal of this book is to expand the resources available for the study of cities, building on the practices of the past and offering an extension of known principles. Using basic tools and disciplined analysis to make observations about cities and streets to expand the knowledge about the complex phenomena of cities.

Notes

1. Leon Battista Alberti (1988). *On the Art of Building in Ten Books*, translated by Joseph Rykwert, Neil Leach and Robert Tavernor. Cambridge, MA: The MIT Press.
2. Sigfried Giedion (1982). *Space Time and Architecture*. 5th edn. Cambridge, MA: Harvard University Press. pp. 82–106.

3. Ebenezer Howard (1946). *Garden Cities of Tomorrow*, ed. F.J. Osborn. London: Faber and Faber.

4. Camillo Sitte (1965). *City Planning According to Artistic Principles*, translated by George R. Collins and Christiane Crasemann Collins. London: Phaidon Press.

5. Le Corbusier (2008). *Towards an Architecture*, translated by John Goodman. London: Frances Lincoln Ltd. pp. 291–307.

6. Jane Jacobs (1993). *The Death and Life of Great American Cities.* Modern Library edn. New York: Modern Library.

7. Matthew Carmona, Steve Tiesdell, Tim Heath and Taner Oc. eds. (2010). *Public Places-Urban Spaces.* London: Architectural Press.

8. Ibid, pp. 6–8.

9. Lewis Mumford (1961). *The City In History.* London: Secker & Warburg. p. 347.

10. Giedion, op. cit., pp. 133–158 & 708–739.

11. Mumford, op. cit., p. 427.

12. Ibid, p. 497.

13. Sitte, op. cit.

14. Ibid, pp. 39–53.

15. Le Corbusier. (1971). *The City of Tomorrow and Its Planning*, translated by Frederick Etchells. London: Architectural Press and Le Corbusier. (1967). *The Radiant City*, translated by Pamela Knight, Eleanor Levieux and Derek Coltman. London: Faber and Faber.

16. Jacobs, op. cit., pp. 5–34.

17. R.K. Jarvis. (2007). Urban environments as visual art or as social settings? A review. In: Matthew Carmona and Steve Tiesdell eds. *The Urban Design Reader.* Oxford: Architectural Press. pp. 28–30.

18. Aldo Rossi. (1982). *The Architecture of the City*, translated by Diane Ghirardo and Joan Ockman. Cambridge, MA: MIT Press.

19. Leon Krier. (1977). The City Within the City. *A+U.* Nov., pp. 69–152.

20. Ian McHarg. (1969). *Design With Nature.* New York: The Natural History Press.

21. Mike Jenks and Colin Jones eds. (2010). *Dimensions of the Sustainable City.* Chester: Springer. pp. 4–5.

22. Patrik Schumacher. (2009). Parametricism – A New Global Style for Architecture and Urban Design. *AD Architectural Design.* 79 (4), pp. 14–23.

23. Spiro Kostof. (1991). *The City Shaped – Urban Patterns and Meanings Through History.* London: Thames and Hudson. pp. 186 & 132.

24. Giedion, op. cit., pp. 91–106.

25. Kostof, op. cit., pp. 216–217.

26. Ibid, p. 152.

27. Ibid, p. 234.

28. Howard, op. cit., pp. 52 & 53.

29. Giedion, op. cit., pp. 789–793.

30. Le Corbusier. (1971). op. cit., pp. 159–178.

31. Le Corbusier. (2008). *Towards an Architecture*, translated by John Goodman. London: Frances Lincoln Ltd. pp. 214–215.

32. Kostof, op. cit., pp. 209–211.

33. Le Corbusier. (1967). *The Radiant City*, translated by Pamela Knight, Eleanor Levieux and Derek Coltman. London: Faber and Faber.

34. Colin Rowe and Fred Koetter. (1983). *Collage City*. London: MIT Press.

35. Kostof, op. cit., pp. 276–277.

36. Volker M. Welter. (2002). *Biopolis: Patrick Geddes and the City of Life*. Cambridge, MA: MIT Press. pp. 60–66.

37. McHarg, op. cit.

38. McHarg, Ibid, pp. 7–17.

39. Elizabeth Plater-Zyberk, Gianni Longo, Peter J. Hetzel, Robert Davis, Andres Duany, and Elizabeth Plater-Zyberk (Firm). (1999). *The Lexicon of New Urbanism*. Miami: Duany Plater-Zyberk Sect A 4.1-4.2. & Co. and Andres Duany, Elizabeth Plater-Zyberk and Jeff Speck. (2008). *Smart Growth Manual*. London: McGraw Hill.

40. Mumford, op. cit., pp. 347–350 and Kostof, op. cit., p. 60.

41. Spiro Kostof. (1991). *The City Assembled – The Elements of Urban Form Through History*. London: Thames and Hudson. pp. 213–214.

42. Mumford, op. cit., p. 349.

43. Mumford, Ibid, pp. 386–391 and Giedion, op. cit., pp. 143–144.

44. Kostof (CS), op. cit., p. 256.

45. Kostof (CS), Ibid, pp. 215–216 and Mumford, op. cit., pp. 345–347.

46. Ibid, p. 230 and Ibid, p. 388.

47. Giedion, op. cit., pp. 762–765.

48. Ibid, p. 775.

49. Sitte, op. cit.

50. George R. Collins and Christiane Crasemann Collins. (1986). *Camillo Sitte: The Birth of Modern City Planning*. New York: Rizzoli. pp. 78–82.

51. Le Corbusier. (1971). op. cit., pp. 11–18.

52. Nan Ellin. (1999). *Postmodern Urbanism*. New York: Princeton Architectural Press.

53. Joseph Stubben. (1907). *Der Stadbau*. Stuttgart: A. Kröner.

54. Jacobs, op. cit., pp. 5–115.

55. Ibid. p. 37.

56. Donald Appleyard. (1981). *Livable Streets*. Berkeley: University of California Press.

57. Bernard Rudofsky. (1969). *Streets for People – A Primer for Americans*. Garden City: Doubleday & Company.

58. Allan B. Jacobs. (1993). *Great Streets*. Cambridge, MA: MIT Press.

59. Andres Duany, Elizabeth Plater-Zyberk, and Robert Alminana. (2003). *The New Civic Art*. New York: Rizzoli.

60. Chicago Department of Transportation. (2013). *Complete Streets Chicago*. Chicago: Chicago Department of Transportation.

61. U.K. Department for Transport. (2007). *Manual for Streets*. London: Thomas Telford.

Chapter Two
The City Section

The use of a large-scale section through a city to investigate qualities and characteristics of the specific urban condition and urban form in general has numerous benefits. The large-scale section reveals vertical structure, basic sectional relationships, the interplay between topography and built form, the scale of the city, the interaction between horizontal and vertical organisation and results in a more developed reading of a city. The vertical structure of a city highlights significant moments of variation in height, while reading this type of relationship shows how this dimension influences the city's spatial character or potentially identifies stages of development. Analysing planimetric urban grain is a valuable method of understanding an urban condition; supplemented with sectional information this analysis becomes spatial, building a more comprehensive understanding and important additional layers of knowledge. The tightly packed plan has a significantly different meaning when comprised of 3-storey buildings, rather than a cluster of towers. If one goal of urban analysis is to generate a clear picture of physical conditions, adding vertical information to large-scale investigations is a critical improvement.

Large-scale vertical relationships entered urban thinking with the work of Patrick Geddes. His use of a progressive scale relating topography and geographic context to forms of economic activity and human settlement introduced the notion of a vertical component to urban analysis. Geddes was pursuing a very particular set of ideas, which are too complex to be discussed in detail in the present inquiry. However, the concept that there was a relationship between the spatial configuration of human settlements and physical features of the local habitat and that these relationships were best communicated in a diagrammatic section has important implications for urban analysis.[1]

The transect diagram, usually referred to as the "Valley Section", was a diagram to communicate Geddes' idea that humans had a natural "ecological" relationship with their surroundings. Geddes believed that there was a natural progression from basic forms of subsistence to the most developed form of urban society. This is reflected in the ordering of the valley section diagram; showing mining taking place in the more elevated mountains, places without built objects for habitation, through the farmers' occupation of the agricultural plain with the small groupings of the town, culminating in the built-up city on the coast. The diagram illustrates Geddes' ideas about the relationship between the physical characteristics of a location, the natural economic occupation for that environment and the form of settlement most appropriate to this combination. These concepts are represented in visual notation using topography, building forms, plant types, tools and occupation names.[2]

The key ideas communicated in the valley section are: the visual representation of Geddes' concept that there is a link between habitat, occupation and settlement form, the presentation of a range of these linkages at various scales in a sequential order and as an interacting and connected whole. Most importantly the diagram proposes a spatial order to this structure of a human modified system of environments.

The linkage between locale, human activity and built form grew out of a complex belief system developed by Geddes, which considered humanities' relationship to life, at the core of which was a belief that the individual and communal were reconciled in the physical facts and the conceptual notions of settlement. Geddes believed that place, activity and culture grew out of and influenced each other, which if properly related result in a natural and balanced human settlement.[3]

Geddes developed the concepts in the valley section influenced by the enlightenment belief in progressive social evolution and the theory of his friend the biologist Charles Flauhault regarding plant association and social species.[4] Geddes ordered the valley section from mountain to coast, progressing through the purported phases of civilisation's development to establish his order as "natural" and to demonstrate the influence of each preceding grouping on the following set, ultimately leading to the final manifestation of culture, the city.[5] Geddes translated the idea of plant association in the valley section, providing a biological basis for his conception of an interconnected network of a settlement that formed an "ecological" system of human habitation across a large area.[6]

While the preceding is a limited summary of some of the major ideas contained in the valley section, of primary importance for this discussion is the spatialisation of these ideas in sectional form. The diagram places the vertical dimension at the forefront in the consideration of the spatial relationships being presented and makes clear that the discussion of human habitation requires the integrated reading of horizontal and vertical information. The diagram demonstrates that topographical variations in combination with human activity influence settlement forms. The sectional character of the diagram also portrays both the coverage and the scale of each type of settlement, which, while still a two-dimensional presentation, contains a different layer of information than plan diagrams. We read the vertical variation within each form of settlement, between the forms and the form against the landscape. In addition to this, while the precise nature of the sequence from mountain top to coastal city may be questioned, the diagram introduces the notion of an ordered progression of height from the dense urban context to less dense rural village. This suggestion that increased density results in increased vertical form as well as a growth in footprint can only be revealed through the sectional diagram. Geddes' valley section also introduces the idea that there is a vertical structure in the built environment; and proposes that vertical relationships are a significant aspect of conceptual models, that in discussing important relationships the vertical must be examined in tandem with the horizontal.

The most significant use of the transect concept in urban design is the New Urbanist deployment for the purposes of urban planning. Andres Duany, of the Miami-based architecture and planning firm, Duany Plater-Zyberk, proposed the use of a transect-based model for generating meaningful relationships in urban planning. The New Urbanist transect is based on a progression from rural to urban, structuring the built environment with a series of six zones of use and density characteristics. The first zone, T1 the Rural Preserve, is an area that is undeveloped due to unsuitability or because it is valued as wilderness. The next zone, T2, is the Rural Reserve; areas where development is limited by the productive use of the land for agriculture, forestry or natural resource extraction. This is followed by zone T3, the Sub-Urban, comprised predominantly of low-rise residential and single-use commercial development. Adjacent to this is zone T4, the General Urban zone, which is made up of denser urban fabric, fundamentally residential in character, but with a wide variety of building forms, from single-family to multi-storey apartment buildings. Moving further in is zone T5, the Urban Centre, which is high density, with residential, retail and commercial mixed together in multi-storey buildings in a tight street pattern. The final zone in the classification system is zone T6, the Urban Core, which has the highest density level, with a mix of uses and civic buildings; the cultural, political and social heart of the city and its region.[7] The system is designed to organise the elements of urban form; plot size, buildings, land use, street network, etc., to produce a coherent urban environment.[8]

Duany argues that the transect is a natural law[9] and that it can be used as a model for organising the built environment into "contextually resonant natural and human environments".[10] The New Urbanists believe that the transect can be used to align human habitation with environmental conditions.[11] Another potent aspect of the New Urbanist conception of the transect is the model's support of "immersive environments", places where all the physical components work together to form a coherent and legible environment.[12] The clarity of the New Urbanist transect and its appeal to a common-sense understanding of how density and urbanism work make it a powerful tool for urbanists.

The New Urbanist transect focuses the use of sectional thinking in a way familiar to architects and designers, using sectional conventions to communicate spatial relationships on an urban scale. While the New Urbanist transect is a diagram of a proposed ideal, a model of how cities should be configured, it also suggests the possibility of using sectional information to understand how cities are actually constituted. The transect concept of reading the distinctions between sectors and recognising both the plan and sectional density of areas within an urban continuum, highlights a seemingly obvious concept, that the spatial character of an urban district and its relationship to other districts has a significant impact on the quality of urban experience. The establishment of a classification method for these changes and the emphasis on using this system to build coherent urban structures point out the need for the analysis of urban form and provides a possible framework for this analysis.

The large-scale city sections included in this book provide a means of examining a wide range of urban forms from cities across the world. The approach used to analyse these cities is not taken directly from the New Urbanist transect model, but it has been influenced by this model. The concept of using city-wide sections to reveal information about a city is an extension of the street section methodology and similarly pursues a more developed understanding through the careful reading of sectional information and comparative analysis. This investigation of vertical data reveals significant knowledge about specific cities, as well as urban forms in a general sense. The information gained has a very narrow focus, but makes a valuable contribution to urban understanding.

City types

To frame the following discussion regarding the use of large-scale city sections, a loose set of city morphology types is outlined as follows: the organic city, the labyrinth city, the 18th-century planned city, the baroque city and the grid city. These terms have been selected because most cities can be broadly identified with one of these terms and they are commonly and widely used to discuss the characteristics of urban form. These terms are by no means definitive or exclusive, nor do they cover all cities; they do however provide a simple form of classification to allow broad comparisons to be made.

The organic city form is found throughout the world and is characterised by the irregular organisation and spatial complexity derived from unplanned growth over an extended period of time. Many cities with this form are heavily influenced by the interaction between built form and natural features.

The labyrinth city is typically associated with Islamic culture and the careful consideration of sacred concerns in constructing the shared space of the city. The intensely controlled nature of this urban form is often lost in the rich visual and spatial quality of the labyrinth city. This city form is protective, serving both the collective needs of fortification and the intimate needs of privacy.

The 18th-century planned city was a response to the density and limitations of the organic city in Europe, with the goal of bringing order to the chaotic, rapidly growing cities of mercantile Europe. The swift development for profit of large tracts of land was facilitated by organised and systematic planning, while also aligning with the cultural trends of enlightenment Europe; it both supported and was supported by a dramatic revision of capital formation and investment.

The baroque city was similarly a response to the medieval organic city, ostensibly based on aesthetic principles in pursuit of a more beautiful urban environment. It is clear that while the rhetoric of ordered beauty, balance and dignity did result in powerful visual and spatial qualities, the straight wide avenues radiating from monumental public spaces also clearly expressed the power and authority of centralised government.

Although the grid has played a role in urban form from Roman cities to imperial China, its most commonly recognised expression is as an instrument of colonial occupation and organisation. The grid's uniformity and extendibility allowed rapid and legible settlement to take place, providing a clear lattice which established control over an unruly locale and which could be filled in over time as needed.

To demonstrate the analytical approach, a city representative of each type outlined above is examined using a large-scale city section. Each specific city is studied for its particular sectional characteristics and the spatial qualities which can be interpreted from examining the section and the plan together. The location for the city-wide section for each city has been selected in relation to the organisational structure of the city in an effort to reveal key vertical information. The section for each city has been drawn to cover the city as widely as possible, cutting through the significant areas and extending through major sectional transitions whenever possible. Seeing each city type with a comparable city-wide section allows similarities and differences to be uncovered and contributes to a broader understanding of city form and space.

Descriptive analysis using city sections

Genoa was selected as an example of the organic city type as its historic core contains the features typical of the organic urban form. The city's development from a small fishing village into a major port, with a trading network throughout the Mediterranean Sea, resulted in prosperity and a strong commercial society. This economic activity took place in the context of a fractious political environment, with the constant need for security. Genoa grew concentrically from the harbour, in a densely packed, unplanned pattern, constrained by successive sets of defensive walls and ultimately the hills surrounding the city. This pattern of growth can be readily perceived by studying the plan of the city. What is not revealed by the plan is the rich interplay between the topography and the built city, or the dramatic verticality of the city. The layers of space that stack up next to each other in this historic city are a consequence of the density forced by the city walls and the response to the topographical features. Steep hills are occupied, while the valley between is filled with multi-storey blocks.

The section through Genoa (fig. 2.1) shows this layering of built form and the response to the topography. Another aspect revealed by the section is the very strong vertical space of the streets in the historic core. Numerous examples of organic fabric share Genoa's density and the narrowness and irregular street

0 100 250 500 1000m

2.1
Genoa City Section

pattern, which is obvious in the city plan, but the singular quality of Genoa's streets is revealed by the section. Tall, 6–7-storey buildings placed with literally an arm's length separating them, creating a powerful spatial consequence. These steep slots of space shown in the section define Genoa's vertical structure as closely packed with high thin buildings layered on increasingly steep hills rising from the water's edge. This verticality and the tightness of the vertical grain result in a small-scale city, with intimate streets and predominantly compact open spaces. The section reads as primarily solid; with minimal circulation spaces into a mass of built form out of which emerges the occasional opening of still tall public space related to the steeple or dome of a church. Reading the plan together with the section of Genoa tells a more complicated story and produces a clearer image of the space, the density of the fabric and the delicacy of its buildings. Being able to see the buildings moving up the hillside, or squeezed together to form a canyon, illustrates the complexity of Genovese space, with its knots of mass and slices of light. Examining this organic city with the section reveals the depth and intricacy of space and form resulting from organic growth. Taken together the plan and section produce an understanding of the urbanism of accretion, accommodation, time and a strong culture.

Examining the space of Genoa with a large-scale section highlights the unique spatial character of the city. The dramatic form and the space of the city, created by the small winding streets and powerful effects of light and dark, generates a distinctive urban environment. Analysing the section and the plan shows the impact of the irregular network, pushed and pulled by topography to produce a layered and intertwined structure. The technical considerations and the need to mitigate the effects of the hot sun clearly played a role in the configuration of the city and particularly in the architectural response, but it is also apparent that the major factor was the limited area and the need for security. This resulted in the occupation of every usable piece of ground in each successive layer within the protective enclosure; causing even sites with challenging slopes to be exploited. The lack of overall regulation and the pressures of the restricted territory have produced a distinctive urban form, with a powerful spatial quality, of local intimate spaces that have a collective sensibility, public places of active communal and commercial exchange.

The Moroccan city of Fès was selected to discuss the labyrinth city form because as a noted centre of Islamic culture it is a strong example of how the focus on protective form results in an intricate maze-like city. Fès was founded as two walled cities, later joined together and expanded and was an important centre for Islamic scholarship, due to the presence of the University of Al-Qarawiyyin. A major area of Islamic legal scholarship is the study of the rules governing the construction of buildings and issues associated with this activity. These rules result from the interpretation of the prophet Mohammed's practices, written records of his words and most importantly the Quran.[13] This body of laws sets out the responsibilities and rights for those building, first and foremost in relation to immediate neighbours, but also within the community at large. Issues ranging from the control of shared public space, to the management of resources, such as sewage or water, are subject to a sacred concern, with the goal being a just and morally sound communal city. A unique feature of Islamic society is the focus on family and the place of the family as the primary religious unit in the religious community. As a consequence of this and a conception of privacy that holds the intimate spaces of the household as sacred sanctuary, the Islamic city is a collection of internally focused modules that gather together to form the fabric of the city. Fès exemplifies this with its dense clusters of walled houses, which form tight, intimate public passages, covered commercial arcades that form a protective layer around mosques and madrasas and very limited open public space.[14]

The large scale section of Fès (fig. 2.2) reveals the basic make up of the city form, a dense continuous mass finely inscribed with delicate vertical incisions. Fès

0 100 250 500 1000m

2.2
Fès City Section

is a horizontal city, consisting of predominantly tight, vertically oriented buildings 3 storeys high, with access spaces squeezed between their walls. The circulation spaces are small and thin, but are relatively low, reading in section as shallow cuts, not deep cracks. The horizontal nature of the city is reinforced by the essentially flat topography. Located on a plain below the Middle Atlas Mountains, the city does not respond to major topographic variations in height, but spreads evenly across the plain, with most of the river flowing through it covered by urban fabric. The relative uniformity of the topography contributes to the horizontal character of the city. The scale of Fès is tight and fundamentally domestic, although it reads as a dense space, the limited height and the little spaces cut into the mass, create a finely grained scale. The scale of the city is the result of many small units being packed together to form a whole. The dominance of 3-storey buildings provides little spatial punctuation in the section of Fès, accentuating the uniform nature of the city. Although there is some vertical variation, this is suppressed in the overall horizontal nature of Fès. While the section shows some open spaces at the edges, the historic core has only thin slots cut into the body of the city.

The use of the large-scale section to examine the space of Fès points out the specific spatial quality of this labyrinth city. The consistency of the form and the scale of the city, coupled with the delicacy of the spaces between buildings, emphasises the intimacy of the city. In conjunction with information provided by the plan, the section reveals the subtlety of the spatial structure, showing the equivalence of the constituent parts on the macro scale and the dominance of enclosed space at the micro scale. There is no doubt that material considerations, such as masonry construction and solar protection, played a role in generating a low rise densely packed urban form; however, it is clear that religious belief in both the conception and the regulation of architecture and community had the most profound impact on the city of Fès. The spatial form evidenced in the section shows the dominance of interior space, while the plan shows the clustering of mass around controllable points of access; both underlining the importance of the private space of the family household and the essentially protective nature of the labyrinth form of Islamic cities.

2.3
Glasgow City Section

Glasgow exemplifies the 18th-century planned city because of its history of using enlightenment ideas in the attempt to control the growth caused by the dramatic increase in the commercial activity of the period.[15] Beginning in the early 18th century laws regulating trade, efforts to improve sanitary conditions, along with planned public buildings and rectilinear streets, were used with the intention of establishing a planned and controlled basis for the growth of Glasgow.[16] Although Glasgow's initial urban form was typical of medieval Scottish settlements,[17] with the city formed along a spine of the high street from the cathedral downhill to the ford of the river, the 18th-century city grew in the opposite direction, spreading from the river's edge uphill and west. Glasgow's grid-iron street pattern, limestone tenements and commercial blocks create a regular and legible urban fabric. The spatial quality of the city reflects the order of the grid, with strong even street frontages, that create contained readable street volumes. Although occupied with buildings dating from the 18th-century to the present, the 18th-century framework has produced a predominantly mid-level city, with buildings forming discrete blocks with permeable bases, resulting in active streets. This gives the public space of Glasgow a formal and regular character.

The section through the city of Glasgow (fig. 2.3) illustrates the effects of the geometric plan, with the evenness of the grid showing in the massing of the blocks and the uniform spacing of the streets giving the city a predominantly horizontal quality. What is also clear from the section is the vertical structure of Glasgow, as the building forms maintain a stable relationship to each other and the city at large. Glasgow's vertical structure is fundamentally constant and ordered, defined by the careful relationship between the mass of building and the open space of the street.

0 100 250 500   1000m

The section also exposes the city's specific interaction with topography. Glasgow's buildings maintain a rough vertical datum, with the buildings on the river being the tallest, and as the city moves uphill building height reduces. This creates a unique spatial experience as the city lowers as one moves uphill away from the river. The spatial discipline of the datum coupled with the controlled geometry of the grid generates the strong horizontal character of the city. The section shows that Glasgow has a moderate scale with a clear understandable fabric of intermediate size. The scale is produced by the uniformity of the grid, the walled streets formed by the perimeter blocks, the relationship to the topography and the medium height of the buildings. The proportion of the building mass to the open space of the street and the overall horizontal orientation creates a physically comfortable scale, in which even the taller buildings have a measured quality, which readily relates to the human body.

Glasgow's originally uniform fabric was punctuated by landmark buildings such as churches or civic institutions; this is less evident in the city today. The city-wide section of Glasgow illustrates the regularity of the city's spatial structure, with some vertical variation caused by more recent multi-storey buildings; however, it is difficult to classify this as spatial punctuation. Contemporary Glasgow is characterised by the evenness of its built form, with limited spatially distinct moments. It is possible to view this as a result of the underlying control of the geometry of the 18th-century conception of the city which was fulfilled in the 19th century and survived the impact of 20th-century interventions.

Using the large-scale section to examine Glasgow reveals the composed and human urban space of the 18th-century framework. With the vertical information in the section, the three dimensional qualities of the regular organisation can be interpreted. The height and mass of the buildings readable in the section show the containment of the streets and the careful proportion of the city form. The even spacing, consistent relationship of building height to topography, balanced composition and humane scale exposed by the city-wide section of Glasgow is the consequence of its 18th-century planning, tied to the enlightenment belief that reason can be used to regulate human activity for the purpose of improving society and material reality.

Because of the sustained application of baroque principles as well as some of the most coherent applications, Paris has been used to examine the baroque city type. Beginning at the end of the 16th century and continuing until the middle of the 19th century, baroque city planning ideas were practised in Paris. The earliest examples were insertions in the medieval fabric, while later additions took advantage of the city's expansion, baroque planning culminated in Haussmann's vast programme of complete transformation.[18] One of the earliest examples, the Place Royale (now Place des Vosges) of 1605–12, used renaissance concepts of order, harmony and balance in the service of a political agenda, asserting the centrality of royal power. This was one of a programme of works to improve Paris, highlighting its significance as the capital and place of royal residence.[19] Although Louis XIV left Paris to create another major baroque composition at Versailles, his reign still saw major baroque additions to Paris. From the Place des Victoires and Place Vendôme, to the new boulevards built on land reclaimed from the removal of city walls, Paris continued to be altered and extended in the baroque manner.[20] The final and most extensive baroque transformation of Paris took place in the mid 19th century, when Haussmann used baroque design principles to reconfigure Paris and create a coherent urban plan that not only expressed power, but demonstrated its effectiveness. The city that resulted from the application of baroque aesthetics is one of vistas, monumental focal points, landscaped streets and geometrically figured public spaces. Paris is a city shaped by the intention of making the public realm a place of light, order and gracious scale. Grand public buildings with open, tree-lined streets laid out in radiating, geometric patterns communicate the hierarchical structure of French society of this era. The transformation from king to emperor changed the economy of power very little, as centralised national authority still controlled France.[21]

Examining Paris with a large-scale section does not reveal the defining features of baroque city planning, as these are more readily perceived in plan. The features of baroque design which are so striking in plan, diagonal avenues, geometric space and symmetrical building forms are not expressed in section. What the section illustrates is the size of the buildings in relation to the un-built spaces and the vertical structure of the city. What can be seen in section is the general horizontal character of the city and the generous quality of the open space framed by the building mass. While the section shows some areas of more density, overall Paris has a great deal of open space, with many instances of wide spacing through buildings. The section also reveals large volumes of space that occur in the baroque avenues, with the typical 6-storey Parisian blocks on either side containing a wide horizontally oriented space. The topography of Paris is relatively flat, giving the city a horizontal quality, with the few elevated pieces of the city providing notable exceptions. This flat topography contributes to the effectiveness of the baroque vistas, allowing long-view corridors, unimpeded by a rising ground plane, to radiate out from a central point in numerous directions, reinforcing the baroque pursuit of expressing the concept of infinite space.[22]

The city section of Paris (fig. 2.4) presents a city of spaciousness, with a generous scale. The proportion of the building mass to the open spaces creates an open quality, but the size of the buildings also generates a sense of formality and weight. The scale is not immense and overpowering, but it is substantial, suggesting permanence and continuity. The spatial punctuation in section comes from the large clear spaces, with the space between the buildings communicating the gracious nature of the city form. The spatial accents arranged in plan translate in section as volumes framed by uniform building masses.

Reading the space of Paris through plan and section allows the dignified scale of the city to be perceived. The openness and grace of both public spaces and the streets is apparent, as are the continuous, uniform and ample building forms. The section clarifies the importance of the ordered relationships so valued by

0 100 250 500   1000m

2.4
Paris City Section

baroque urban thinking, by illustrating the continuity of the urban form and the balance between space and mass. While the full drama of the geometric plan motifs of baroque urban design can never be fully appreciated in two-dimensional drawings, the volume and scale revealed in the section help generate a sense of the monumental space of Paris.

Chicago is a prime example of the urban form that results from the application of a grid. Chicago's grid was initially applied as a tool for regulating nature, but ultimately was used as a device for organising land development for economic benefit. Beginning at the edge of Lake Michigan and spreading west, successive waves of growth were absorbed by the expandable mechanism of the grid. The grid's main features (extendibility, flexibility, uniformity, connectivity and readability)[23] all made the grid an effective means of dividing new areas of land for speculative development, structuring the explosive physical growth of Chicago. Initially Chicago's grid was filled with low wooden buildings, but after the fire in 1871 and the demands of continued growth, experimentation in structural engineering and building technologies ultimately led to the skyscraper and Chicago's grid took on a vertical dimension.[24] It is tempting to see the skyscraper as the embodiment of the grid's extendibility in vertical form. The urban form that was generated by the vast spreading horizontal grid centred on a high rise core was a new conception of urbanism, with immense impact on urban thinking and cities around the world. Chicago's incredible verticality, wide streets and the regular rhythm of its blocks creates a very particular urban quality. The streets are vertical, but they are not dark and packed, as the wide roadway and ample sidewalks provide a sense of openness, unlike the tight canyons of some cities.

The vertical structure revealed by the large-scale section of Chicago (fig. 2.5) reflects the city's pattern of growth, the impacts of location and the insertions of transportation infrastructure. The eastern edge of the section is occupied by a flat area of parkland, between the waterfront and the core of tall buildings. The towers are clustered between this waterfront park and the channel of the Chicago River. Immediately west of the river is a mixed layer of towers and mid-level buildings contained by the river to the east and the below grade expressway to the west.

The City Section

Moving further west from the expressway is an area of 6–8-storey buildings that transition to the 1–3-storey buildings that extend to the city's edge. The section shows the height of Chicago's core and the points of transition to the horizontal fabric that constitutes the majority of the city, revealing both the height of the buildings and the sectional elements that structure these changes. These minor topographic variations are important urban thresholds, demonstrating the significance of the relationship between topography and built form that is made apparent by the section. The section provides a vivid, graphic portrayal of the dramatic juxtaposition of the vertical thrust of the densely packed downtown against the extreme horizontality created by the flat topography and the regularity of the low- and mid-level grid of buildings stretching to the west. It is this remarkable verticality set within a vast flatness that gives Chicago its unique spatial identity. Another spatial characteristic exposed by the sectional analysis is the openness of Chicago's urban form. The section shows the way in which the uniformity and size of street spaces created by the grid form and set in a flat topography creates an open, spacious urban construct. The scale of Chicago made evident in the section is immense, a consequence of the giant scale of the core and the vast scale of the miles of low buildings that spread to the west. Both the large size of the centre and the low scale of the fabric share the wide street spaces of the grid, creating a proportion of open space to building mass that emphasises a large scale, one vertical, the other horizontal. Between the towers, tall, wide volumes express a verticality that is not constrained or squeezed. In the miles of 1–3-storey buildings the same wide street spaces communicate a broad extendable, horizontal scale.

0 100 250   500   1000m

2.5
Chicago City Section

Chicago's spatial punctuation is reserved for the spike at its centre. Rising against the flat lake to the east and the low matt of buildings to the west, this grouping of high buildings dramatically marks the economic, cultural and physical heart of the city. This punctuation and its significance for the city are made clear in the section.

The information provided by examining Chicago using a large-scale plan and section makes explicit the effects of the grid as an organising device. The simplicity and directness of the grid supplies a frictionless operability, allowing rapid identification and registration. Large areas of land can be organised quickly into a readily communicable system of ownership. The neutrality and uniformity of the grid are evident in Chicago's spatial structure, with its large area of coverage and the manner in which the increment of its grid accommodates both the vertical and the horizontal. The grid's qualities can also be noticed in the openness generated by the proportion of street space and building mass and sense of scale this creates; vertical and large with civic impact in the tall core and relaxed, without boundaries in the horizontal expanse surrounding the centre. Chicago is identified as big, broad and robust; its grid form contributes a great deal to this perception.

By examining the five cities above with the section, the spatial characteristics of the specific city and to some degree each basic type of city can be more thoroughly understood. The section provides vertical data which shows how high buildings are, as well as how close together they are, from this the room of the street can be comprehended, or the lack of spatial definition can be seen. By looking at the whole city, the typical massing and pattern of openness can be discovered. Unique points of transition can be noted and the relationship between distinct areas revealed. Because the proportion of buildings and of open space is represented, the scale of a city can be determined. This and other information is essential to understanding the physical configuration of a city, contributing to a more complete urban reading. Without the vertical dimension shown in a section, significant aspects of an urban form are missing and critical spatial properties are difficult or impossible to determine. In addition to the expansion of knowledge in relation to individual cities, broader information regarding city type or urban form in general can be developed. In examining Chicago the module of its grid and spacing of building illustrates the impact of the most basic regulatory mechanisms and also suggests how the careful modulation of these can be used to shape spatial qualities, or how possible insertions will affect wider spatial structures. This knowledge extends the understanding of how grid systems affect urban contexts, providing additional clues about how cities work. Comparing the large-scale sections of two cities can also lead to valuable knowledge, for example contrasting Glasgow to Chicago and investigating the similarities and differences makes apparent useful data about both cities' physical form and spatial character. The vertical variation created by Glasgow's topography is contrasted with Chicago's flatness, revealing how the grid organises form and space in response; Glasgow's contained form reinforced by rising topography and a datum of building mass, while Chicago's spread responds to the flat expansion of the prairie away from the lake. This comparison illustrates the grid's capacity to both define and to expand, demonstrating the systematic basis of the grid and the variations of spatial rhythm that can result. Genoa's tight vertical streets can be scrutinised with the grand scale of the Parisian avenue, the intimacy of one placed in context by the monumentality of the other. Both virtues and limitations are exposed and the possibilities of various configurations can be considered. The sections can indicate how light and mass work together at an urban scale to form coherent spaces or how existing urban situations that do not work might be revised. Examining urban form with city-wide sections to explore individual conditions, typological character, underlying urban structures and wider urban principles, makes an important contribution to building a deeper and more fully rounded body of knowledge about cities. It provides a clear and flexible means of investigating the physical aspects of cities at the macro scale. While the physical configuration of cities is a narrow portion of a wide and complex range of factors, the direct impact this has on how cities are used and experienced, emphasises the importance of understanding this material and the value of all additional knowledge that can be gathered.

Notes

1. Patrick Geddes. (1968). *Cities in Evolution*. London: Ernest Benn Ltd.
2. Volker M. Welter. (2002). *Biopolis: Patrick Geddes and the City of Life*. Cambridge, MA: MIT Press. p. 60.

3. Ibid, pp. 31–34.

4. Ibid, pp. 61–62.

5. Ibid, p. 64.

6. Ibid, p. 70.

7. Elizabeth Plater-Zyberk, Gianni Longo, Peter J. Hetzel, Robert Davis, Andres Duany, and Elizabeth Plater-Zyberk (Firm). (1999). *The Lexicon of New Urbanism*. Miami: Duany Plater-Zyberk & Co. Sect A 4.1-4.2.

8. Andres Duany, Elizabeth Plater-Zyberk and Jeff Speck. (2008). *Smart Growth Manual*. London: McGraw Hill. p.1.4 and *Ibid,* pp. A4.1–A4.2.

9. Andres Duany. (2002). Introduction to the Special Issue: The Transect, *Journal of Urban Design,* 7 (3), p. 253.

10. Ibid, p. 255.

11. Charles C. Bohl and Elizabeth Plater-Zyberk. (2006). Building Community across the Rural-to-Urban Transect [The Transect]. *Places*. 18 (1), p. 8.

12. Ibid, p. 9 and Emily Talen. (2006). Help for Urban Planning: The Transect Strategy. *Journal of Urban Design*. 7 (3), p. 294.

13. Besim Selim Hakim. (1986). *Arabic-Islamic Cities – Building and Planning Principles*. London: Kegan Paul. p. 16.

14. Stafano Bianca. (2000). *Urban Form in the Arab World – Past and Present*. London: Thames and Hudson. pp. 34–40.

15. Andor Gomme and David Walker. (1987). *Architecture of Glasgow*. London: Lund Humphries.

16. Tom M. Devine and Gordon Jackson. eds. (1995). *Glasgow: Beginnings to 1830*. Manchester: Manchester University Press. p. 114.

17. Ibid, p. 22.

18. Lewis Mumford. (1961). *The City In History.* London: Secker & Warburg. pp. 653–682 & 765–822.

19. Leonardo Benevolo. (1980). *The History of the City*, translated by Geoffrey Culverwell. London: Scholar Press. p. 655.

20. Ibid, pp. 664–666.

21. Spiro Kostof. (1991). *The City Shaped – Urban Patterns and Meanings Through History*. London: Thames and Hudson. p. 216.

22. Mumford, op. cit. pp. 386–391.

23. Kostof, op. cit. p. 116.

24. "Chicago." *Encyclopædia Britannica. Encyclopædia Britannica Online.* Encyclopædia Britannica, Inc., 2013. Web. 12 Aug. 2013. <http://original.search.eb.com/eb/article-61249>.

Chapter Three
The Street

Although human settlement occurs without streets it is possible to suggest that the street is the fundamental "city" element, the building block of cities. The city can be defined as a physical, social, economic and political entity that grows out of the shared civic conception that individual actions must be moderated for the benefit of the community. If cities are the largest manifestation of this civil understanding, then the street is the physical manifestation of this idea. The street is a delineated area for common use, framed by a collection of individual structures, whose purpose is to serve the function of circulation and exchange; social and material. The process through which streets are determined has taken innumerable forms throughout history, from the carefully planned to the seemingly arbitrary; however, they all begin with an agreement that individual privileges are limited for social benefit in a particularly defined concrete space.[1] A cluster of buildings owned by separate individuals without a recognised public space, which everyone can use, is a settlement, but not a town or urban entity. This is not to deny the definition of community to those places without a defined public space; it is to assert that the physical recognition of the shared, communal place is essential to the definition of town or city. Possibly this is fundamentally an issue of scale. When those sharing a territory belong to a single family or are small enough in number that social intimacy is strong enough to regulate behaviour, the formal recognition of the civic may not be necessary. However, when the size and make-up of the group expand beyond this, communal understanding is required and the definition of public space is necessary. Making clear to everyone what space they are allowed to move in and through freely and where individual private space begins.[2] This foundational nature of the street, coupled with the fact that physically without the street cities could not exist, places the street at the centre of all urban discussions.[3] From the earliest examples of urban design in Europe, through the renaissance, the baroque period, the late 19th-century advocacy for medieval patterns and even in the Modernist attempts to refashion the Street, the design of streets has been at the heart of urban design.

In addition to the strictly utilitarian and physical role that streets play, the street is also a social instrument. The street's practical provision also facilitates social engagement at many levels. Streets provide the place to interact; with those we know and those we don't. From commercial exchange, arranged entertainment, accidental meeting, to people watching,[4] the use of streets for social interaction and the importance of streets in creating a vital community has been noted by numerous authors, forming a major branch of urban design theory and research. While the scope of this book does not allow a complete review of this literature, the following summary illustrates the significance of this aspect of the street for those examining and designing streets.

Most famously Jane Jacobs made lengthy and persuasive arguments for the place of the street in the communal life of city residents. Stating that the street acted as a social glue, with people understanding complex layers of information regarding behaviour and communication, and the street being a critical mechanism of social regulation.[5] In his book, *Streets for People*, Bernard Rudofsky argues that the street is the historical stage for the mundane and the remarkable, the personal and the communal.[6] Donald Appleyard's research for *Livable Streets* pointed to the important role that the space of the street played in the social life of communities, demonstrating how vehicular traffic impacted social interaction on streets and how these impacts affected people's perceptions about the street they lived on and their sense of community.[7] Another important early contribution to the growing understanding of the street's social value was *Public Streets for Public Use,* this collection of essays makes the case that streets are a communal asset, and that quality of life is directly affected by the way streets support social exchange.[8] Jan Gehl's work in Copenhagen and the resulting publications detail the way public spaces and streets can provide for social interaction. Gehl's analysis of how sight, sound and communication affect social exchange and how the opportunity for social activity creates a place of community, was supported by extensive quantitative research over many years.[9] Gehl's careful analysis of social behaviour resulted in the classification of "outdoor activities", a range of social contact types and the importance of social interaction to people and society. Working with this information the research went on to describe how the physical characteristics of a public space helped or inhibited the various types of social exchange and outlined strategies for designing spaces which support social interaction.[10] A major concern for all these books is to highlight the damage vehicular traffic causes to streets and an insistence that focusing on how people use streets for social interaction is critical to improving urban spaces. These books and many more have helped develop a consensus that streets are not solely functional, that the previous focus on vehicular concerns in the design of streets is detrimental to cities and that streets should be designed to accommodate everyone who uses them. This limited discussion of work examining the social aspects of streets is not intended to be comprehensive; this is not the purpose of the book, but merely meant to outline the development of contemporary urban thinking and the significance given to the street and its examination.

Given the street's importance for urban design, a large body of material has been developed to analyse streets and to provide guidance for their design to both design professionals and to communities. These range from advocacy proposals put forward by urban designers and architects, best practice guidelines from professional bodies, policy documents implemented by government bodies, to research and books produced by academics. Particularly relevant to this book are attempts to examine and define streets, to build an understanding of the physical aspects of the street as an urban element.

Since the 1960's, the realisation that the life of cities was in large part dependent upon the life of streets has been an important concept in urban theory.[11] A slow process of rethinking the street has been taking place, with an increase in efforts by a variety of urban advocates to influence policy makers and the general public. The list of these groups is extensive, and the following are just a few examples for the purpose of illustrating the role they have played and continue to play in the formulation of street design.

Advocacy

One of the leading advocates for changing government policy regarding a wide variety of issues related to the built environment in the U.S. is Smart Growth America. This collection of groups, from specific issue advocates to industry groups, works to protect and improve the physical environment at the national, state and local levels in the U.S. and has been a strong voice for changing the approach to development policy in the United States. The organisation campaigns for development that preserves resources and places social value above economic benefit.[12] One example of the organisation's activities is the National Complete Streets Coalition (NCSC). The goal of Complete Streets is to create streets that provide a comprehensive and integrated transportation network. The coalition argues for such policies at all levels of government and provides resources for those pursuing the implementation of Complete Streets policies. These policies are predicated on the belief that streets which are full of people engaged in a wide variety of activities create a more vibrant community than the monotonous, loud, dirty and frequently dangerous streets dominated by vehicular traffic. Complete Streets' policy establishes planning, design and management guidelines that aim to provide equally efficient and safe transportation resources for everyone: pedestrians, bicyclists, mass transit users, private vehicles and commercial traffic. By placing the focus on an integrated and comprehensive system which gives equal value to all user groups in the community, these policies seek to manage resources efficiently to encourage a broad range of social activities in public space and to maximize social benefits for a community. The model legislation formulated by the NCSC brings together a group of policies and best practices compiled by practitioners and government bodies to formulate a coherent approach to planning and designing a transportation system for the full spectrum of user groups.[13] These advisory documents contain design parameters for the physical make-up of streets with guidance regarding sidewalks, bike paths, roadway width, intersection design and other elements.[14] The success in recent years by advocacy groups like the NCSC in creating changes, in government policy at all levels, new professional standards, revised attitudes from industry groups, and altered expectations from the general public, is remarkable and a positive step forward. This has resulted in a widening acknowledgement that streets are essential to social well being and that they require careful consideration and this has had important consequences for the discussion of street design.

Another important voice for revising street design is the Congress for New Urbanism. This organisation was founded by a group of architects and urban designers to promote alternatives to automobile-based development and has had an immense impact on the field of urban design. The limits of the current discussion preclude an in-depth exposition of the complete New Urbanist programme or the extensive literature surrounding it. What can be said is that this group has been extremely successful; with numerous aspects of their agenda being adopted by government bodies from various countries, significant influence in academic and professional circles, the generation of a large body of research and many real world examples.[15] In publications such as *The Lexicon of New Urbanism* and *Smart Growth Manual*, New Urbanist principles addressing the full range of planning issues are presented. Central to the New Urbanist position is the belief that development and planning policies that are based on single-use zoning and heavy automobile usage create poor environments for people, which are wasteful and destructive. The basic principles of New Urbanism are that the built environment should include:

- Liveable streets arranged in compact walkable blocks.
- A range of housing choices to serve people of diverse ages and income levels.

- Schools, stores and other nearby destinations reachable by walking, bicycling or transit service.
- An affirming, human-scaled public realm where appropriately designed buildings define and enliven streets and other public spaces.[16]

Much of the design approach is based on the careful examination of precedents, with numerous design principles modelled on historic places. The leading proponent of New Urbanism, Andres Duany, strongly advocates use of the transect as a method for organising design decisions, using the rural to urban transect to establish "a sequence of human habitats of increasing density and complexity, from rural hinterland to urban core".[17] Of most relevance to this discussion is the New Urbanist interest in the street, with detailed proposals for all aspects of street design. The books cover street networks, street configuration, physical parameters, streetscape, street frontage details and parking.[18] While there has been extensive criticism of New Urbanism for a purported historicist viewpoint, these street design proposals contain a great deal of valuable data about the physical components of streets and considerable understanding of how these components work together to form coherent public spaces. These books provide a wealth of useful information for the analysis and design of streets and warrant close study by all those interested in street design. Particularly relevant for this book are the analyses of street frontage and the use of sectional diagrams to classify frontage typology and define terminology. These diagrams are used to illustrate concepts regarding form and do not explicitly discuss spatial issues; however, they do point to the value of the section as a tool for examining and communicating important spatial information about streets.[19]

Professional expertise

Also contributing to discussions surrounding the design of streets are practitioner associations and organisations made up of government officials. These groups operate at various levels from the national to the local, and contribute both through advocacy and by providing expertise to members and consultation to interested parties, such as individuals or citizen groups. Organisations such as the American Association of State Highway and Transportation Officials or the Local Government Commission, campaign publicly, organise events and provide expertise to government officials involved in planning and development. Practitioner associations such as the Institute of Transport Engineers or the American Society of Landscape Architects play a similar role, providing expertise for their members, government bodies and the wider public, while also engaging in efforts to disseminate their positions as widely as possible. These groups are an important source of knowledge and generate interest in issues regarding the built environment.

As an organisation established to assist government officials involved in community development at the local level, the Local Government Commission (LGC) provides technical assistance, organising help, training, design services, publications and resource materials.[20] One programme established by the LGC is the Center for Livable Communities, whose mission is to help local officials in efforts to carry out "resource efficient local and regional land use planning".[21] The LGC has published a variety of books on the subject of neighbourhood design and sustainable communities. The fundamental principles of the LGC align with the New Urbanist agenda, advocating for dense mixed-use walkable neighbourhoods based on traditional models. The LGC's position on streets is outlined in *Street Design Guidelines for Healthy Neighbourhoods*.[22] The book is a short guide to the design of streets which can provide adequately for the range of users, and is based on the analysis of traditional neighbourhood streets from around the United States. The book classifies streets into six types and uses sectional diagrams to provide dimensions for roadways, planting strips, bike lanes and sidewalks. The diagrams also define the appropriate purpose and land use for the street types.[23]

An example of a practitioner association with a strong influence on the discussion of street design is the Institute of Transport Engineers (ITE). The ITE is one of the oldest and most established organisations dealing with transportation issues. Founded in 1930, it is a standards development organisation for the U.S. Department of Transportation and leading voice for the technical development of transportation resources.[24] This role and the ITE's dissemination of professional expertise and public awareness programmes place it at the heart of transportation efforts in the U.S. Policies and standards embraced by the ITE have a great deal of influence on professionals, government officials and policymakers. In 2010 the ITE in conjunction with the U.S. Federal Highway Administration, the U.S. Environmental Protection Agency and the Congress for the New Urbanism, produced the report *Designing Walkable Urban Thoroughfares: A Context Sensitive Approach*.[25] The manual is designed for professionals involved in the design of streets, presenting the principles of context sensitive and walkable streets, with design guidelines for achieving these type of streets. The guidelines in the manual give detailed information for the design of a range of street types; from general planning principles, to criteria and recommendations for streetsides, travelled ways and intersections.[26] The report is supported with visual material: photographs, tables, and plan and section diagrams; to clarify and expand the text. One of the goals of the document is to increase awareness of the flexibility in the standards contained in the American Association of State Highway and Transportation Officials' policy handbook, *Geometric Design of Highways and Streets*, known as the "Greenbook".[27] The "Greenbook" is the source of legal standards used in roadway legislation throughout the U.S. and as such influences all levels of road design from national to local. Another major goal of the context sensitive solutions method presented in the report is to establish a multi-disciplinary approach and community involvement in the planning process.[28] The adoption and dissemination of these principles and guidelines by the ITE is a significant development and reflects an increasing acceptance of arguments for street design which supports a full spectrum of users, reversing the previous focus on maximising road and street design for vehicles. This change in approach by the technical designers of streets has important consequences for streets and those who study and design them.

Government guidance

As government bodies control policies and legislation which regulates the construction and modification of streets, official government guidance documents for the design of streets are incredibly important in the discussion of street design.

There are numerous documents and reports produced by agencies at all levels, but for the purposes of this discussion two examples have been selected: the New York City Street Design Manual and the United Kingdom Dept. for Transport's *Manual for Streets*. The two documents cover very similar material, with many shared principles and contain comprehensive information regarding the design of streets, the obvious difference being the context. The N.Y.C. *Street Design Manual* references the range of streets specific to New York, while the U.K. Manual for Streets is intended primarily for those involved in the planning and design of residential streets.

The N.Y.C. *Street Design Manual* is intended to provide "policies and guidance to city agencies, design professionals, private developers and community groups for the improvement of streets."[29] The manual starts from the premise that the safety of all users is most important and that street design requires that the needs of users be treated equally, also stressing the community benefits that result from high quality street environments, such as economic gains, improvements in public health and increased social engagement.[30] After outlining the policy goals and the planning process,[31] the manual goes on to provide design guidelines for streets, the use of materials, guidance for lighting streets and information regarding the use of street furniture.[32] The document is predominantly text, with text-based tables and photographs of examples to support the descriptions in the text. The value of the manual for this conversation is the information supplied regarding the relationship between the accommodation of pedestrians, bicyclists and social activity and vehicular traffic. The manual allows the full range of design considerations to be reviewed for a range of urban situations, from dense commercial to strictly residential. While the inclusion of sectional diagrams would enhance the spatial analysis, the wide array of streets discussed and the collection of design options provides a useful resource for the analysis of streets and ultimately a valuable design tool.

The U.K. Dept. for Transport report, *Manual for Streets*, like many of the guidance documents discussed, begins with the recognition that streets play an important social role, demonstrating the assimilation of the research and academic thought from the field of urban design. Prior U.K. government research showed that much of the previous policy, regulation and design guidance often resulted in poor quality streets with numerous negative impacts.[33] The manual hopes to address these issues by providing a common reference resource for the planning and design of streets, which places all users and the social life of streets at the heart of the process.[34] The document is organised in three sections: Section A – Context and Process, Section B – Design Principles and Section C – Detailed Design Issues. Section A begins by setting out the goals and the main changes of approach being recommended. The manual is intended for use on the design of residential streets and discusses the importance of collaboration in the process.[35] Some of the most significant changes advocated are: placing pedestrians first, stressing the need for a collaborative process, recognition of the street as a place for social exchange and the promotion of inclusive environments.[36] In describing the context for the manual's recommendations, a summary of the history of road design is presented, highlighting the deficiencies of vehicle-dominated design thinking and the importance of high quality streets to the community.[37] The manual outlines the planning and design process, detailing the various stages and information typical for each stage, with a discussion of design codes and auditing processes; pointing out improvements to the outcomes if the recommendations are followed.[38]

Section B discusses the design principles underpinning the manual, describing organisational concepts, the connectivity and the permeability of street networks, the characteristics of walkable neighbourhoods and different street types.[39] This is followed by an outline of the value of high quality public space and its benefits.[40] Basic urban design principles are described, with a discussion of street dimensions and how design can affect social interaction.[41]

In Section C more detailed information is provided, beginning with a discussion of the requirements of various users, followed by street geometry recommendations to facilitate the full range of uses.[42] There is also a detailed discussion of the influence of street design factors on vehicle behaviour and the importance of minimising vehicle speeds in creating desirable community streets.[43] Also included is information regarding the requirements for parking bicycles, cars and motorcycles, with design guidance for accommodating parking while maintaining the visual quality and liveability of streets.[44] This is followed by detailed discussions of traffic signs, street furniture, materials and management issues and the impact of these on the perceptions and experiences of users.[45]

Again, as with the documents discussed previously, the *Manual for Streets* is a valuable tool for designers and urbanists. The manual summarises the current consensus of best practice for providing liveable, socially active streets, and, with the included design strategies and solutions, is a useful resource for understanding streets and the role they play in communities. Particularly valuable is the translation of general principles to the U.K. context, with the discussions specific to U.K. streets revealing the importance of careful adjustments to generic concepts. The manual also contains illustrations that can be helpful in the analysis of existing conditions or design proposals.

Academic resources

Another important source of information is academic research, with an increasing body of detailed literature being developed continuously. It is not the intention of this book to provide an exhaustive review of this literature, but to summarise two examples relevant to the specific discussions of the book. Both books contribute valuable insights to the understanding of urban streets and provide analytical methods for examining streets that are very useful.

Vikas Mehta's book, *The Street: A Quintessential Social Public Space*,[46] sets out an argument for the place of the street in the social life of a community and through careful observation and research of specific streets, develops a systematic description of social behaviour and the array of components that foster this behaviour. As well as providing both a thorough exposition of the street's role in social exchange and a summary of the history of the street, the book also examines environmental and ecological psychology and some aspects of human behaviour research, paying particular attention to territoriality and proxemics and social distance.[47] From this the book suggests that understanding human needs, both required and supplemental, can provide guidance for the design of sociable streets.[48]

Using direct observation, interviews and surveys, a large body of information was gathered about three streets in the Boston metropolitan area. The research was aimed at determining how people socialised, where they socialised and what mix of elements support this social activity.[49] Using the research data the streets were ranked by the amount of social activity taking place.[50] One of the core ideas of the book is a typology of social behaviour, with three classifications: passive sociability, fleeting sociability and enduring sociability. Passive sociability is described as being in a public place among other people without direct engagement. Fleeting sociability is classified as brief chance encounters between people who know each other in a limited way, such as neighbours or regular customers at local shops. Enduring sociability is defined as instances of longer social exchange between people who know each other well on a personal or communal level.[51] Mehta also points out that all these forms of social engagement are very important, playing a role in establishing social understanding in individuals and the social parameters of public places.[52]

Mehta continues by describing the various requirements needed to support the mix of these social behaviours, carefully analysing the street research to identify those factors which lead to sociable streets. These factors include a sense of safety, community, environmental comfort, physical comfort, practicality, environmental control, sensory pleasure and opportunity for social interaction.[53] Using the data gathered, each of these factors is examined, the physical characteristics described and the perception of the users explained.[54] Another aspect explored is the role of independently owned businesses in creating an identifiable place.[55] Also discussed in some detail is the influence of territorial behaviour. Outlining that territorial displays by businesses, the way users are able to modify these territories and how particular physical characteristics can influence territorial definition Mehta describes the role that the control of territory plays in creating sociable places and encouraging social interaction.[56]

Careful statistical analysis of eleven characteristics of the three streets allowed the influence of each characteristic to be determined, resulting in the groupings of some and the isolation of two into four factors.[57] This set of factors affecting social behaviour were defined as: factor one, the combination of those characteristics which are impacted by businesses and land use, factor two contains five physical attributes of the street with measured effects, factor three recognises the influence of seating provided by businesses and factor four counts identified community places.[58] Finally the four factors are described as representing land use qualities (factor one), physical qualities (factors two and three) and social qualities (factor four).[59] The research revealed that the mix of these four factors had a strong influence on the degree of sociability of specific locations on the three streets.[60] When all four factors are present that segment of the street is transformed from a circulation space to a social space.[61] From this analysis an objective means of measuring "place" is constructed, leading to the definition of three distinct qualities which contribute to the establishment of an identifiable place that has social meaning – continuity, adaptability and personalisation.[62] These three qualities are described in detail, accompanied by an argument that the creation of place that these qualities enable is critical to the social well being of city residents.

This is followed by a discussion of street culture, using an investigation into a street in India to illustrate possible changes and presents a set of guidelines for the planning, design and management of streets.[63] The guidelines propose that streets should be: viewed as gathering places, attractive to all users, provide community places, be economically diverse, offer sensory stimulation, allow local control and receive management support from government.[64] Each guideline is supported with detailed suggestions and arguments.

The book concludes with a discussion of the three aspects of sociable streets identified previously: social, behavioural and physical, arguing that each aspect must be understood and considered in efforts to make successful sociable streets. Finally the particular value of sociable neighbourhood streets is discussed and the assertion that such streets are critical to urban residents, local communities and society at large, especially in light of our increasingly urbanised world.

The book is a valuable resource for the examination of streets, carefully describing the importance of streets, their history, discusses much of the significant literature of public space, examines environmental behaviour research and some applicable psychological theory. The rigorous empirical research provides a wealth of information about the relationship of social behaviour, land use and the physical attributes of streets. Of particular value to the purposes of this book is the analysis of the physical characteristics of streets and the impact these have on behaviour. By showing a correlation between where and how long people occupy specific parts of the street, the importance of physical elements and the identification of a range of these which can encourage social activity and influence perception. The most important physical support of social exchange identified by the research was seating, either public, commercial or the opportunistic use of building elements or street furniture.[65] Sidewalk width was also shown to be a critical characteristic, with wider sidewalks being more heavily used and perceived as more pleasant.[66] The research revealed that the sidewalk could be divided into three zones of activity. Zone one, immediately adjacent to the building edge, was used to move into or out of buildings, read signs, view window displays, use utilities (such as public phones or bank machines) or as a place to sit, lean, talk or watch the street activity. The research showed that these types of activities increased when architectural features such as steps, corners, bay windows, niches, canopies or awnings provided the chance to sit and stand or offered shelter from the rain or sun. This zone also attracted children interested in the shop windows or by opportunities to play. The second zone, in the middle of the sidewalk, was identified as the circulation space of the street, predominantly used for movement, with people occasionally stopping briefly if necessary. Zone three, situated next to the roadway, was used for stationary activities and social interaction: sitting, eating and drinking, talking, group socialising, playing, reading, sleeping and people watching. On the streets studied this zone contained the majority of the fixed and movable seating, street furniture, landscape elements and traffic and utility infrastructure.[67] These observations directly inform discussions regarding the operation and spatial understanding of sidewalks and pavements by demonstrating that architectural facades and the physical objects that populate sidewalks and pavements have a critical impact on the experience and spatial perception of streets. The influence of these elements on the spatial structure of streets will be discussed later.

Another observation made by Mehta that is relevant to this book regards the influence of visual stimulation created by the architecture and other physical components of the streets examined. With research revealing that architectural articulation, fenestration, shop displays, canopies, awnings, signage, street furniture and landscape elements, influence user perception, attraction and avoidance, social behaviour and place identification.[68] This relates to the analysis of the physical elements of streets at the heart of the discussions later in Chapter 5, informing the analysis and underlining the value of detailed knowledge of this aspect of streets.

Mehta's book also discusses the permeability of the facades that contain the street and the impact this has on the character of the street. Pointing out that permeability is more than transparency, but requires strong visual, auditory and olfactory interaction between the interiors and the exterior space of the streets to support the active engagement of street users. Mehta cites research regarding the importance of sensory stimulation in shopping behaviour and pedestrian pleasure, pointing out the role of the architectural features, fenestration and displays in providing this stimulation. Mehta's research showed that permeability increased social activity and pedestrian interest, particularly for children.[69] The concept of permeability and Mehta's research which shows the effect of the level of permeability on social behaviour and interest is significant for a central argument of this book: that interior spaces adjacent to the street form part of the street space and that analysing the permeability of streets is essential to understanding how streets function.

While there is a great deal more to be learned from Vikas Mehta's *The Street: A Quintessential Social Public Space*, those aspects examined indicate the value of his research and the relevance to the current investigation. Although the emphasis of the book is on the impact of programme or land use in creating meaningful social spaces, the book does provide detailed empirical research showing that physical features influence the perception and experience of streets. This research indicates which physical attributes warrant analysis and provides guidance for the processing of the results, suggesting the level of influence of various factors. Importantly certain aspects of the research examined above expand and support principles contained in the analysis proposed later in Chapter 5. The focus on social behaviour does limit the exploration of other issues, such as spatial experience or a more structured analysis of the physical elements that do not directly relate to street level activity. Also, although the visual information presented has many strengths, a more extensive diagrammatic exposition would improve communication, making some issues more comprehensible, for example when photographs are used to illustrate the discussion of zones of activity[70] or permeability.[71] The photographs do provide information related to the discussion, but diagrams would be clearer and could extend the analysis. These minor points do not undermine the contributions of the book but highlight a difference in focus. *The Street: A Quintessential Social Public Space* makes critical observations regarding social behaviour, proposes a compelling thesis regarding the influence of land use and business ownership on the creation of socially meaningful places and while the focus is on neighbourhood commercial street, most of the research and concepts are directly relevant to many urban streets. These ideas are supported with thoughtful research that synthesises material from urban theory, environmental behaviour and psychology, expanding and adding to the knowledge and understanding of streets.

One of the most important resources for the study of streets is the book *Great Streets*[72] by Allan B. Jacobs. In the book Jacobs outlines the place of the street in the city and the importance of the street in urban life. Jacobs argues that the physical aspects of streets are critical to their success. The book provides an invaluable body of comparative data about streets, analysis of urban organisation and detailed discussions of several factors in the shaping of streets. The book uses the comparative analysis of existing streets to expand knowledge about how streets work and an insistence that good streets are designed and must be maintained.[73]

Great Streets is divided into four sections. The first section contains detailed analysis and drawings of specific streets organised thematically. Section two contains a collection of streets selected as models of particular street types. Section three is a discussion of street organisation, with a set of partial figure ground drawings of cities from around the world. The final section provides detailed descriptions of the characteristics observed on great streets, forming a proposed set of qualities needed for successful street design.

Section one begins with the examination of a street of personal significance for Jacobs, a residential street he lived on, a meaningful street for him, setting the tone of the book. For while this is a book full of information about streets and cities, there is a strong human quality at the centre of the book. Streets are presented using descriptive analysis, with the facts explained to portray the experience they shape, with everyday events and occurrences used to contextualise this information. The residential street, Roslyn Place, is described as a space with specific physical properties around a narrative framework of the lives and interactions of the residents. This description is accompanied by a scale plan and section and perspective sketches of the street. These drawings illustrate the information in the text, but also allow the reader to analyse the street.[74]

Following this opening analysis, Jacobs examines in detail selected streets to discuss significant themes, using the model established in the first analysis. He examines organic streets, European boulevards, damaged streets, tree-lined streets, street compositions and three individual instances with particular qualities: a residential boulevard, a promenade and the Grand Canal in Venice as a water street. These thematic discussions establish the terms for the short analysis of individual streets in section two and articulate arguments for the set of principles for good street design detailed in section four.[75]

The second section of the book contains a collection of streets from cities around the world, with brief descriptive notes, scale drawings and sometimes perspective sketches. Again the streets are classified by the type or use and organised to facilitate comparative analysis.[76] The streets presented range from ancient streets, through commercial and residential streets to the special condition of one-sided streets. The street descriptions provide basic information about the street, highlight particular characteristics, describe spatial qualities, social activity, landscaping, street furniture and the impact these have on the experience of the street. This collection has been compiled as a means of learning about streets and is intended as a resource for the design and construction of good streets.[77] The inclusion of analytic drawings at the same scale for each street allows the space of the street and the elements which shape it to be examined and to be easily compared with other street drawings included.

Section three of the book is concerned with street patterns, consisting of partial plans of thirty-nine cities.[78] Jacobs points out that the organisation of streets is influenced by numerous factors and can contribute to understanding important aspects of individual cities and cities in general. He briefly discusses comparing existing street patterns, which have resulted in successful urban form, to design proposals for new streets or districts, suggesting that the strengths of proven models can improve the proposed designs. He also stresses the importance of understanding the context for a specific street and that the analysis of the organisation, block size and scale of the city form in which an individual street is situated, reveals information essential to understanding the street. Using the comparative method, he explains the way in which the context can affect the perception and experience of a street, explaining that the same street form has radically different consequences in different street patterns. Jacobs argues that understanding street patterns and the impact they have on individual streets contained in them can help in the analysis and design of streets.[79] Again, as with the collection of street drawings in section two, the selection of city plans is intended as a resource for comparative analysis. With each plan of one square mile drawn at an identical scale, reduced to figure ground, the main features of the street pattern for each city are readily communicated and direct comparisons are possible. Jacobs states that if the goal is to learn more about "the physical, designable characteristics"[80] of streets, then understanding the relationship between the individual street and the street pattern is critical.

Jacobs outlines the forms of information revealed through the comparative analysis of the figure ground drawings, discussing similarities and differences, topography and natural features, organisation and structure, historical factors, density, two-dimensional scale, variation in scale, design concepts and some additional observations about specific cities. Through the discussion of these aspects of the analysis, the details of the methodology emerge and the benefits are articulated. Specific characteristics revealed through the comparisons generate a more developed understanding of specific cities, as well as information and ideas regarding cities in general.[81]

The final part of the book, *Great Streets* is an attempt by Jacobs to make explicit the factors that make great streets. Some of these factors are seen as requirements, others as valuable additions which markedly improve streets, while still others are considered beyond the control of designers. Again, Jacobs argues that streets are the critical component of urban environments and that while their purpose is movement, their role as a stage for social interaction is vital. Accepting that much of what makes a street successful cannot be designed, he still insists that physical attributes are important and that conscious design of these attributes is necessary for successful streets.[82] Jacobs describes a set of required qualities, asserting that not all great streets possess these qualities, but that their presence usually indicates a successful street, if not a guarantee; stating that a great street requires the skilful combination of these qualities through considered design.[83] The essential qualities include: accommodation of people, physically comfortable, spatially defined, visually stimulating, transparent at street level, consistent, maintained and construction with quality and design.[84] In examining the non-essential qualities, Jacobs argues that while a street can be great without these, they significantly improve a street. These attributes are: trees, distinct starts and defined finishes, details, stopping places, accessibility, diversity of uses, limited length, slope, restricted parking, contrast and adaptability.[85] Believing that knowledge about how to create good streets can be developed through the analysis of existing great streets, Jacobs has constructed a reference for designers, providing a body of information, a set of detailed discussions which examine this information in a distilled set of operational proposals for using this information.[86] All of the issues discussed in this section expand the understanding of streets, developing additional layers of attributes and relationships, also providing a disciplined means of examining how these interact. The careful consideration and the analysis of existing examples helps manage the complexity of streets, demonstrates a useful method and reveals valuable principles for the study and design of streets.

In his conclusion Jacobs argues that good streets are critical to healthy, liveable cities. He states that while circulation and access are important functions, streets play an important social role and supply public space for interaction, expression, community and socialisation. To fulfil this role streets must work for people, inviting use and supporting a variety of activities by a wide range of users. Certain characteristics and qualities are required for streets to succeed and the careful consideration of these can improve existing streets and help shape high quality new ones. He also emphasises that comparative analysis and the examination of models can provide invaluable knowledge and lead to an understanding of the intangibles of good streets. Finally Jacobs believes that good streets are designed to be good and that they are taken care of, seen as special and valued over time.[87]

Great Streets is a classic text in the field of urban design, of particular value for the investigations in this book. The careful examination of streets, especially their physical attributes, establishes a basis for discussion, providing a framework and a vocabulary which can be used to analyse streets and to explain key concepts and relationships concerning streets. Beginning with the space of streets and explaining how the components – street wall, pavements, trees, street furniture, etc. – are configured to form and articulate streets, critical ideas such as enclosure, definition, visual stimulation, coherent design, connectivity, management, social activity and inclusivity are discussed.[88] Demonstrating how the physical characteristics of streets contribute to the experience and perception of streets, Jacobs underlines the importance of understanding these aspects of streets and how this knowledge can be used by designers. By outlining the critical principles and requirements for streets to successfully meet functional and social needs, critical concepts regarding streets and urban environments are revealed.[89] In some cases this reinforces core ideas of urban design, such as human scale or the need to support social exchange; however, these ideas are developed through the analysis of examples, such that the concept has more specificity, e.g. the general rule regarding the proportion of street height to width.[90] In other instances concepts frequently discussed, often in qualitative terms, are examined for their experiential consequences, for example the impact of trees on streets, where Jacobs details the physical phenomena of light patterns, colour, shadow, leaf movement, spatial rhythm, shade, light penetration, etc., describing how these improve physical comfort, provide visual stimulation and generate spatial complexity, creating a rich experience.[91] Many of these ideas are referenced in the discussion which follow and are developed and extended through application.

One of the most valuable aspects of the book is the collection of drawings, both of streets and the figure ground drawings of street patterns. These drawings are a valuable resource, providing information about a very wide range of streets and street patterns. These can be used to analyse the characteristics of individual cases, showing the effects of specific configurations and attributes. Examining the plan and section of Regent Street reveals the cubic volume and the sweeping form of the street created by the 1:1 height to width ratio as it bends around the arc in plan, or the layers of space created on Kurfurstendamm by trees, pavement and canopies.[92] A similar resource is provided later in Chapter four of this book and the new methodology presented in Chapter five can be used to study the drawings in *Great Streets* in combination with those in Chapter four, allowing more value to be derived from both sets of drawings.

The value of the drawings in *Great Streets* is enhanced through the use of comparative analysis. The book has been designed to be used this way and throughout the book Jacobs demonstrates the methodology. In some instances this is done in an implicit fashion, such as when he compares the street height to width ratios of the Via Del Corso with the Via Dei Grecci, to discuss the oppressive quality of the Via Del Corso.[93] At other times he uses comparative analysis in an explicit, structured way to explore a particular point or illustrate a principle, e.g. when analysing two wall sections to discuss facade articulation,[94] or in his analysis of Boston maps to explain the changes in urban scale illustrated by the change in block sizes and street patterns.[95] Comparative analysis is shown to be an effective tool and Jacobs argues the careful use of this methodology develops useful knowledge and that it is necessary to improve the design of streets and urban environments.[96] Comparative analysis is at the centre of this book, with a detailed methodology described and demonstrated in Chapter five. Like *Great Streets* a central argument of this book is that comparing existing streets is essential to understanding and designing streets.

The core position of *Great Streets* is that information and knowledge about physical streets can improve the design of streets. While accepting that much of what leads to successful streets is outside of the realm of design, Jacobs argues that physical attributes play a critical role and that more in-depth knowledge of the physical components and their impacts is essential. Again this book shares this position, being founded on the belief that streets need to be carefully designed to work and that much of what makes an existing street good is often taken for granted or ignored. Physical characteristics are important to street design, more detailed knowledge is beneficial and the disciplined examination of precedents is valuable.

While *Great Streets* is an essential text, there are some limitations, centred mainly on the specialist nature of the book. Much of the book is reliant on tacit knowledge, making it difficult for readers who have limited experience with urban design theory. For example the core principles presented in section one are embedded in the detailed descriptions of specific streets and could be more explicitly communicated. So while experienced readers will recognise these issues, less knowledgeable readers may focus on the descriptions of individual streets and miss the general principles being articulated.[97] Many aspects of the text are precise, but at other times qualitative description is left unarticulated. For example when Jacobs discusses slope as an attribute that improves a street, he suggests that there is a benefit to changes in elevation along a street, but only generally describes what this might be.[98] The book would also be improved by the inclusion of more analytical diagrams, particularly as those that are included are very useful. Many more complex points would be clarified by diagrams in addition to the textual descriptions, for example in the illustration of human scale, point of view and horizontal spacing the diagrams are effective, but a set of volumetric diagrams comparing streets with different height to width ratios would strengthen the explanation.[99] Although the examination of streets is very wide ranging, some areas could be more fully explored; such as permeability. Jacobs devotes a small section to transparency and does explain the impact on the street, providing some details regarding entryway spacing and fenestration. However, while discussing examples of poor visibility, he passes over their drawbacks rapidly and does not expand on how the loss of visual and physical permeability detracts from streets.[100] The issues raised here are of particular interest as they are relevant to many of the critical concerns of this book, such as making tacit knowledge explicit, presenting an analytical methodology based on diagrammatic analysis and arguing that the ground-floor spaces adjacent to the street are critically linked to the space of the street. The significance of *Great Streets* to this book cannot be overstated, as many of the central positions of *Great Streets* are extended and developed in the following chapters. *Great Streets* is a foundational text, making vital contributions to the field of urban design and to the growing body of knowledge about streets.

A spatial continuity

If one of the major concerns of urban design and architecture is to develop vibrant inclusive urban environments, with streets being the most common and consequently most important elements, then strategies which increase activity and the enjoyment of streets are crucial. One possible adjustment to the commonly accepted conception of streets is to conceive of the street as a composition of linked spaces, with interior spaces that are accessible from the street viewed as necessarily part of the room of the street. If architecture and urban design are primarily concerned with meaningful relationships between spaces both interior and exterior, certainly the relationship between the exterior space of the street and the interior spaces adjacent to it should be conceived as an essential relationship. The careful consideration and design of this critical interface can radically improve the space of the street, creating more interest, activity and interaction.

Ever since Jane Jacobs challenged modernist design strategies and the 19th-century social welfare conceptions of the street which underpinned them, the idea of the street as a positive urban component has grown. It is now a central tenant of urbanism that vital streets, full of activity, used by a mix of people for as much of the day and night as possible, are essential to healthy cities. Jacobs observed that populated streets, with defined public–private boundaries and a mix of uses created social interaction and performed important social functions, from the basic provision of needs, to safety and a sense of identity and community.[101] Jacobs' identification of the need for the interior spaces to condition and affect the public space of the street, her "eyes on the street",[102] underlines a basic urban relationship; adjacent spaces are related and a considered well-designed relationship supports human activity and social interaction. Most importantly streets that result from this are superior and are necessary for a healthy urban environment. As mentioned above, Allan B. Jacobs emphasises the need for a connection between the interiors along a street and the public way as a critical requirement for a successful street. Using examples from cities around the world, Jacobs points out the contributions that visual connections between the interior and the sidewalk make to the experience and perception of a street. On vibrant streets which attract people and activities, such as the Paseo de Garcia in Barcelona, the shop windows are described as part of the public space,[103] or the example of the Boulevard Saint-Michele, Paris, where shop windows and an area for exterior displays create interest and encourage the imagination.[104] Jacobs also discusses the damage caused by poor visual connections between interior and exterior spaces, describing the reduction in the sense of security and the lack of community identity.[105] A recent book by Stipo, a group of Dutch architects and urban designers, *The City At Eye Level: Lessons for Street Plinths*,[106] also discusses the importance of the street level spaces to the success of streets. The authors argue that the ground level of a building must be designed and managed to provide functional, social and psychological value. The book uses case studies to demonstrate that the design of ground-floor spaces that are human scale, people centred, mixed use, adaptable and visually stimulating can create streets that attract people, activity and social interaction; building community and vital new neighbourhoods and interventions that can rehabilitate damaged or problematic streets.[107] As discussed earlier in the chapter, Vikas Mehta's research documented the impact of transparent and permeable street fronts, with more people using, gathering and staying for longer on the portions of streets which had visually and physically connected street frontage. Mehta found that people identified this attribute of a street as desirable and that people preferred to use these sections of a street. Mehta also documented the increase in social exchange on parts of a street which had stronger interior and exterior connections, with the higher usage rates contributing to more social interaction. These more desirable and active parts of the streets also held people for longer, with the duration of stay measurably increased.[108] This provides empirical support for the intuitive understanding that the greater visual stimulation of transparent and permeable street fronts create more desirable and active streets. Similar findings were reported by Jan Gehl, et al., in "Close Encounters With Buildings", as the observations established that the physical features of ground-floor facades, principally visual connection, had a measurable impact on people's behaviour.[109] Gehl and his colleagues compared the behaviour of pedestrians on sections of streets with blank facades with the behaviour on sections with visually connected and permeable facades. The research showed that people engaged open, visually stimulating frontages at much higher levels than blank, closed facades. People turned to look as they passed and stopped to view shop windows. People used these areas to stop for optional activities, such as resting, eating, smoking or talking. This increase in activity also attracted more people, as Gehl frequently points out in all his work, "people attract people".[110] This pattern of behaviour was even more pronounced at night, with people engaging lighted transparent facades at much higher levels than dark, closed frontages.[111] This is followed by case studies to demonstrate models for regulating ground-floor design in both historic and new urban environments, from which basic principles for ground-floor facade design are derived. These principles stress the need for a mix of public uses, architectural detail, visual transparency, physical permeability, human scale, sensitivity to context and architectural features such as steps, niches and doorways.[112] The article ultimately argues that the design of the ground-floor street frontage has a significant impact on how a street is used and that the careful deployment of simple design strategies can improve streets.

With both intuition and research pointing to the need for interactive and visually compelling ground floors adjacent to streets, it is interesting to reconsider some basic ideas about how buildings and streets interact. Pre-modern conceptions of the boundaries between the street and the interiors of buildings were predicated on the clear definition of interior and exterior. Windows and doorways marked the end of interior space; interior space was discrete and legible, with the space of the street being a separate space with distinct characteristics. Modernist design principles pursued the eradication of this type of discrete boundary, proposing a more continuous vision of space; one where the interior moved out into the exterior and the exterior was drawn into the interior space. However, this fundamental conception of space was disrupted in relation to the street. When it came to streets modernism saw them as contributors to the dirty, dark, overcrowded, chaotic and violent 19th-century industrial city. In agreement with contemporary progressive thinking, modernism identified traditional streets as a major cause of urban problems, proposing an alternative urban environment without streets. Instead of streets which coupled movement, commerce and social interaction, modernism proposed that buildings be located in a landscape, with a direct contact to a natural environment and that movement be through a dedicated network of roads.[113] The moral pursuit of improving living conditions and eliminating perceived ills, coupled with the modernist aesthetic agenda, prevented the examination of a modernist conception of the relationship between urban exterior and interior. What is proposed is an extension of contemporary notions of continuous space to the street. Architects and urban designers should rethink the separation of ground-floor interiors from the room of the street. Those responsible for the configuration, construction and management of urban space must see the ground-floor spaces along a street as contributing to the urban environment, pursuing a public space of the street that is both exterior and interior. Architects must design the ground floor of urban buildings to address the public space of the street, extending the activity of the interior out into the street. Most importantly, owners must understand the public nature of the ground floor and their responsibility to the public space of the city. If streets are to perform their critical role in the life of cities, there must be a joint effort to pursue the active engagement of ground-floor spaces with the streets they form.

The design of ground-floor spaces should utilise the sophisticated tools of architectural practice to generate high-quality and meaningful solutions. The careful modulation of thresholds, boundary conditions and spatial compositions can generate strong physical and visual connections between interior and exterior spaces. Architectural design which pursues urban relationships and considers the impacts of design choices on the street can lead to interesting and desirable streets, which attract use and support a vital urban environment. If architects conceive of the street as a room which the interior space they are designing is connected to, rather than that moment where their design stops, a completely different approach to the design issue opens up. Most of the architectural solutions are self evident and based on fundamental architectural principles, such as scale, threshold, composition, tectonics, materiality and spatial definition. The important alteration is the removal of the simplistic distinction between the interior space and the street. Once they are seen as two parts of one whole, the design problem is transformed and the possibility of meaningful, interrelated interiors and exteriors is greatly improved. Streets where the interior and exterior are designed to complement and enhance each other can only result in more vital streets, which will improve urban space.

The most important contributor to a vibrant urban environment is the active street and the integrated design of the street and the ground floor is the best means of achieving this. The street is a civic room; the activity of the ground floor should necessarily overlap with the activity of the street. The blurring of interior and exterior space extends the architectural conception of a spatial continuum in an instrumental manner to urban thinking. The design of the relationship between the interior and the street is the most important task for an architect in an urban context and methodologies for understanding and designing active streets are essential tools for urban designers, architects and those who assess their designs.

Elements of the street

To establish a basis for the analysis of the physical characteristics and spatial qualities of streets, a basic vocabulary of terms will be developed in reference to existing models. While there are numerous variations of many of these terms and a lack of consensus about some, the goal is to define useful terminology for the analysis which follows in Chapter five.

The primary elements of the street are: the roadway, the sidewalk/pavement, street furniture and landscape features and the street wall. The roadway provides for the movement of vehicles, the sidewalk accommodates pedestrian activity, the street furniture and landscape features support the use of the street and the street wall forms the edges of the room of the street. Each of these elements is comprised of various components, with the variations of these components distinguishing the individual street.

The roadway is often a dominating feature of a street, consequently requiring examination, focused on the number of circulation channels, their width, the provision for parking, the plan form and the surface. Single-channel roadways are the most common and result in clear spatial structures, whose modulation is influenced by the subtleties of the combined elements. Multiple-channel roadways create spatial layering, with interlacing volumes and more complex relationships. The width of the roadway plays a major role in determining the volume of the street, with narrow roadways creating tight, vertical spaces and wider or multiple channels creating more open, horizontal conditions. The width of the roadway combined with the width of the sidewalk/pavements and the height of the street wall defines the enclosure or the room of the street.[114] Allan B. Jacobs states that widths exceeding four times the height of the street wall provide poor spatial definition and that most good streets have height to width ratios in the range of 1:1.1 to 1:1.25.[115] Four examples: (Fig. 3.1–3.4) Polk Street, San Francisco, South State Street, Chicago, Rue Talaa Kebria, Fès and Bath Street, Glasgow, demonstrate the variation in the width of roadways and the relationship between this width and the height of the street wall. The height to width ratio for Polk Street is 1:1.78, South State Street it is 1:1, for Rue Talaa Kebria 1:.48 and for Bath Street it is 1:2.17. These different height to width ratios produce volumes that range from vertical in Fès to horizontal in Glasgow. As the major component of the horizontal dimension, the roadway width is an important consideration in the analysis of the street.

Streets designed to prioritise vehicular movement have geometries with negative impacts on other users, with wider roadways and larger corner radii creating poor spatial definition, higher speeds and less natural pedestrian movement patterns.[116]

The Street

To design streets which support a full range of users and provide safe attractive places for people, the roadway design must constrain vehicular movement and illicit driving behaviour that is responsive to non-vehicular users.[117] Parking provision also influences roadway width and the pedestrian experience of a street. The portion of the roadway designated for parking can take many forms and have either positive or negative impacts. Carefully configured parking can provide a visual and physical barrier between moving vehicles and pedestrians, supporting a pleasant and active street. While poor parking arrangements can damage streets, limiting pedestrian movement and emphasising the dominance of vehicles, creating a place that is unwelcoming to people.[118] The form of the roadway is critical to the spatial character of a street. Curved streets limit visual depth, bending to close the space of the street. A straight form allows continuous lines of sight and open connected spaces. Straight street forms can have rhythm, proportion and balance, while curved plans can create visual diversity and stimulating spatial composition.[119] The surface of the roadway also influences the perception of the street. Most roadways are paved with asphalt or concrete, which are efficient and cost-effective surfaces, allowing rapid installation and ease of maintenance. These materials are used primarily for their suitability for motor vehicles and cost benefits. While these are important considerations, the materials have serious limitations, particularly in relation to creating distinctive streets. The ordinary character and uniformity have

3.1
Polk St., San Francisco

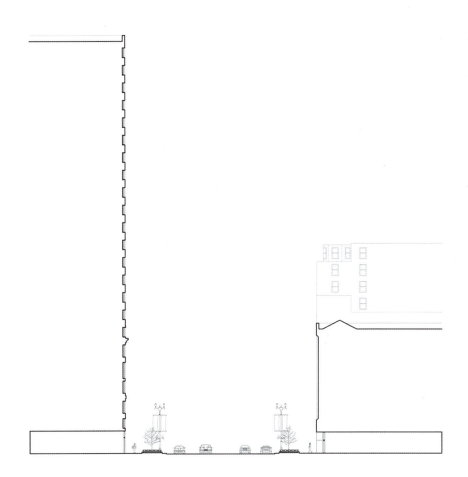

3.2
South State St., Chicago

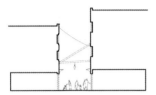

3.3
Rue Talaa Kebria, Fès

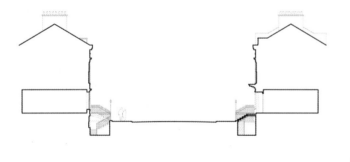

3.4
Bath St., Glasgow

limited visual and tactile qualities. Cobblestones, bricks, or other roadway surfaces can create a range of physical stimulation, adding interest and pleasure to the experience of a street.

The change in priorities for street design that have followed the recognition that populated, active streets are essential to the economic, cultural and social health of cities has led to an expanded understanding of the uses and activities that can take place on sidewalks/pavements. Beginning with Jane Jacobs describing the sidewalk of her neighbourhood to Jan Gehl's research into use patterns and pedestrian behaviour, or Allan B. Jacobs' evocations of the vitality of life on the pavements of great streets, there has been a steady effort to understand the complexity of this critical urban space. One fundamental concern is the organisation of sidewalk space, from suggested systems in design manuals,[120] to others developed by researchers such as Vikas Mehta.[121] All these share basic characteristics, denoting a zone against the roadway, a zone of movement and a zone at the building's edge. These zones vary in width and layout in relation to the type and configuration of the street, but the main divisions remain. In all of these models, the zone immediately adjacent to the building is identified as the place of interchange and informal social activity; people move in and out of buildings, window shop, stand, lean, sit, talk and smoke.[122] It is also the area which businesses use to expand into, placing displays, temporary signs, tables and chairs or decorative enhancements.[123] The centre zone is typically designated as the zone for pedestrians, allowing people to circulate along the length of the street. The zone against the roadway contains the street furniture and landscape elements. This is the area where light poles, street signs, fire hydrants, telephone poles and other infrastructure items are located, also the zone where many of the public amenities are situated: trees, benches, planters and bus stops. This is the section of the sidewalk/pavement where the models differ, with some models seeing this as a place to accommodate increased activity. The San Francisco city design manual, *SF Better Streets*, divides this into two distinct zones (the furnishing zone and the edge zone) and even suggests an additional zone, termed the extension zone, where sidewalk activities can expand into the roadway space.[124] For the purposes of this book the sidewalk/pavement will be divided into four zones: the transition zone, that area next to the street wall, followed by the circulation zone occupying the centre of the sidewalk/pavement, next to this is the amenities zone and finally the curbside zone, where the sidewalk/pavement meets the roadway (Fig. 3.5). The differentiation in terms is not merely semantic, but essential to accurately portray the functions of these areas.

The transition zone is defined by its physical and visual exchanges, with the movement between the interior and exterior expressed on many levels. It is the place where the change from open public space to enclosed space occurs and the various devices and methods of transition have significant impact on the perception and experience of an individual street. The transition zone can range from the simple tight wall plane of entry thresholds, such as in Fès (Fig. 3.3), to the horizontal and vertical layers in the steps and porches that span light wells on Bath Street in Glasgow (Fig. 3.4). The configuration and use of the transition zone has a major impact on the experience of a street, with an infinite number of arrangements, all of which can be appropriate if carefully designed.

The circulation zone is much more than a "pedestrian clearway";[125] as both William Whyte and Vikas Mehta's research confirmed, people also use this part of the sidewalk to stop for short conversations and other short duration social

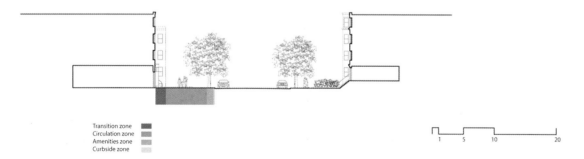

Transition zone
Circulation zone
Amenities zone
Curbside zone

1   5   10   20

3.5
Sidewalk Zones

interaction. It is primarily a place of movement, but not always in a strictly functional sense.[126] The sidewalk/pavement width is the most prominent aspect of the circulation zone, specifically the relationship of width to the pedestrian load. Narrow pavements can cause overcrowding or be difficult to use for even individual users; conversely they can be part of an intimate human scaled street. Wide pavements can be abandoned and empty or busy and vital with large flows of people. Identifying the characteristics and extent of this zone is essential to building a comprehensive understanding of a street.

The term amenities zone is used to stress the importance of understanding the consequences of street furniture and landscape elements, both functional and spatial. Be they straightforward functional components, beautification efforts or public provision, these objects are placed on the street, in the public right of way, as a benefit for one group of street users. This means they are subject to consideration for all of their impacts and must be evaluated in the context of the complete street composition. The amenities provided influence the space and use of the sidewalk/pavement and the street as whole. On South State Street in Chicago there are large planters, trees, benches, light poles and banners (Fig. 3.2). This gives the street a civic quality, structures the space of the pavement, offers a physical and visual barrier between the vehicular traffic and pedestrians and provides opportunities for social interaction. All this is at a large scale, generating the environment of a grand commercial street; appropriate both to number of people who use the space and the size of the tall buildings which form the room of the street. On Polk Street in San Francisco the street trees and light poles also carry out many of the same spatial, visual physical functions at a more intimate scale, giving the street a more local identity (Fig. 3.1).

The curbside zone has been given this label to acknowledge it as a threshold between the vehicular and pedestrian users. The quality of the curbside zone is almost solely dependent on the configuration and properties of the material used to designate this boundary. Wide granite blocks, which can be occupied by a single person, can serve as a place to stop and review the street or for a moment of private reflection. Narrow concrete curbs are purely functional and rarely go beyond being a simple line dividing the roadway and the pavement. Low small stone curbs make a fine distinction between the roadway and the sidewalk/pavement and can encourage a more casual separation, in which pedestrians move between the sidewalk and the roadway freely. While how this boundary is used can depend on cultural factors or the traffic context, the physical properties heavily influence the behaviour of both pedestrians and vehicle drivers. High, utilitarian curbs designed with standardised features generate a lifeless boundary; curbside zones which are treated as important threshold moments, with quality materials and generous forms, contribute to a more distinctive definition. This is not to insist that a raised curb is required, but to suggest that whatever the nature of this boundary, blurred, ordinary or generous, this division between users is a major issue for all streets.

With recent interest in creating sidewalks/pavements that foster and support a wide range of activities and which possess notable qualities, a variety of new sidewalk treatments have been proposed. While this book is intended as an analytic resource and not a complete account of street design, it is worth briefly discussing some of these street design ideas. These elements are aimed at providing space for desired activities, allowing pavements to move beyond the simply functional and to become places which people enjoy using. These elements are typically alterations to the geometry of the sidewalk to provide more room, either for movement or to allow spaces for stationary activity. Curb extensions are designed to facilitate pedestrian movement, by reducing the radius at intersections to shorten the crossing distance and improve visibility. Curb extensions also reduce vehicle speeds by narrowing the roadway and can be used to visually integrate the parking lane into the pavement. Other innovative sidewalk treatments involve extending the pavement areas to accommodate planting, storm water management and even creating small parks or mini plazas.[127] Many of these strategies are aimed at creating pavements that replicate the successful pavements of existing streets or retrofitting existing streets to prioritise people over vehicles. Their main impacts are to provide more space for people and a coherent design which focuses on improving the visual, physical and social experience of those using the sidewalk/ pavement.

Another aspect of sidewalks/pavements to be considered are the material properties: surface, curbs and edge treatments. The materials used to pave and detail sidewalks have a direct effect on the users, in a visual, tactile and qualitative way. At a basic level sidewalk surfaces meet the need for level and smooth surfaces to allow all users access and to move freely and safely. The edge and curb treatments need to mark boundaries, provide access and withstand the impacts of use. As with roadways, the common use of asphalt and concrete provides a cost efficient means of meeting these functional requirements. Special paving and details can also be used, making the sidewalk/pavement more distinctive, providing definition and visual enhancement. Decorative paving and high quality detailing, such as brick, patterned paving, stone slabs, granite curb stones or cobblestone edging signal care and quality and provide visual stimulation, differentiating a street and giving it an identity. Paving treatments can also be used to emphasise pedestrian priority, marking paths and crosswalks, requiring vehicular traffic to adapt to pedestrian users. Paving can be used to demarcate and accent specific areas of the sidewalk, supporting uses and activities contributing to the development of a vital public space. Sidewalks also play a role in various other issues such as drainage or beautification. The treatment of the details required by these functions is very important to creating a coherent streetscape. The various municipal design manuals provide guidance regarding paving, access crosswalks, stormwater management and planting considerations.[128] A careful survey of these provides a wealth of information in relation to these issues, while intended as design guidance, these manuals are very helpful in the analysis of existing streets as well. Also important is the examination of the appropriateness of materials and design strategies to the particular conditions of a street, as maintenance is critical to the success of a design and higher quality materials and workmanship require a commitment to upkeep, as the neglect of distinctive materials is more apparent and has greater impact.[129] Again the scope of this book does not allow for extensive coverage of sidewalk design; however, a sensitivity to these issues is required during the examination of streets and an awareness of these sidewalk/pavement elements will deepen the analysis. An attention to sidewalk/pavement use, organisation, design, materials and details is critical to a comprehensive reading of a street. Reference to current best practice is a powerful tool for evaluating a found condition; both to see what may be missing and elements that are present that may not be included in current practice.

Street furniture and landscape elements are significant components of the sidewalk/pavement space and have numerous impacts on streets. These impacts can be negative and positive, with ill-considered and careless placement causing visual confusion and physical problems or disciplined design creating a unified aesthetic, functionally improved and more attractive space. As the emphasis on streets as places for people has grown, attention to the design issues regarding street furniture and landscaping has increased. While it is critical to carefully locate all objects in a streetscape design, there is a hierarchy, with certain elements having higher priority. One of the most significant elements of a streetscape are trees. Not all streets have trees, but if there are trees, they have a dramatic effect. The size, the spacing and canopy coverage of trees influence a range of spatial relationships, such as definition, rhythm, directional emphasis and layering. Trees can create edges and enclosure or permeable boundaries and punctuating moments. Trees also have a major impact on light, providing visual stimulation and shade, with the movement of branches and leaves noted as particularly important in making streets desirable.[130] Although difficult to quantify or define precisely, trees also have an emotional and psychological consequences, with people viewing the natural forms and colours as beautiful and pleasant. Trees also contribute to a sense of place, creating the range of effects discussed, but when in relation to a specific place the result is a unique environmental experience. For these and other reasons trees are important components of the streetscape and require attention in the analysis of streets. Of particular relevance for the discussions in this book are the spatial outcomes and the influence of trees on the spatial relationships of a street.

Lighting is also an important element of the streetscape, with both the design character and the performance being significant in the experience of the street. Well-designed lighting creates a sense of security, an inviting atmosphere and adds visual richness. Like trees, the rhythm of lines created by light poles have a spatial impact, both forming layers and leading the eye along the street.[131] It is also important to note that distinctive lighting fixtures which are visually appealing contribute to the individuality of a street, lending identity and being a strong indicator that the street is a valued public space. Lighting designs should also consider the qualities being created, with light levels, directionality and rendering being designed to create inviting environments.[132] This means lighting for pedestrians as well as vehicles, with pedestrian lighting being scaled and shaped for people. This can result in multiple layers of lighting and more complex spaces on streets. The placement of light poles and fixtures is therefore an important design factor and the analysis of existing streets should be carefully considered, especially in regard to the spatial effects on a street.

Seating is very important to the liveability and vitality of a street, being a major attractor of activity and people. Streets which have purpose-built public seating are much more likely to be used by people and this contributes heavily to the attraction of other people.[133] When designed seating is coupled with casual opportunities, such as planters, bollards, steps or architectural features, a street becomes a place where people collect, stop to rest or to watch the activity going on around them. Streets with seating, both public and private, purpose built or opportunistic, are streets where people stay for longer periods.[134] It has been noted that the duration of the activities taking place is a critical factor in creating a sociable public space.[135] Not every street will have seating, but if seating is present, the location and relationship to trees, roadway, street wall and significant destinations are important. Seating in conjunction with shade is more attractive and it is more desirable if it is buffered from vehicular traffic. Most importantly seating should allow the life of the street to be observed, as this is a major attraction of sitting on a street.[136] Combinations of these three characteristics are even more effective at encouraging people to stop and enjoy a street. Examining a street to determine if there are opportunities for sitting is a critical aspect of analysing a street's spatial character, as seating adds territories, boundaries and spatial events to a street, creating a more complex spatial composition.

These three main elements of street furniture and landscaping are followed by a long list of supplemental components which have less impact but remain important. Planters, bollards, street signs, parking meters, bicycle racks, small retail stalls, utility infrastructure and fire hydrants, must also be considered for the effect they have on the streetscape and the use of the street. These elements support the use of the street in numerous ways, providing utility, safety and information to pedestrians, bicyclists and vehicular traffic. Streets must be designed to include these amenities, with the amount, location and type of amenity being determined by the patterns of use on the particular street. In analysing a street, the presence and location of these various elements and the relationship between them and other components should be noted. As with trees, lighting and seating, these streetscape elements can have spatial and functional impacts, creating distinct places on streets or supplementary layers to the dominant zones of the sidewalk and as such their examination is essential. The critical point regarding the analysis of the streetscape is that every object should be considered in relation to all the others and to the whole street. While there is no doubt many streets studied will have haphazard relationships between streetscape elements, it is also the case that many will have good relationships, whether by design or happy accident.

The final component of the street is the street wall, which forms the edge of the room of the street. The fundamental aspects of the street wall to consider are: vertical definition, the relationship of the base to the room of the street, the characteristics of the facade above the base and the roofscape created by the top of the street wall. All street walls determine the nature of the street edge, but the variation in the way this happens is the result of how the elements above are configured and combined. How the street edge is formed makes a major contribution to the character of a street. The space of the street, its visual vitality and physical operation are consequently heavily influenced by the qualities of the street wall.

The vertical quality of the street wall in combination with the width of the roadway and sidewalk/pavement form the spatial volume of the street, but the street wall determines the enclosure. The level of enclosure is the result of the height and continuity of the street wall; with high continuous street walls creating greater enclosure than lower street walls or streets whose vertical edge is poorly defined, with large gaps or single-storey buildings placed incoherently within plots.

Streets with limited enclosure, created by low or discontinuous vertical edges lack spatial definition, which is critical for a street, as fragmentary or ineffective enclosure leads to weakly formed space, lacking containment and spatial identity[137] (Fig. 3.6). Not all street walls are identical and not all vertical enclosure is formed by a consistent line of facades; many very good streets have buildings recessed from the property line and still others are formed by a series of buildings with spaces between them (Fig. 3.7). The crucial point is the coherence of the space formed by the street wall and the other components of the street. Horizontal spatial definition is not inferior to vertical spatial definition, as Bath Street in Glasgow proves (Fig. 3.4). What is required is legible and consistent spatial definition. This point is made by numerous relaxed residential streets, which have single family houses set back from the roadway and spaced irregularly on varied plot sizes[138] (Fig. 3.7). The space of such streets is coherent and contextually suitable. The houses form a legible pattern, the room of the street is defined by the facade, the porches, the lawns and the trees, forming a residential room, appropriate to its use. A similar configuration in a more urban context, with different use patterns and spatial identity would read as incongruous and disconnected from its surroundings.[139] The more common problem is the singular or partial alteration of a prevailing pattern of enclosure, with an individual building that is set back with side yards, or a development inserted into a dense fabric that ignores the scale

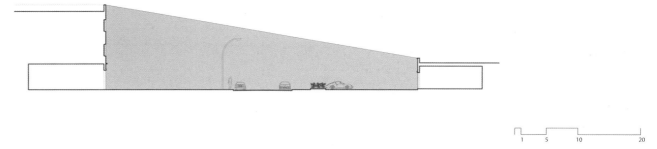

1   5   10   20

3.6
Poor Spatial Definition

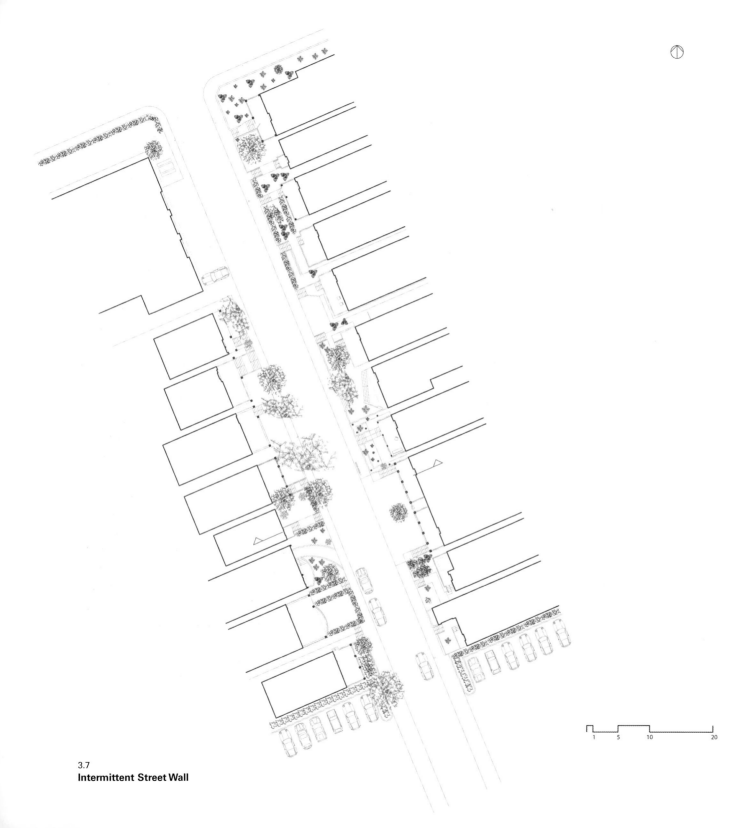

3.7
Intermittent Street Wall

massing and frontages that surround it. When analysing the space of the street, determining the character of the street wall and the enclosure it creates is a critical aspect of the examination.

The base of the street wall has a variety of important functions; structuring the essential interaction between the interior and the exterior spaces of the street, modulating the edge of the street room, supporting street activity, providing visual stimulation and is central to the identity of the street. How each of these functions is accomplished should be examined, with the specific characteristics identified. This detailed knowledge allows significant relationships between the base of the street wall and the other components of the street to be evaluated.

As argued previously interaction between the interior and the exterior spaces of a street is crucial to vital urban environments. The physical properties of the base of the street wall are obviously key to the way this interaction occurs. Simplistic solutions, such as large glazed surfaces or historically referenced entryways cannot adequately address this function of the base, as they often lack meaningful architectural qualities, resolving into flat surfaces or poorly scaled symbolism. Building rich, effective spatial interaction relies on careful architectural judgement and skill; composition, proportion, materiality, scale, spatial layering and much more are required. Analysing existing street bases to understand how this is accomplished supplies valuable information. The section through Polk Street in San Francisco (Fig. 3.1) illustrates this, as the threshold between the pavement and the interiors are manipulated, creating a rich interplay between the inside and the outside spaces of the street. On one side of the street the entryway is placed under the overhang of the upper building wall in a recess and up a set of stairs, while across the roadway the opposing interior's boundary is a large window, under a projecting bay window, and whose sill allows passersby to view the interior. These seemingly mundane arrangements actually have complex spatial consequences. The exterior presses into the interior, as the recess of the steps pushes through the interior boundary, but the recess and the steps form a place for interior activity to spill out into the space of the street. The interior overhangs the exterior, with the bay projecting out into the volume of the street, forming a pocket of space for exterior social activity; such as window shopping, talking, sitting or smoking. All of this is accomplished while the necessary distinctions are maintained, with appropriate levels of privacy and control created. This is just one example of the way the careful manipulation of architectural elements (steps, bays, thresholds and windows), allow the base of the street wall to encourage interaction between the interior and exterior so important to vital streets.[140] Existing streets should be analysed to build a catalogue of these strategies and a vocabulary for designing and understanding this crucial aspect of the street wall base and the street as a whole.

Related to the function of structuring the interaction between the interior and the exterior, is the role the base of the street wall plays in modulating the edge of the room of the street. It is the base of the street wall which forms the edge of the exterior habitable space of the street and the manner in which this edge is configured has numerous impacts on the street. Streets which have street wall bases that are articulated, with a varied profile and architectural elements such as steps, window sills, planters, etc., attract social interaction.[141] When this edge is visually and physically permeable it is more stimulating and more pleasurable for those using the street, increasing the activity level and duration of use.[142] The characteristics of the street wall base also contribute to the perceptions of security, as the permeability affects activity levels and the atmosphere of the street. Permeable street fronts attract people and at night project light into the street; these factors increase the sense of security.[143] The base of the street wall is also that part of the street wall which pedestrians have the most direct interaction with, both visually and physically. It is the edge that most relates to the pedestrian's field of vision and also the threshold crossed when entering or leaving the interior spaces of the street.[144] On Bath Street in Glasgow the base of the street wall is a rich interplay of space, circulation, view and light provision (Fig. 3.4). The ground floor is raised such that those inside can observe the street, but from the pavement only light and a sense of interior activity can be perceived. The interior enclosure is also set back from the pavement to allow light to penetrate to the basement level. This light well has a variety of consequences; requiring a set of steps and a small porch for ground-floor access necessitates a railing along the pavement and creates a spatial layer between the facade and the pavement. The architectural sequence which results creates visual interest, spatial complexity, practical provision and experiential richness. Again examining existing streets to understand how this critical portion of the street wall works across a range of situations reveals valuable knowledge for those interested in streets.

As discussed previously the base of the street wall can also support the activity of the street. The physical characteristics of the architecture play a role in how people perceive and use this portion of the street. Blank walls with little formal variation encourage pedestrians to continue moving and discourage visual interest.[145] When the base of a building has architectural quality, with scale, articulation and spatial variety, it is attractive on numerous levels. This portion of the street is where casual social activity takes place, standing, smoking, window shopping, stopping to talk on the way in or out of the building.[146] Bases with formal, visual and spatial variety attract more of this behaviour.[147] Research has shown that people are attracted by other people, they use spaces with people in them more readily.[148] Consequently a street wall base which supports this crucial social activity potentially attracts more people, increasing the vitality of the street. Analysing a street wall to determine how success-fully it supports social interaction is an important part of building a complete picture of a street and existing streets are a valuable resource for this type of investigation.

The base of the street wall is one of the major visual components of the street, particularly in relation to pedestrians, whose field of vision is limited to the ground floor.[149] This is the zone of the facade revealing the interior and with signs and displays aimed at attracting pedestrian attention. This is also where personalisation of the street takes place, with businesses using plants, decorations and advertising to distinguish the space they occupy.[150] The architectural resolution of the street wall base can contribute to visual stimulation as well. Openings, doorways, facade articulation, details and materiality help to create a visually attractive street.[151] Visually stimulating streets are more heavily used and recognised as more pleas-urable.[152] The base of the street wall is central to the visual character of a street and the identity of a street is heavily influenced by its qualities. This is supported by research which shows that people retain more information about this portion of the street and are able to construct more accurate descriptions of it.[153] The specific combination of colour, form, scale and spatial configuration generates the individuality of a street. Especially as many commercial streets contain a similar set of nationally and internationally branded stores, the physical features of the base help to distinguish the street from others with very similar retail outlets. On urban residential streets the individuality of the base is equally important, specifically in cities with strong typological and stylistic continuity. While no doubt street trees and other streetscape features and spatial character contribute to the identity of a street, it can be argued the base of the street wall has the most significant impact on the identity of the street. The careful assessment of the base of the street wall to determine its visual qualities and properties extends the knowledge of a street and is an important aspect of a street analysis.

Although the facade above the street wall has less direct visual impact on the street, the features and details of this portion of the street wall still influence the perception and experience of the street. The scale and proportion of the facade play a major role in defining the scale of the street space, often signalling the nature of the street: commercial, institutional or residential. The materials and architectural expression generate the backdrop for the life of the street. Even when the majority of the visual information and experience of the street is at ground level, the broad sense of the street is established above the ground floor. A wide commercial street with an active retail environment at its base is set within a 19th-century masonry framework, with large openings in deep articulated architraves, building the overall image of the street in which the specific events of the street take place. The play of light across the surfaces of a facade and the shadows formed by architectural features and details create visual stimulation, contributing to the sensory experience of the street.[154] The relationship between open and closed portions of the facade has an impact on the space of the street. Large opaque street walls, with a regular pattern of medium to large openings, such as a 19th-century perimeter block development, have a contained and balanced street space. The street space created by large expanses of glass, with projections and recesses in the facade and light and reflections activating surfaces, can be dynamic and layered. How much of the facade is open and the arrangement of these openings is an important characteristic of the street wall. The combination and configuration of the facade above the base influences the nature and character of the spatial enclosure of a specific street. There is frequently variation in the facades of individual buildings and the observation of these variations and the examination of the relationships between the different facades can reveal significant information about the space of the street. Analysing the facades along an individual street and across a range of streets offers a wealth of information and forms another aspect of a comprehensive examination of streets.

One final consideration in the analysis of the street wall is the roofscape, the top edge of the street wall that articulates the moment where the street space touches the sky. The nature of this edge and the manner in which it terminates the street wall has significant impact on the spatial perception of the street. While this edge is remote from the activity of the street, this boundary of the street enclosure is an important visual component of the street. Consistent rooflines, either flat or with repetitive forms, create a stable volume and a planar reading of the sky, strengthening a room-like quality of a street. However, the sky is also the outside of the room, the space beyond and the roof edge is the line that marks the end of the street space. When this line is relatively constant, changes are noteworthy, towers, steeples, and domes which push past this line denote significant moments in the city and become landmarks. When this edge is irregular, with buildings of varied height, architecturally articulated roofs and service infrastructure, the space of the street is extended. The pushing and pulling of roofscape elements creates a dynamic and changing edge and spatial pockets, layers and openings activate the space of the street, drawing the eye along the edge with this visual activity. The space of the street has a less planar top and instead becomes a more fluctuating volume. The street is an outdoor room and its enclosure is in dialogue with the space outside of this room; the next volume along, the room it joins at an intersection and the wider space it sits within and the visual threshold of the roof edge is one of the elements that establishes the relationship to this wider space. Is the street volume contained, with strong definition, or does it push up into the sky with a variable envelope? Of course there is an infinite range of possibilities between these two conditions. The strength of this visual effect is influenced by the distance of the top edge of the street wall from the ground. A low consistent edge emphasises the sky as the top surface of the street space, higher roof lines reduce this effect, with the sky reading as a line of light. When an irregular roof line is close to the ground the space of the assembled objects is accentuated, when the edge is pushed high above the street the objects are flattened into silhouettes, reducing the depth of this edge. These variations in the roof edge are the result of numerous factors, from economic forces or technical limitations to aesthetic considerations or regulatory guidelines. Whatever the nature of this edge, from consistent deep cornices to the up and down of individual towers, this edge draws the upper perimeter of the street and is a key visual characteristic of all streets.

Another critical concept in the discussion of streets is scale. The scale of a street is to a large degree the consequence of the relationships established by the components discussed above. How these elements come together to form the street and most particularly the size of the space they form determines the perceived scale of the street. Without attempting an exhaustive discussion of this complex topic, it is necessary to have an operable definition of human scale. For the purposes of this discussion human scale is defined as objects and space that are scaled in relation to the human body and perceptual faculties. A human scaled street has physical features and proportions that correspond to the human body and perception.[155] The human scale street has a visual and experiential order that can be related to the human body as a unit of measure; doorways and window openings are close to the size of the human body and building heights allow visual and verbal contact. The street wall is divided both horizontally and vertically, allowing visual and physical engagement.[156] Horizontal divisions include multiple entryways that encourage interaction and choice, window openings that provide visual stimulation and architectural divisions that minimise monotonous expanses of blank wall. Vertical layers are proportioned to the human body, with ground floors that fit into the human cone of vision, floor heights that relate to the enclosure of the body and an articulated surface that generates visual interst.[157] The human scaled street provides enclosure that is proportioned to the human body as spaces that are too wide are perceived as uncomfortable and alienating, while those that are too tall can be oppressive.[158] For example Jacobs states that most great streets have a height to width ratio of 1:1.1 to 1:1.25, with a ratio of 1:4 being the maximum for clear definition and enclosure.[159] While Gehl argues that too much width prevents the visual contact necessary for intimate emotional experience.[160] Human scaled streets have a spatial definition that contains and is coherent, that is not overwhelming or too expansive. Human scale is also expressed in the material qualities and details of the street wall and streetscape, with texture and craftsmanship evidencing human skill and consideration.[161] The complexity of the topic of human scale in relation to streets requires a more extensive examination, but this summary provides a reference point for the discussions in this book.

The basic components of the street have been examined to provide the terms and context for the analysis of specific streets and the proposed methodology. Each of these elements makes an important contribution to the physical character of the street and consequently to the perception and experience of the street. The careful assessment of each of these components and the consideration of the relationships between them is essential to developing a thorough understanding of a street. While not every street contains all these components, e.g. roadway, sidewalks/pavements, street furniture, etc., and some components examined have less relevance for certain streets, the framework holds for most streets. All streets have a shared space for movement, vertical elements, which have a base, middle and a top edge and these things have spatial consequence. Examining the specific combination of these features reveals critical information about an individual street which can be compared to other combinations to construct broader understandings about streets in general.

The chapter has been concerned with the street and its place in contemporary urban thinking. Through the summary of historic ideas, key debates and current consensus, the significance of the street has been confirmed. A range of resources, from government guidelines to academic research, have been reviewed to establish a broad picture of current concerns and approaches to the topic of streets and their design. This has culminated in the outlining of a terminology to frame the examination of streets. The analytic method being proposed is predicated on the use of scaled plan and section drawings, with a particular emphasis on the diagrammatic evaluation of sectional drawings. The core argument is that the physical elements and their configuration have a fundamental impact on the experience of a street. Many of these physical attributes can be analysed through observation, photography, diagrams, sketches and perspective drawings, including the spatial characteristics. However, disciplined sectional analysis provides precision and a level of detail that is noteworthy. The knowledge revealed through the combination of accurate horizontal and vertical information has significant value in evaluating spatial configurations. The focus on very specific information in analytic drawings allows critical relationships to be explored. Fundamental issues such as: scale, proportion, layering, overlapping, penetration, expansion, compression, pattern, composition, repetition and much more can be examined in a rigorous fashion. The use of scaled drawings also allows comparative analysis, through which similarities and differences can be assessed and unique characteristics highlighted. The examples included allow these comparisons to take place across a range of street types from cities around the world. The results of this approach have value for designers and urbanists, contributing to a more comprehensive understanding of streets and will help to develop strategies and techniques for integrating the interior spaces of the street into the exterior room of the street.

Notes

1. Spiros Kostof. (1992). *The City Assembled – The Elements of Urban Form Through History*. London: Thames and Hudson. p. 189 and Joseph Rykwert. (1982). *The Necessity of Artifice: Ideas in Architecture*. London: Academy Editions.
2. Ibid, p. 194.
3. Ibid, pp. 194, 220 & 243.
4. Allan B. Jacobs. (1993). *Great Streets*. Cambridge, MA: MIT Press. p. 5.
5. Jane Jacobs. (1993). *The Death and Life of Great American Cities*. Modern Library edn. New York: Modern Library.
6. Bernard Rudofsky. (1969). *Streets for People – A Primer for Americans*. Garden City: Doubleday & Company.

7. Donald Appleyard. (1981). *Livable Streets.* Berkeley: University of California Press.

8. Anne Vernez Moudon. ed. (1987). *Public Streets for Public Use.* New York: Van Nostrand Reinhold.

9. Jan Gehl. (2011). *Life Between Buildings: Using Public Space.* Washington: Island Press. pp. 103 & 168.

10. Ibid, pp. 171–197.

11. J. Jacobs, op. cit.

12. http://www.smartgrowthamerica.org/about – accessed 02-08-13.

13. http://www.smartgrowthamerica.org/complete-streets/changing-policy/model-policy/model-state-legislation/ – accessed 02-08-13.

14. Ibid. One of these documents, the Institute of Transportation Engineers, *Designing Walkable Urban Thoroughfares*, will be discussed in more detail later.

15. In fact New Urbanist thinking is central to the positions advocated by Smart Growth America.

16. http://www.cnu.org/who_we_are – accessed 02-08-13.

17. Elizabeth Plater-Zyberk, Gianni Longo, Peter J. Hetzel, Robert Davis and Andres Duany. (1999). *The Lexicon of New Urbanism.* Miami: Duany Plater-Zyberk & Co. Sect. 1.4.

18. Ibid.

19. Ibid. H1.1 & H1.2.

20. http://www.lgc.org/whatwedo/index.html – accessed 03-08-13.

21. http://www.lgc.org/center/about/center.html – accessed 03-08-13.

22. Dan Burden, Michael Wallwork, Dave Davis, Sharon Sprowls and Paul Zykofsky. (1999). *Street Design Guidelines for Healthy Neighbourhoods.* Sacramento: Center for Livable Communities.

23. Ibid.

24. http://www.ite.org/aboutite/index.asp – accessed 04-08-13 and http://www.standards.its.dot.gov/About/ProgramPartners – accessed 04-08-13.

25. Institute of Transportation Engineers. *Designing Walkable Urban Thoroughfares: A Context Sensitive Approach, An ITE Recommended Practice.* (2010). Washington: Institute of Transportation Engineers.

26. Ibid. pp. 114–203.

27. Ibid. p. 3.

28. Ibid. p. 3.

29. New York City Department of Transportation. *Street Design Manual.* (2009). New York: New York City Department of Transportation. p. 17.

30. Ibid. p. 19.

31. Ibid. pp. 17–42.

32. Ibid. pp. 45–198.

33. U.K. Department for Transport. *Manual for Streets.* (2007). London: Thomas Telford. p. 6.

34. Ibid. p. 6.

35. Ibid. p. 12.

36. Ibid. p. 13.

37. Ibid. pp. 15–16.

38. Ibid. pp. 23–38.

39. Ibid. pp. 41–49.

40. Ibid. p. 51.

41. Ibid. pp. 52–60.

42. Ibid. pp. 63–77.

43. Ibid. pp. 79–97.

44. Ibid. pp. 99–113.

45. Ibid. pp. 115–136.

46. Vikas Mehta. (2013). *The Street: A Quintessential Social Public Space.* London: Routledge.

47. Ibid. pp. 7–65.

48. Ibid. pp. 64–65.

49. Ibid. pp. 67–96.

50. Ibid. pp. 92–93.

51. Ibid. pp. 97–115.

52. Ibid. pp. 99–100.

53. Ibid. p. 120.

54. Ibid. pp. 117–148.

55. Ibid. pp. 148–152.

56. Ibid. pp. 159–164.

57. Ibid. pp. 165–174.

58. Ibid. pp. 166–172.

59. Ibid. p. 171.

60. Ibid. pp. 171–174.

61. Ibid. p. 174.

62. Ibid. p. 177.

63. Ibid. pp. 181–202.

64. Ibid. pp. 188–202.

65. Ibid. pp. 129–131.

66. Ibid. pp. 131–133.

67. Ibid. pp. 84–89.

68. Ibid. pp. 134–135.

69. Ibid. pp. 137–138.

70. Ibid. p. 90.

71. Ibid. p. 138.
72. A. Jacobs, op. cit.
73. Ibid. pp. 2–11.
74. Ibid. pp. 15–19.
75. Ibid. pp. 20–131.
76. Ibid. p. 135.
77. Ibid. p. 134
78. Ibid. pp. 202–268.
79. Ibid. pp. 202–204.
80. Ibid. p. 202.
81. Ibid. p. 268.
82. Ibid. pp. 270–271.
83. Ibid. p. 271.
84. Ibid. pp. 271–292.
85. Ibid. pp. 293–308.
86. Ibid. pp. 271–308.
87. Ibid. pp. 311–314.
88. Ibid. pp. 14–131.
89. Ibid. pp. 270–308.
90. Ibid. p. 280.
91. Ibid. pp. 293–295.
92. Ibid. pp. 14–254.
93. Ibid. p. 87.
94. Ibid. p. 285.
95. Ibid. pp. 261–266.
96. Ibid. pp. 270–271 & 313–314.
97. Ibid. pp. 13–131.
98. Ibid. p. 305.
99. Ibid. pp. 277–281.
100. Ibid. pp. 285–287.
101. J. Jacobs, op. cit.
102. Ibid. pp. 29–54.
103. A. Jacobs, op. cit. p. 43.
104. Ibid. p. 286.
105. Ibid. pp. 286–287.
106. Meredith Glaser, Mattijs van't Hoff, Hans Karssenberg, Jeroen Laven and Jan van Teeffelen. eds. (2012). *The City At Eye Level: Lessons for Street Plinths.* Delft: Eburon.

107. Ibid. pp. 61–71, 180–191 & 122–133.

108. Mehta, op. cit. pp. 137–143.

109. Jan Gehl, Lotte Johansen Kaefer and Solvejg Reigstad. (2006). Close Encounters With Buildings. *Urban Design International*. 11 (1), pp. 29–47.

110. Ibid. p. 37.

111. Ibid. p. 38.

112. Ibid. pp. 44–46.

113. Le Corbusier. (1967). *The Radiant City*, translated by Pamela Knight, Eleanor Levieux and Derek Coltman. London: Faber and Faber. pp. 119–126.

114. Reid Ewing, Susan Handy, Ross C. Brownson, Otto Clemente, and Emily Winston. (2006). Identifying and Measuring Urban Design Qualities Related to Walkability. *Journal of Physical Activity and Health*. 3 (Suppl 1), p. S226.

115. A. Jacobs, op. cit. pp. 279–280.

116. *Designing Walkable Urban Thoroughfares,* op. cit. pp. 45–47 and *Manual for Streets*, op. cit. pp. 89–90.

117. Federal Highway Administration. *The Effects of Environmental Design on the Amount and Type of Bicycling and Walking*. (1992). Washington: National Bicycling and Walking Study, US Federal Highway Administration. p. 13.

118. Plater-Zyberk, et al., op. cit., *Designing Walkable Urban Thoroughfares*, op. cit. and *Manual for Streets*, op. cit.

119. Camillo Sitte. (1965). *City Planning According to Artistic Principles*, translated by George R. Collins and Christiane Crasemann Collins. London: Phaidon Press. p. 61.

120. http://www.sfbetterstreets.org/design-guidelines/sidewalk-zones/ – accessed 09-09-13 and http://www.seattle.gov/transportation/rowmanual/manual/4_11.asp – accessed 09-09-13.

121. Mehta, op. cit. pp. 84–90.

122. Gehl, et al., op. cit. p. 30 and Jan Gehl. (2011). *Life Between Buildings: Using Public Space*. Washington: Island Press. pp. 147–151.

123. Mehta, op. cit. pp. 138–144.

124. http://www.sfbetterstreets.org/design-guidelines/sidewalk-zones/ op. cit. p. 98.

125. http://www.toronto.ca/planning/urbdesign/streetscape/index.htm – accessed 10-09-13.

126. Mehta, op. cit. p. 89 and William H. Whyte. (1980). *The Social Life of Small Urban Spaces*. New York: Project for Public Space. pp. 19–21.

127. http://www.sfbetterstreets.org/design-guidelines/sidewalk-zones/ op. cit. p. 6.

128. *Street Design Manual*. op. cit. pp. 116-131, http://www.sfbetterstreets.org/design-guidelines/sidewalk-zones/ op. cit. pp. 211–215 & 192–203 and http://wx.toronto.ca/inter/plan/streetscape.nsf/paving?OpenView – accessed 10-09-13.

129. A. Jacobs, op. cit. p. 300.

130. Ibid. pp. 282–283.

131. Ibid. pp. 298–299.

132. Gehl. (2011). op. cit. p. 165.

133. Ibid. pp. 23 & 155–164.

134. Mehta, op. cit. pp. 129–131.

135. Gehl. (2011). op. cit. p. 77.

136. A. Jacobs. p. 27 and Gehl. (2011). p. 159.

137. Ibid. pp. 277–281 and Ibid. p. 69.

138. A. Jacobs, op. cit. pp. 174–183.

139. Plater-Zyberk, et al. op. cit. Sect H.

140. Gehl. (2010). op. cit. p. 187.

141. Mehta, op. cit. pp. 122–124, 128 & 169 and Gehl, et al. op. cit. pp. 30–31.

142. Mehta, pp. 137–138, Gehl, et al. pp. 37–39 and Jan Gehl. (1986). "Soft Edges" in Residential Streets. *Scandinavian Housing and Planning Research*. 3 (2), p. 92.

143. Gehl, Kaefer and Reigstad. op. cit. pp. 37–38.

144. Ibid. pp. 32–34.

145. Ibid. pp. 37–39.

146. Mehta, op. cit. pp. 149–153.

147. Mehta, p. 128 and Gehl, et al. p. 30.

148. Whyte, op. cit. p. 19 and Gehl. (2011). op. cit. p. 23.

149. A. Jacobs, op. cit. p. 279 and Gehl, et al. op. cit. p. 33.

150. Mehta, op. cit. pp. 138–143.

151. Mehta, p.135, A. Jacobs, op. cit. pp. 281–285 and Gehl, et al. op. cit. p. 30.

152. Mehta, pp. 119–120, 122–125 & 135 and Gehl, et al. pp. 34–35 & 37.

153. Gehl, et al. p. 34.

154. A. Jacobs, op. cit. pp. 283–285.

155. Ewing, et al. op. cit. p. 226.

156. Gehl, et al., op. cit. pp. 34–35.

157. A. Jacobs, op. cit. pp. 283–285 and Gehl, et al. p. 34.

158. Gehl. (2010). op. cit. p. 41 and Gehl. (2011). op. cit. p. 69.

159. A. Jacobs, op. cit. pp. 279–280.

160. Gehl. (2010). op. cit. p. 76 and Gehl, et al., op. cit. pp. 30–35.

161. Gehl, et al. pp. 32–35.

Chapter Four
Cities and Streets: The Data Set

0 100 250 500 1000m

4.1A
Amsterdam City Plan

0 100 250 500 1000m

4.1B
Amsterdam City Section

Amsterdam, The Netherlands   Lat. 52°22′26″ N – Long. 4°53′22″ E

Founded in the late 13th century and becoming a prominent medieval trading port through the 14th century, Amsterdam developed around the river Amstel and alongside the Ijsselmeer, in the Northwest of the Netherlands. The city sits in a flat plain and is the product of centuries of human alterations of the landscape, beginning with the damming of the river, through the construction of its distinctive canal network and land reclamation projects and extending to the construction of the North Sea canal in the 19th century. Radiating from the city's medieval core, successive rings of canals are lined with 4–5-storey brick buildings, forming tight streets and a dense urban form. The spatial character of the city is low scaled and intimate, with vertical street walls and an active ground plane due to the level changes created by the canals. This central part of the city is surrounded by 19th- and 20th-century extensions, with more expansive and rectilinear planning.[1]

Oude Hoogstraat, Amsterdam

Oude Hoogstraat is oriented East to West, in the core of medieval Amsterdam. As in much of the centre of Amsterdam the street wall is formed by 4–5-storey brick buildings, with a narrow roadway (2.9 meters/9 feet 6 inches) and small bands of pavement (2 meters/6 feet 6 inches) on either side. The result is a vertically oriented space, with the continuous street wall creating a clearly defined space. Generally the ground-floor spaces connect directly to the street, with large openings and regular entryways, creating a permeable street wall base. The street is designated for pedestrian use, with the roadway used for bicycles and emergency and service vehicle access. The street is an intimate and human scaled street, with subtle spatial qualities and material articulation.

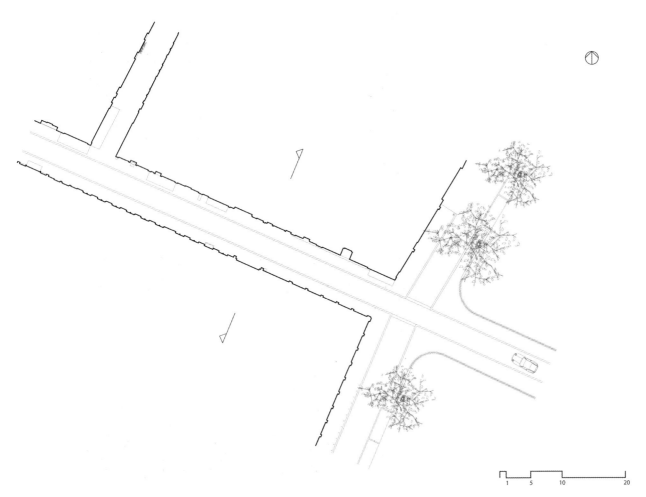

4.1 C
Amsterdam Street Plan

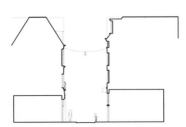

4.1 D
Amsterdam Street Section

4.1 E
Amsterdam Photo

4.2 A
Bangkok City Plan

4.2 B
Bangkok City Section

Bangkok, Thailand   Lat. 13°45'00" N – Long. 100°31'00"E

While there had been previous settlements in the area, Bangkok was established
as the capital in 1782 and developed as the primary trading port of the country.
The city straddles the Chao Phraya river, spreading over the flat plain of the river
delta. Originally the city was accessed primarily by water, with either the river or

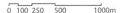

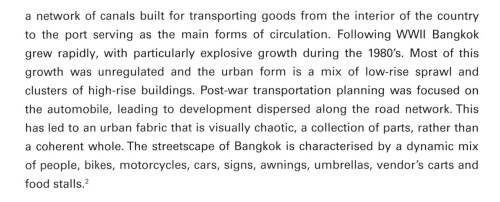

a network of canals built for transporting goods from the interior of the country to the port serving as the main forms of circulation. Following WWII Bangkok grew rapidly, with particularly explosive growth during the 1980's. Most of this growth was unregulated and the urban form is a mix of low-rise sprawl and clusters of high-rise buildings. Post-war transportation planning was focused on the automobile, leading to development dispersed along the road network. This has led to an urban fabric that is visually chaotic, a collection of parts, rather than a coherent whole. The streetscape of Bangkok is characterised by a dynamic mix of people, bikes, motorcycles, cars, signs, awnings, umbrellas, vendor's carts and food stalls.[2]

Thanon Khao San, Bangkok

Thanon Khao San is a short street on the Northern edge of the historic core of Bangkok, which runs East to West. The space of the street is formed by a series of layers in front of the street wall, with the base of the street wall being modulated by a mix of open shops, food stalls, vendor's carts and cars. Above this is a profusion of signs, awnings, and balconies. The height of the street wall varies from single storey to six storeys, with the predominant height being 4 storeys. The roadway is typical for a small commercial street, with room for parking and vehicles to travel in both directions (8.7 meters/28 feet 6 inches). In practice this is modified by the presence of vendors and vehicles. The pavements are moderately sized (4 meters/13 feet) and occupied by a variety of retail stalls, selling food, handicrafts, and a variety of merchandise. This creates a very layered street space, with direct interaction between the ground floor spaces and the exterior of the street. The small-scale nature of the market stalls and vendor's carts breaks up the linear space of the street, generating an array of choices and an extremely vital visual environment. This is strengthened by the overhanging balconies, awnings and signs that project into the space, which activates the space above the ground floor. The unregulated nature of this street results in a place which is lively and full of sensual experiences.

4.2 C
Bangkok Street Plan

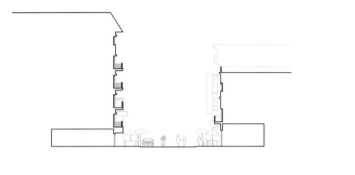

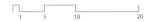

4.2 D
Bangkok Street Section

4.2 E
Bangkok Photo

4.3A
Beijing City Plan

4.3B
Beijing City Section

Beijing, China   Lat. 39°54′27″N – Long. 116°23′50″E

Beijing is a very ancient city, with human settlements dating back to the Neolithic period and numerous earlier cities occupying the site with the current city dating from the 15th century. Situated on the plain below the Yan and Jundu mountains and between the Yongding and the Chaobai rivers, Beijing has little topographical variation. The original city plan was a square, with a main North-South axis,

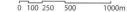

establishing a rectilinear street pattern. The traditional city consisted of low rectangular urban fabric, which has been radically transformed since the end of WWII, particularly in the last thirty years. This has been predominantly medium- and high-rise development, with both residential and commercial towers replacing the traditional low-rise typology. The spatial quality in much of the city is post-war urbanism, with towers that ignore the street in commercial districts and multi-storey apartment blocks set in landscaped plots in residential areas. The streetscape

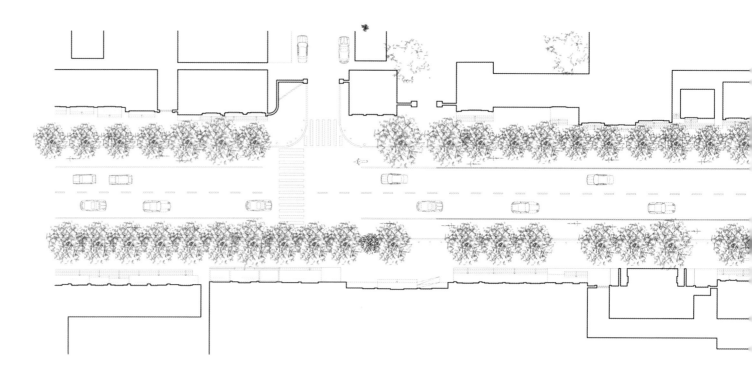

4.3 C
Beijing Street Plan

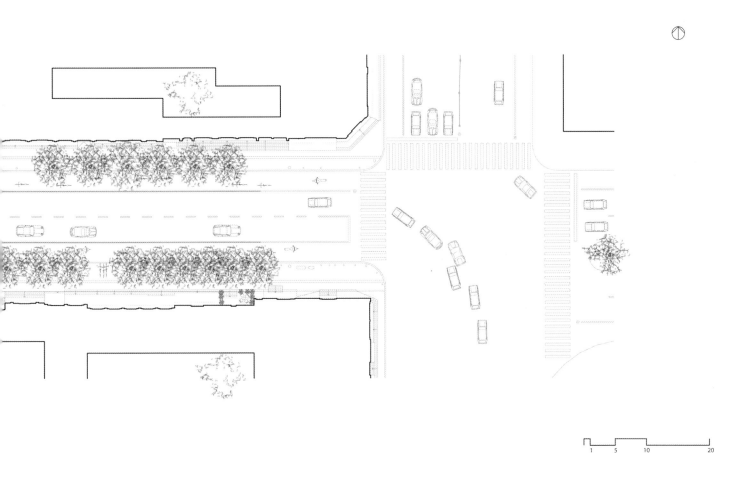

can be fragmentary, with tower bases, rather than a consistent street wall and many streets are very broad, dominated by vehicular traffic and lack strong spatial definition.[3]

Gulou East Street, Beijing

Running East to West, the street's Western end is the Northern terminus of the city's North-South axis. This is marked by two ancient monuments: the Bell tower and the Old Drum tower. The street is bordered by single-storey buildings raised half a storey above the pavement, with the ground floor reached by steps. The street has medium-width pavements (4.5 meters/14 feet 9 inches) with a row of trees in the amenity zone separating the pedestrian pavement from a bicycle lane (3 meters/9 feet 10 inches) followed by a two-lane roadway for vehicular traffic (7.8 meters/25 feet 7 inches). This forms a wide horizontal space, with multiple layers of space, with the trees and the low street wall creating three major spaces, the centre space that combines the roadway and bicycle lanes which is defined by the trees and the two spaces for pedestrians on either side created by the low street wall and the row of trees that line the pavement. These main spaces break down into layers as well, with the bicycle lanes modifying the roadway and the pedestrian spaces modulated by the trees and the steps leading to the interior spaces.

4.3 D
Beijing Street Section

4.3 E
Beijing Photo

4.4A
Boston City Plan

4.4B
Boston City Section

Boston, United States   Lat. 42°21'30"N – Long. 71°03'35"E

Founded in 1630 by Puritans from England on the Shawmut peninsula, Boston is situated between the Charles River and Massachusetts Bay. The topography of the area is the result of glacial activity, with waterways carved by glaciers and glacial deposits forming hills and islands in the waters surrounding the city. Boston is also a chronicle of the various stages of urban development in the United States, originally comprised of a dense organic street pattern surrounding the harbour in the 17th century, followed by the succeeding phases of development using landfill and dams to expand the city, first with the regular, tight 18th-century streets of Beacon Hill, to the 19th-century grid of the Back Bay and the late Baroque boulevard of Commonwealth Avenue and the "Emerald Necklace" parks planned by Frederick Law Olmstead. This was followed by post WWII urban renewal, the construction of the Central Artery and commercial high-rise development of the 1960's and 1970's, which dramatically altered the scale and form of the city. Most recently the Central Artery/Tunnel Project, known as the Big Dig, has removed the elevated highway underground and replaced it with a network of urban parks. Boston's spatial character is indicative of this layering of urban models, a former mercantile waterfront developed for commercial and leisure activity, a central business district of large monolithic towers, tight streets lined with small-scale brick buildings, a mix of historic landmarks, surrounded by a patchwork of 3–4-storey residential neighbourhoods.[4]

Newbury Street, Boston

In the Back Bay area created by landfill in the 19th century, Newbury Street is oriented Northeast to Southwest, with a street wall formed predominantly by 3–4-storey brownstones. Originally a residential street, in the 20th century the ground floors of most of the street have been re-purposed for retail uses, with the upper floors occupied by residential apartments. The street has very wide sidewalks (roughly 8 meters/26 feet), portions of which are occupied by small yards, street trees and light poles in the amenity zone, a fairly typical roadway (12 meters/34 feet 4 inches) of two lanes with a parking lane on either side and various forms of transition between the exterior and interior spaces of the street. In some instances the ground floor is raised half a storey and occasionally there is a retail unit underneath with the yard at the lower level. This results in a rich transition zone, with a wide variety of uses and spatial qualities; from private yards, shop front seating areas to spots for informal social exchange. The strong spatial definition of the street wall enclosure, coupled with this varied transition zone, creates a vital public space, filled with people circulating, shopping and socialising.

4.4C
Boston Street Plan

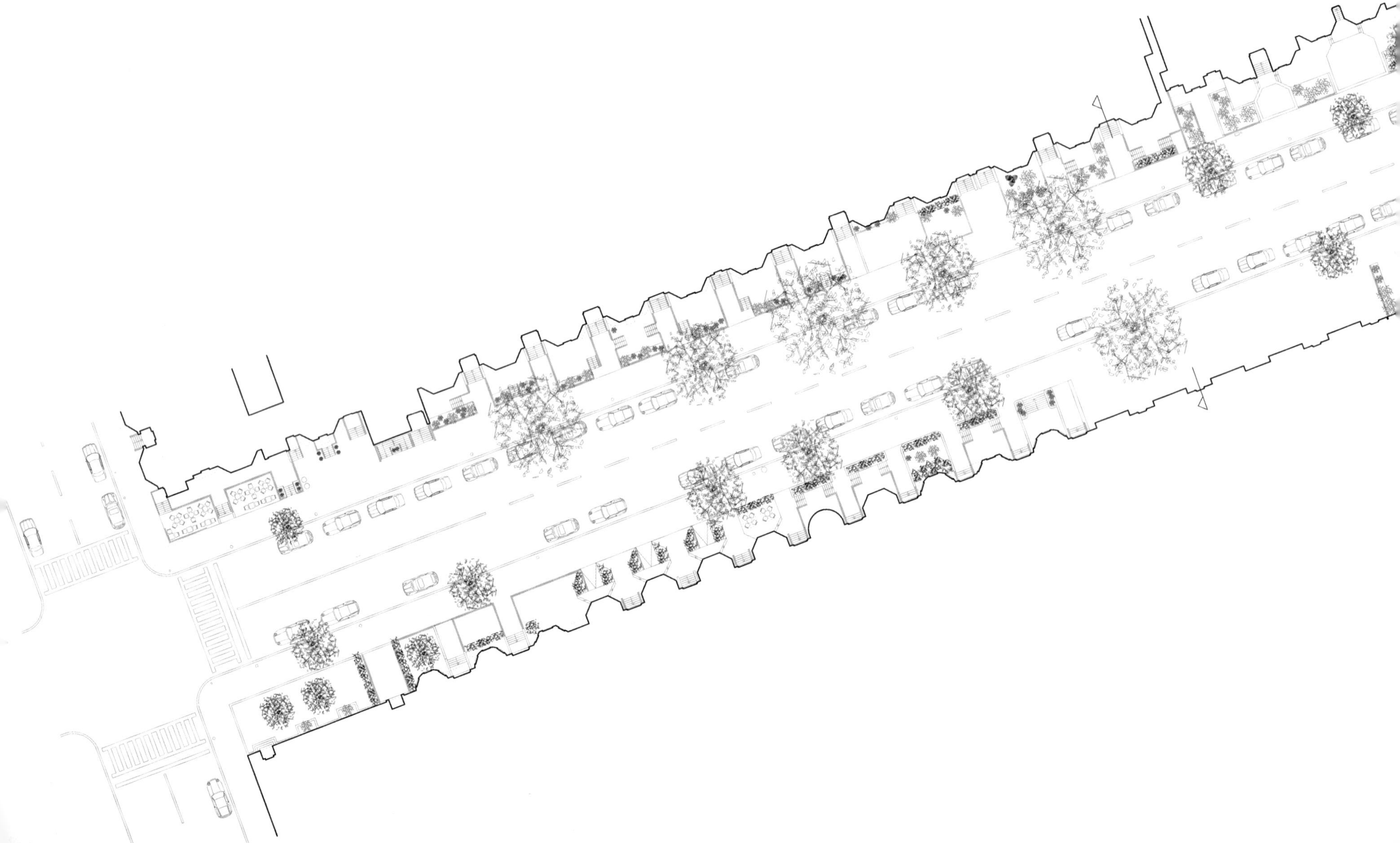

4.4 D
Boston Street Section

4.4 E
Boston Photo

4.5 A
Buenos Aires City Plan

4.5 B
Buenos Aires City Section

Buenos Aires, Argentina   Lat. 34°36′47″ S – Long. 58°22′38″ W

While an earlier settlement existed on the site, Buenos Aires was permanently established in 1580 on the Southern shore of the Rio de la Plata, the wide estuary of the Parana and Uruguay rivers that spreads out to the Atlantic Ocean. The city sits on the Northern coastal edge of the flat agricultural plains of Argentina, intersected with numerous small watercourses, with little variation in elevation. The city is characterised by its division into identifiable districts bordered by wide avenues, with a street pattern that is generally gridded between the diagonals of the

```
         0  100 250   500        1000m
```

```
         0  100 250   500        1000m
```

avenues. There is a mix of 19th-century neo-classical and 20th-century modernist architecture, with streets typically lined with mid-level blocks interspersed with high-rise residential towers. Buenos Aires has an open spatial quality, often described as European in both scale and aesthetic, as the street wall is consistent and the roadways are broad. The city also includes large areas of informal settlements, without organised infrastructure or official recognition. These areas are organic in form, with tight, narrow streets of 1–2-storey structures. The contrast of this very limited urban provision with the quality of the regulated districts raises significant social, environmental and urban issues.[5]

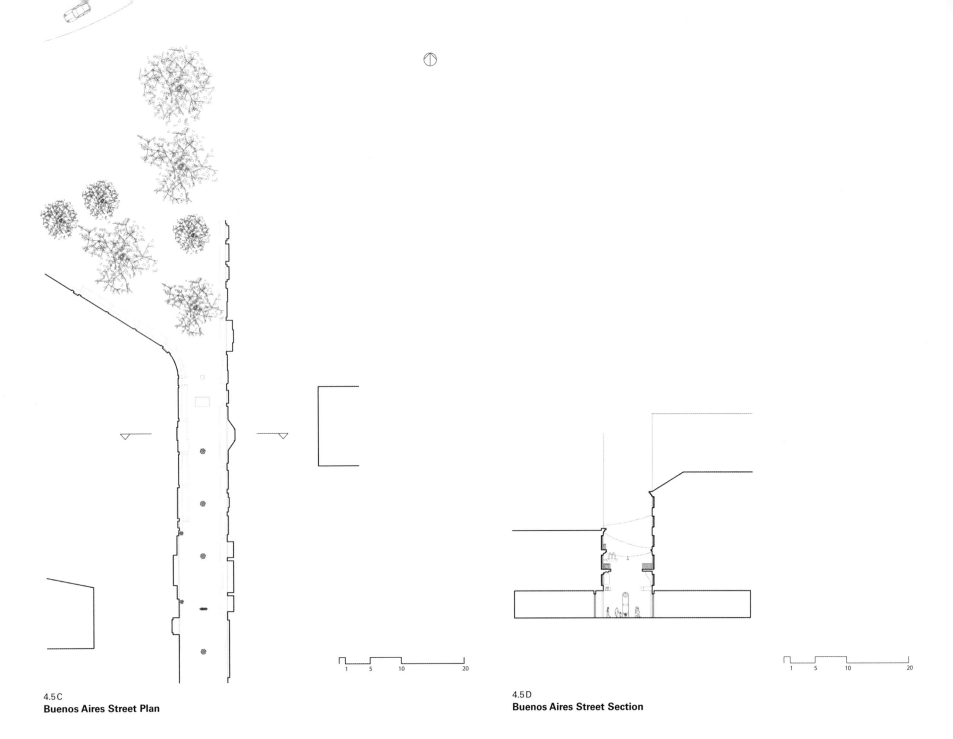

4.5 C
Buenos Aires Street Plan

4.5 D
Buenos Aires Street Section

Calle Florida, Buenos Aires

In the heart of Buenos Aires, running North-South, Calle Florida is a pedestrian street, lined with retail stores at pavement level. As with other streets in Buenos Aires, the street wall varies, with buildings on Calle Florida ranging from 3 storeys to mid-level blocks up to 14 or 15 storeys. The pavement between the street walls is small (7.6 meters/25 feet) which creates a tall vertical spatial enclosure. The face of the street wall is highly articulated by various elements: balconies, awnings, canopies, signage and lighting. The base of the street wall is varied, with recesses, shop windows and entryways. There is a strip of street furniture and planters near the centre, with the occasional retail kiosk, providing informal seating and opportunities for casual social interaction. This combination of enclosure, street amenities, a visually stimulating street wall and both horizontal and vertical spatial layering, creates an active urban space with a strong identity.

4.5E
Buenos Aires Photo

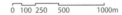

0 100 250   500   1000m

4.6A
Cape Town City Plan

0 100 250   500   1000m

4.6B
Cape Town City Section

Cape Town, South Africa   Lat. 33°55′00″ S – Long. 18°25′00″ E

Cape Town was settled in 1652 to provision ships by the Dutch East India Company. The colonial city occupied the flat lands located between the coast of Table Bay and the base of Table Mountain. The contemporary city has spread into the flat plain to the East and into the foothills of both Table Mountain and Signal Hill. The core of the city is organised by the grid dating from the colonial period, with wider primary streets and a secondary division of smaller streets. There is a mix of historic low-rise buildings and a range of mid-level and high-rise towers, with development of industrial and residential areas to the East horizontal in form. After WWII a network of freeways was built and a raised motorway was built along the waterfront of the city centre. The influence of post-war planning principles which prioritise vehicular traffic has led to a somewhat disjointed urban fabric, which often lacks spatial definition. The spatial character of the city is horizontal, with the consistent street wall of the pre-war city interrupted by post-war towers, set back buildings and parking provision.[6]

Long Street, Cape Town

Running South-West to North-East, Long Street is a secondary street in the colonial grid of Cape Town. The street contains buildings that range from colonial through 19th-century to contemporary structures, with a variation in building height, street wall bases and facades as a result. The North-Eastern end of the street is predominantly mid-level contemporary development 6–10 storeys, with some 20-storey towers. As the street continues South-West the scale reduces and the pre-war mixture of 2-4 storeys re-emerges. The roadway width is moderate (12.4 meters/40 feet 8 inches) with room for 2 lanes of traffic and a parking lane on either side. The pavements on either side of the roadway are a fairly typical width (3.5 meters/11 feet 6 inches) and often have outdoor seating supplied by the adjacent businesses. There are frequent instances of outdoor porches on the upper floors which overhang the pavement, to form an arcade which provides shade from the sun. Many of the historical arcades have fine architectural detailing, creating an engaging visual streetscape. The street generally has a strong spatial enclosure, with an active street wall base, while some of the larger buildings damage the scale relationships of the street.

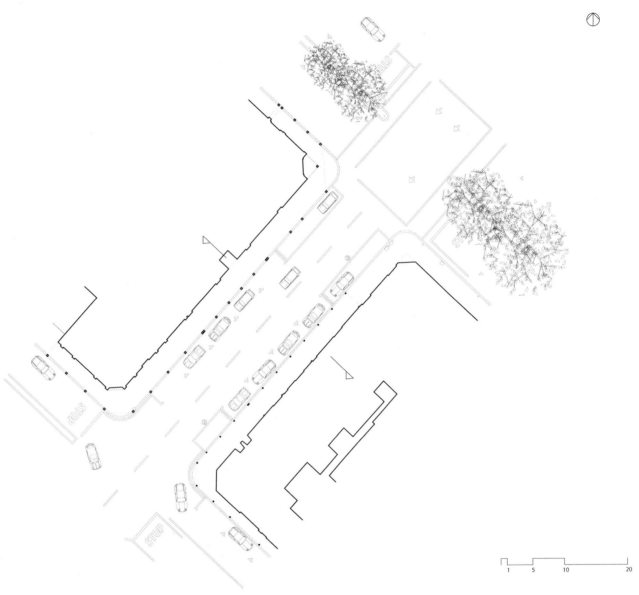

4.6C
Cape Town Street Plan

4.6D
Cape Town Street Section

4.6E
Cape Town Photo

4.7 A
Chicago City Plan

4.7 B
Chicago City Section

Chicago, United States   Lat. 41°51'00" N – Long. 87°39'00" W

Founded at the mouth of the Chicago River in the early 19th century, Chicago grew rapidly in the middle of the century due to its role as a railway terminus, connecting the interior and West of the U.S. to markets on the East coast. Chicago spreads out from the Western shore of Lake Michigan on a flat glacial plain; the city's horizontal form is defined by the regularity of the surveyor's grid, the expansiveness of the prairie echoed in the extendibility of the grid. The streets formed by this grid have wide roadways, designed for the rapid movement of vehicles, seen primarily as the instruments of commercial circulation. The city is predominantly low rise, with large areas of 2–3-storey detached residential buildings, but famous for the cluster of high-rise buildings in the central business district. Beginning in the late 19th century, Chicago became the laboratory for high-rise architecture, first pushing load-bearing masonry to the limits and then experimenting with and systematising the steel-framed multi-storey building. This remarkable vertical core contrasted with the horizontality of the grid and the lake divided by the regular rhythm of wide streets produces an open spatial quality. The city has a large scale, with an urban form that communicates strength and resilience and the streets share this character, whether residential or commercial, and are practical and active.[7]

South State Street, Chicago

South State Street runs North-South through the centre of Chicago's "Loop", the central business district and is one of the city's earliest and most prominent commercial streets. The street wall is formed by primarily mid-level blocks ranging in height from 10 to 20 storeys. The roadway is wide (17.5 meters/57 feet 4 inches) accommodating 4 lanes of traffic, with a small median demarcated with road markings and the sidewalks on either side of the roadway are ample (6.65 meters/21 feet 9 inches), which creates a broad space between the street walls. The street wall varies in height, consequently the height to width ratio is not constant, but is most consistently 1:1, creating a broad volume of space. The sidewalks are populated by large planters, trees, benches, light poles and banners, which layer the space of the pavement, provide places for people to stop, add visual stimulation and buffer the pedestrian zone from the vehicular traffic on the roadway. The room of the street is at a commercial scale, with capacity for large flows of people and vehicles and the full range of activity these uses bring.

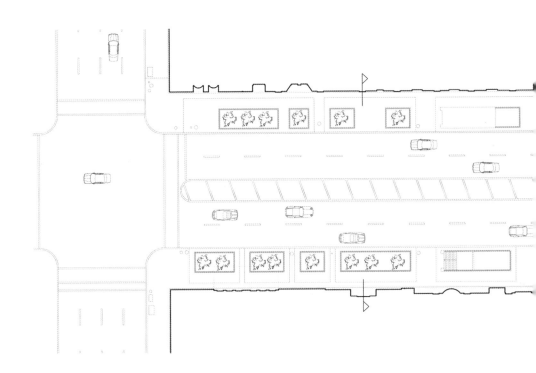

4.7 C
Chicago Street Plan

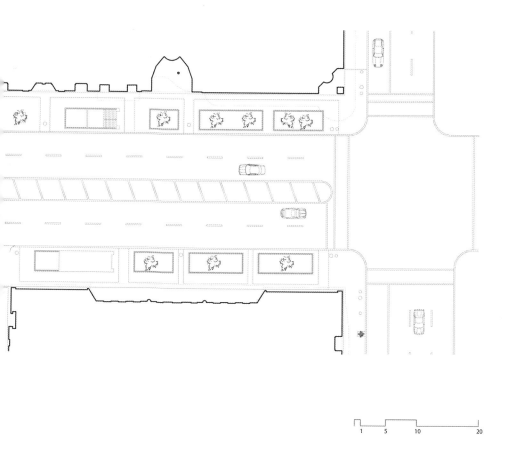

1   5   10   20

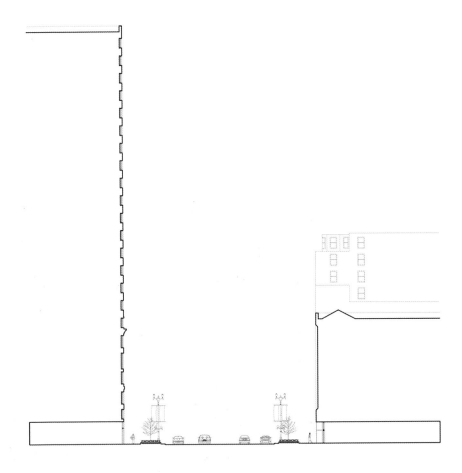

4.7 D
Chicago Street Section

4.7 E
Chicago Photo

4.8A
Copenhagen City Plan

4.8B
Copenhagen City Section

Copenhagen, Denmark   Lat. 55°40'33" N – Long. 12°33'55" E

In the early 12th century a small settlement was fortified, leading to the establishment of a more substantial town, which through trade and royal patronage
became the city of Copenhagen. The city is spread across parts of two islands,
Zealand and Amager, with the navigable waterway between them forming the
historical harbour. The topography is flat, and the city is interspersed with various
inlets, water channels and lakes, which have been used for industrial, commercial,
military and leisure purposes. The city is generally low rise, with buildings ranging

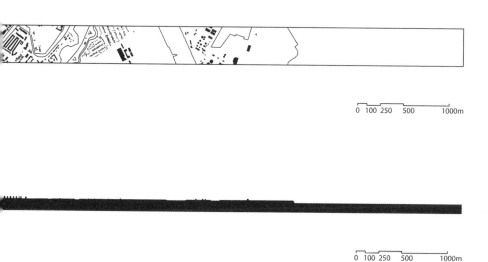

0 100 250 500 1000m

0 100 250 500 1000m

from 3 to 5 storeys, of brick, concrete and stone, with majority of the urban fabric dating from the late 18th century to the present. Copenhagen has numerous architectural monuments, from northern European baroque palaces and churches to neo-classical examples of the national romantic period. The street wall typically forms a consistent enclosure and the spatial character of the city is modest, with many small-scaled streets and public places enclosed by subtly modulated facades. Since the 1970's the city has been pursuing the pedestrianisation of the historic centre of the city. This has led to an increase in the vitality and social use of the city, making Copenhagen a model for people-centred urbanism.[8]

Vimmelskaftet, Copenhagen

In the heart of the historic city, Vimmelskaftet is oriented East-West. The roadway and pavements are unified into a single surface, which must be shared by vehicles, bicycles and pedestrians. This surface is thin (5.6 meters/18 feet 4 inches) and

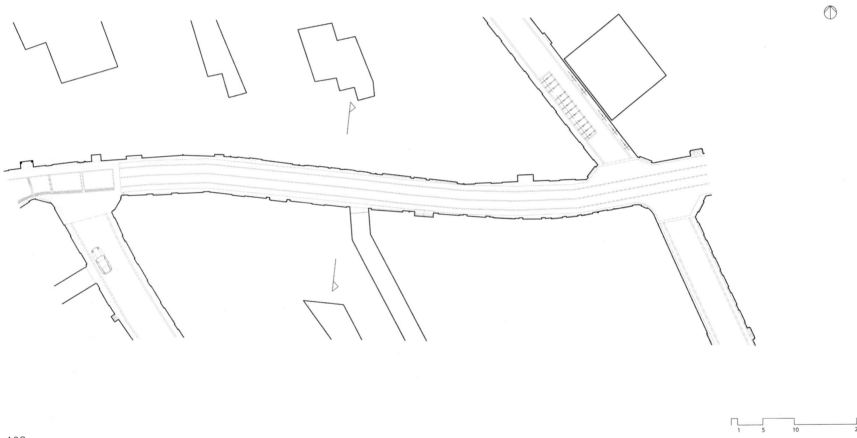

4.8 C
Copenhagen Street Plan

enclosed by 3–4-storey buildings, which results in a vertical space that is modified by variations in the facades, signage and awnings. The base of the street wall integrates the interiors of the street into the exterior space of the street, as most of the interior spaces are level with the pavement and many of the ground-floor elevations are glazed with regular doorways. The street curves gently in plan, creating a space that closes as the eye moves along it, producing an engaging visual experience as the individual facades fold around the bend. The mix of architectural styles, materials, colours and textures results in a visually stimulating urban space.

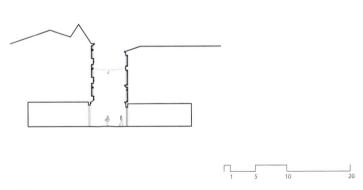

4.8D
Copenhagen Street Section

4.8E
Copenhagen Photo

0 100 250 500 1000m

4.9A
Fès City Plan

0 100 250 500 1000m

4.9B
Fès City Section

Fès, Morocco   Lat. 34°02'13" N – Long. 4°59'59" E

Fès is the result of the union of two settlements in the 11th century, the first founded on the East bank of the Wadi Fès at the end of the 8th century and the other on the West bank in the early 9th century. Fès has been a significant place of Islamic culture, with the oldest mosque in North Africa and as the site of the University of Al-Qarawiyyin, a historic centre of Islamic scholarship. Located on a flat plain at the base of the Mid-Atlas mountains, there is little elevational variation, with just a slight incline from the centre of the Medina out to the edge of the historic city, away from the watercourse of the river. The city is comprised of 3–4 storey masonry buildings, with the occasional vertical of the characteristic square minarets of North Africa. The urban form is the result of religious laws derived from the Quran as discussed in Chapter 2, this leads to the labyrinthine quality, with narrow tight streets, designed to protect the privacy of the family groups that live there. The city is horizontal in overall form, with streets that have a vertical definition. The small scale of the streets creates intimate spaces, densely populated with commerce and social interaction.[9]

Rue Talaa Kebira, Fès

Running Southwest to Northeast through the core of the city; the Rue Talaa Kebira, like much of the historic city, is a pedestrian street with no vehicular traffic. The pavement is narrow and varies in width (from 5 meters/26 feet 4 inches to 3 meters/9 feet 10 inches) enclosed by stucco faced street walls, with simple openings, awnings, many overhangs over entryways and occasionally elements that bridge the street. While the city is low in form, the density and the narrowness of the street produce a vertical spatial experience. Many of the ground floor spaces are shops, which open directly onto the pavement and frequently use part of the public space to display products, creating a lively and visually stimulating space. The narrow space is animated by light and the variation of form as the street wall moves in and out along the length of the street. The spatial quality of the street is dense and dynamic, as the close walls frame the variations of form and light.

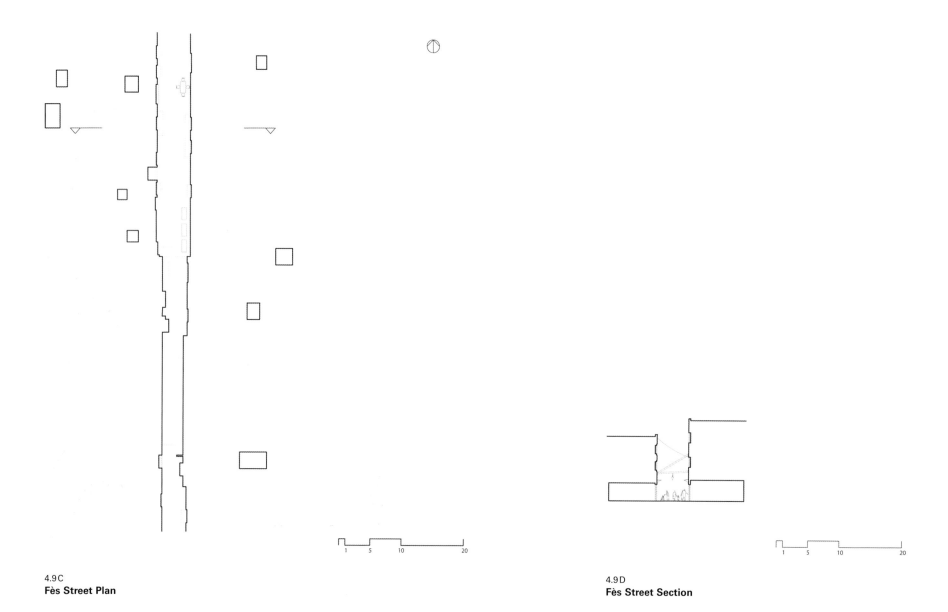

4.9 C
Fès Street Plan

4.9 D
Fès Street Section

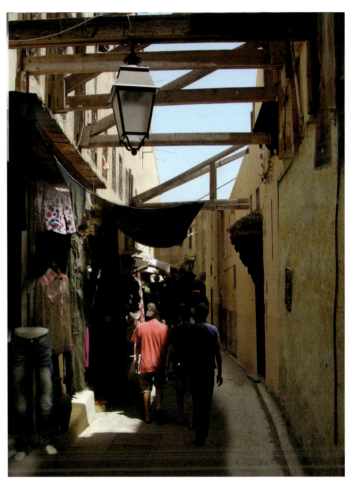

4.9 E
Fès Illustration

0 100 250 500   1000m

4.10 A
Genoa City Plan

0 100 250 500   1000m

4.10 B
Genoa City Section

Genoa, Italy   Lat. 44°24'22" N – Long. 8°56'01" E

The city of Genoa has very ancient roots, its natural harbour making it a prosperous
fishing and trading port of the Roman Empire, later becoming one of the most
powerful mercantile cities of the renaissance, with a trading network throughout
the Mediterranean basin. The city is located on the West coast of the Italian
peninsula, as the coast bends West at the top of the Ligurian Sea and occupies the
flat coastal strip around the harbour and the foothills of the Apennine Mountains.
The city's structure is the result of successive stages of concentric growth outward

from the harbour, with the compression of defensive walls and the surrounding hills causing a compact organic urban form, which was added to with sections of regularised street patterns after the demolition of the city walls. The density and the dramatic topography has resulted in a vertical city in the historic core, with tall 7–8 storey buildings packed tightly together and rising up steep slopes. This central area of the city is a complex web of very narrow streets, with small public spaces carved out around neighbourhood churches. The various levels of the city stack the tall vertical streets into a knotted cluster of dark slots of space and thin lines of blue sky overhead. This finely grained network is filled with the commercial and communal life of the city, creating vibrant social streets, the essential public places of Genoa.[10]

Via San Bernardo, Genoa

The Via San Bernardo runs Northwest to Southeast from the edge of the waterfront through the heart of the medieval city and has been an important commercial street throughout its history. The street is lined with 5–7 storey masonry buildings, with a thin paved strip of circulation between them (+/–3 meters/9 feet 10 inches). The base of the street wall is punctured by regular openings into ground floor shops or small courtyards accessing the upper levels. The interior spaces along the street are directly connected to the exterior, with at most a single step at the threshold to accommodate the slope of the street. The facades are predominantly solid painted stucco walls, with small punched openings at each floor. This simple surface is relieved by occasional architectural details, operable timber shutters, wall mounted light fixtures and religious icons set in niches. The street is predominantly used by pedestrians, but motorcycles and service vehicles also operate on the street, which requires everyone using the street to be conscientious of the shared nature of the space. The tall volume of the street has powerful sense of enclosure, producing an intense spatial compression in a space filled with activity and movement, generating a lively, stimulating social urban place.

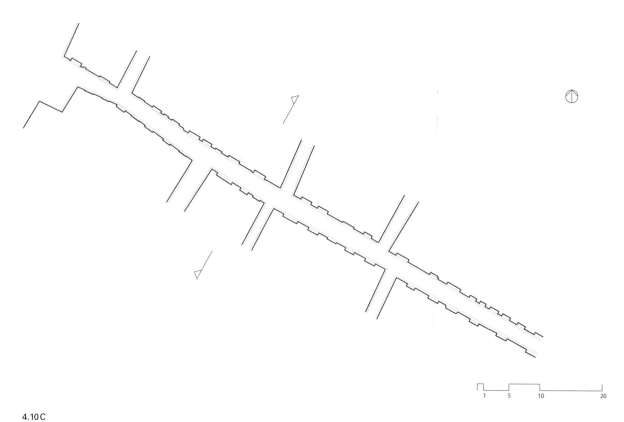

4.10 C
Genoa Street Plan

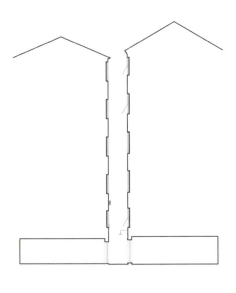

4.10 D
Genoa Street Section

4.10 E
Genoa Photo

4.11 A
Glasgow City Plan

4.11 B
Glasgow City Section

Glasgow, Scotland   Lat. 55°51′54″ N – Long. 4°15′27″ W

Glasgow became an established settlement in the 6th century with the founding of a religious community by St. Kentigern on the hill above the ford of the river Clyde. The city sits on both the North and South bank of the river, with the commercial centre on the North side and a large expansion in the 19th century on the South side. Glasgow's topography is the result of the river and glacial deposits, with the Northern portion of the city rising away from the river with a series of hills formed by glacial deposits, while the South side is flatter, there are still hills, if somewhat lower and further apart. Glasgow grew rapidly during the industrial revolution and the city's urban form reflects this, with a rectilinear overlay onto a medieval pattern.

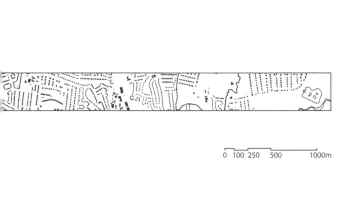

0 100 250 500   1000m

0 100 250 500   1000m

The medieval city was first extended with orthogonal streets in the 18th century, with a further formal grid extension to the west added in the early 19th century. The city is predominantly formed by 3–4 storey masonry perimeter blocks, with taller 19th century buildings in the commercial centre interspersed with 20th century towers. After WWII Glasgow underwent a period of economic decline, leaving many industrial sites vacant along the river, recently developed with luxury housing. This period also included various attempts at urban renewal, resulting in clearances of dense low rise neighbourhoods, which were replaced by point towers both in the city and at its edge, as well as seeing the construction of a motorway at the western edge of the city centre. These changes to the city have affected the spatial quality of Glasgow, with the intact urban 19th century fabric having a strong spatial enclosure and a coherent sense of place, while the impacts of the redevelopment are felt as poor urban relationships and disjointed spatial qualities.[11]

Bath Street, Glasgow

Bath Street is oriented East-West in the early 19th century extension to the west of Glasgow's commercial centre. While the Eastern and Western ends of the street include mid level 20th century buildings, much of the street is lined with limestone Georgian terrace houses, forming a contained horizontal volume, as the consistent street wall is set back from the pavement to allow light to penetrate to the basement level. The overall proportions and features of the street are generous; commensurate with the quality of the buildings, the pavements are a comfortable width (3.25 meters/10 feet 6 inches) with cast iron fencing on low stone walls at edge of the light wells and cast iron lighting fixtures lining the 4 lane roadway (14.17 meters/46 feet 6 inches) and the limestone facades are finely designed with rich classical architectural detailing. The set back of the street wall and the architectural sequence of the raised ground floor reached by a flight of steps set within a fence line and topped by a small porch framed by columns, creates a rich layering of both vertical and horizontal space. Bath Street, designed as a gracious residential street, now accommodates uses ranging from commercial office space, restaurants, retail and hotels.

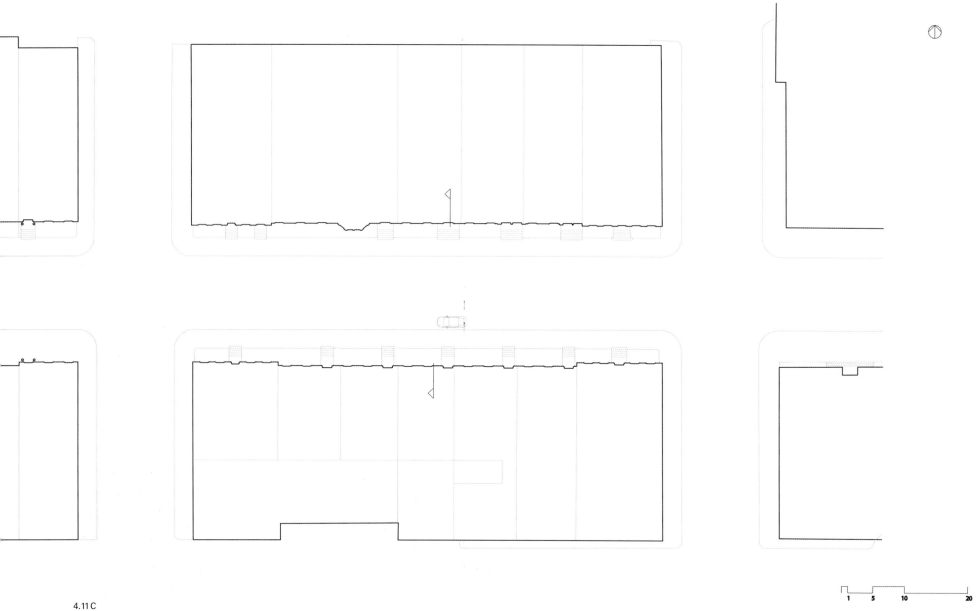

4.11 C
Glasgow Street Plan

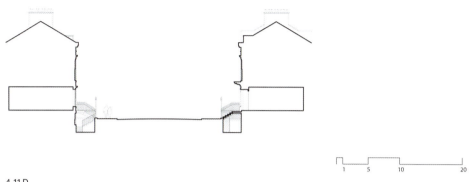

4.11 D
Glasgow Street Section

4.11 E
Glasgow Photo

4.12 A
Lagos City Plan

4.12 B
Lagos City Section

Lagos, Nigeria   Lat. 6°27′11″ N – Long. 3°23′44″ E

Originally a fishing and trading village, Lagos became a major centre of the slave trade, colonised by the Portuguese and later the British. The city began on Lagos Island in the Lagos Lagoon and has spread to the mainland and the other islands around it, becoming the largest city in Nigeria. The earliest part of the city is on the North-Western point of Lagos Island, with irregular street pattern and 1–2 storey buildings, in relatively poor repair. To the South-East is the central business district, with a rectangular street layout with buildings dating from the colonial period to contemporary high rise development. Lagos has been growing rapidly since the

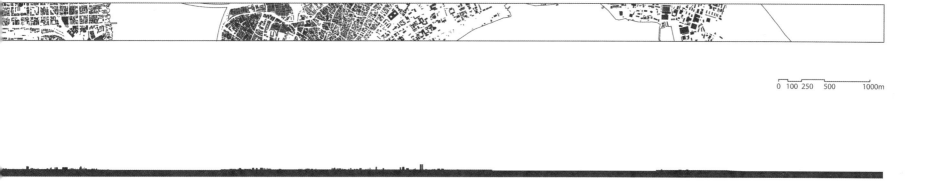

0 100 250 500 1000m

0 100 250 500 1000m

1960's and 1970's, with large roads and bridges connecting the sprawling metropolitan area. The city lies on flat land, very close to sea level, with an urban form that is primarily horizontal outside of the central commercial core. Large areas of the city are made up of unregulated and underserviced settlements; these areas are comprised of small, densely packed single storey structures with narrow circulation routes. The spatial character of the city is defined by the informality of the streetscape and the low scale of most of the urban fabric, with the public space of the city bursting with a vital mix of commerce, social activity and flows of people and vehicles.[12]

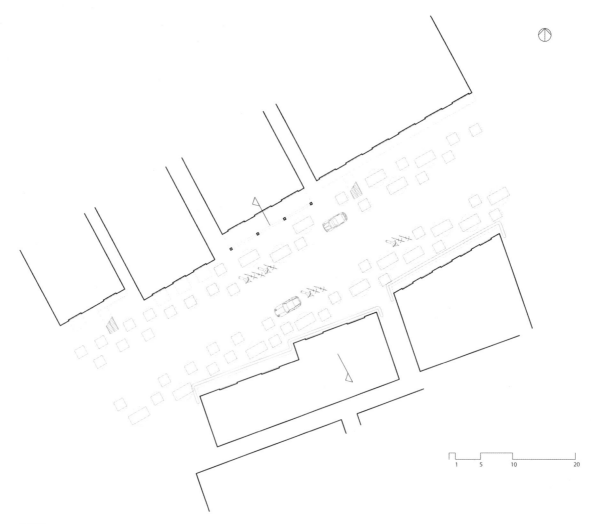

4.12 C
Lagos Street Plan

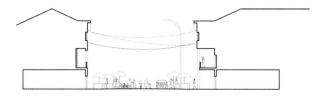

4.12 D
Lagos Street Section

4.12 E
Lagos Photo

Computer Village, Lagos

Computer village is located on the North-Eastern side of the mainland, in a district next to the airport and is oriented South-West to North-East. The roadway is unpaved and varies in width (from approx. 17 meters/55 feet 9 inches to nearly 23 meters/75 feet 6 inches), as the street edge is composed of irregularly placed 3–5 storey buildings. The open space between the buildings is divided informally into five zones, with a central circulation space bordered on both sides by an area of vendors and small market stalls covered by individual umbrellas and a space for access to the interior spaces. The street is a bustling market, where pedestrians, bicycles and vehicles mix. A layer of umbrellas, stalls and carts along the edge closes down the centre and creates a low spatial enclosure at the heart of the street, with a back drop of a varied street wall that has buildings of different heights and spaces between them. The facades of the building are articulated by balconies, awnings, recessed entryways and advertising. The movement of people, the multiple zones of vertical and horizontal space, the displays of merchandise and the collection of stalls and tables, create a high level of visual stimulation and a vibrant urban place.

4.13 A
London City Plan

4.13 B
London City Section

London, United Kingdom   Lat. 51°30'30" N – Long. 0°07'32" W

London was founded in the 2nd century as a Roman colony and has been a major trading and cultural centre throughout history. The city is located in South-Eastern England, originally situated on the Northern bank of the river Thames, the city now straddles the river and has spread over a massive area, covering 607 square miles (1,572 square km). The topography of the city is flat, as it sits in the broad river valley, with little elevational change, except for low hills at the edges of the city. London has a varied street pattern, with organic medieval, 18th century grids, monumental boulevards, and numerous patch works of irregular streets and its organisation is poly-centric, with districts for politics, finance, entertainment,

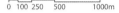
0 100 250 500   1000m

0 100 250 500   1000m

and shopping. London's urban fabric is largely 18th and 19th century 2–4 storey brick buildings, with numerous 20th century insertions. The City of London, home of London's financial district, is an increasingly vertical cluster of towers which occupy the medieval street network and as the city spreads away from this vertical grouping it is horizontal in character. Post WWII development in London followed modernist planning principles, with large high rise housing estates set in green fields, and the development of the road network for the efficient circulation of automobiles. While many streets were damaged by this, the city's streets have a predominantly strong spatial definition, with consistent street walls that are aligned with the pavement. Starting in the late 20th century the city has undergone a great deal of urban redevelopment, much of which has utilised urban design strategies aimed at producing a vital public realm. While not always successful, these efforts have dramatically improved the overall quality of the city's public spaces, creating a complex, varied and intense urban environment.[13]

Charlotte Street, London

Charlotte Street is oriented South-East to North-West and is located in the Fitzrovia district in London's West End, which was developed in the 18th century. Like much of the surrounding area, it is formed by mainly 3–4 storey brick buildings, with some 5–6 storey 20th century structures at the Northern end. The street is modest in scale, with a roadway of medium width (9.4 meters/30 feet 10 inches), with a pavement area that is also modest (4 meters/13 feet). An interesting feature of the street is the variation in the base of the street wall and the transition zone of the pavement. In some instances there are small areas treated as front yards or as terraces for the interior space, in other cases the pavement is pulled away from the face of the building to allow light to penetrate below ground, while many interior spaces open directly onto the pavement. The street has a clear spatial definition, with the volume of the street reading as a contained whole. The street has a human scale, with many of the ground floor interior spaces directly integrated into the spaces of the street, with material qualities and architectural details that engage the eye.

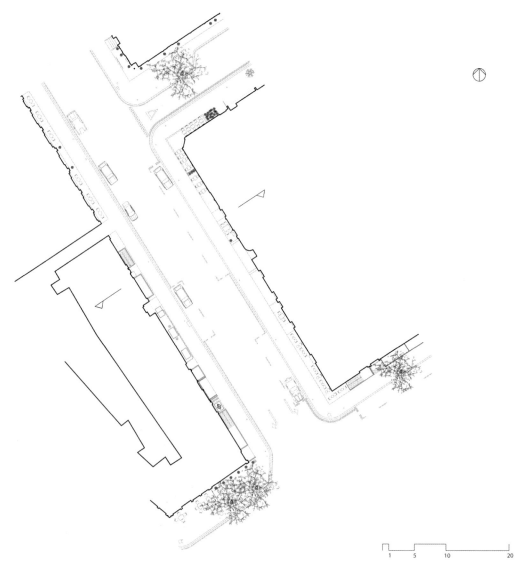

4.13 C
London Street Plan

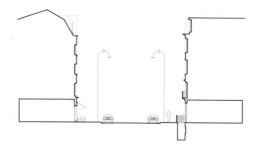

4.13 D
London Street Section

4.13 E
London Photo

4.14A
Mexico City City Plan

0 100 250 500 1000m

4.14B
Mexico City City Section

0 100 250 500 1000m

Mexico City, Mexico   Lat. 19°25'42" N – Long. 99°07'39" W

Mexico City was founded on the site of the destroyed Aztec city, Tenochtitlán, by Spanish conquistadors in 1521. The city is located in the highland Valley of Mexico, which was once filled with lakes and is surrounded on three sides by mountains. Originally the city was on an island in Lake Texacoco, but as the city grew the lake was filled in and drained. The extreme edges of the city meet the foothills of the mountains, but for the most part the topography of the city is flat, with the exception of some low hills. Mexico City is one of the largest and most populous cities in the world, growing rapidly for the last six decades and the city spreads horizontally over a vast area. The historic core has a colonial grid street pattern and is surrounded by gridded extensions that are cut by large diagonal avenues, most of which are surface highways. The city is comprised of mainly 3–4 storey buildings, with clusters of towers along main thoroughfares, predominantly the Paseo de la Reforma and near the Bosque de Chapultepec. The spatial quality of the city is dynamic and vibrant, with open, straight streets, architectural variety and colour. The streets are crowded with activity, vendors, people circulating, and a huge amount of vehicular traffic and the streetscape is generally an enclosed volume with a consistent street wall. The city also has many informal settlements, where open land or former green areas have been occupied unofficially. These areas lack many basic services and have contributed to a growing set of problems associated with Mexico City's explosive growth.[14]

Calle De Mesones, Mexico City

The Calle De Mesones is a small street that runs East to West in the heart of the historic city, just South of the Plaza de la Constitución. The street is formed by a 2 storey street wall, mainly of 19th century vintage and colonial in style. The base of the street wall typically opens directly onto the thin pavements (2meters/6 feet 6 inches) which flank the narrow roadway (6 meters/19 feet 8 inches). The combined width of the pavements and the roadway in relationship to the 2 storey street wall produces a nearly 1:1 height to width ratio, creating a stable volume of enclosure. The street has trees and light poles in amenity zone next to the curb and while these do restrict the space of the pavement, they also add vertical components to the street space. The transition zone of the pavement is frequently used to display products and some of the entry ways are recessed, blurring the boundary between the interior and the space of the street. Above the ground floor the street wall is animated by awnings, signage and balconies, generating visual stimulation above the pavement level. The street has a small scale, with an active visual field and the mix of spatial qualities, material character and social activities, forming a vital street.

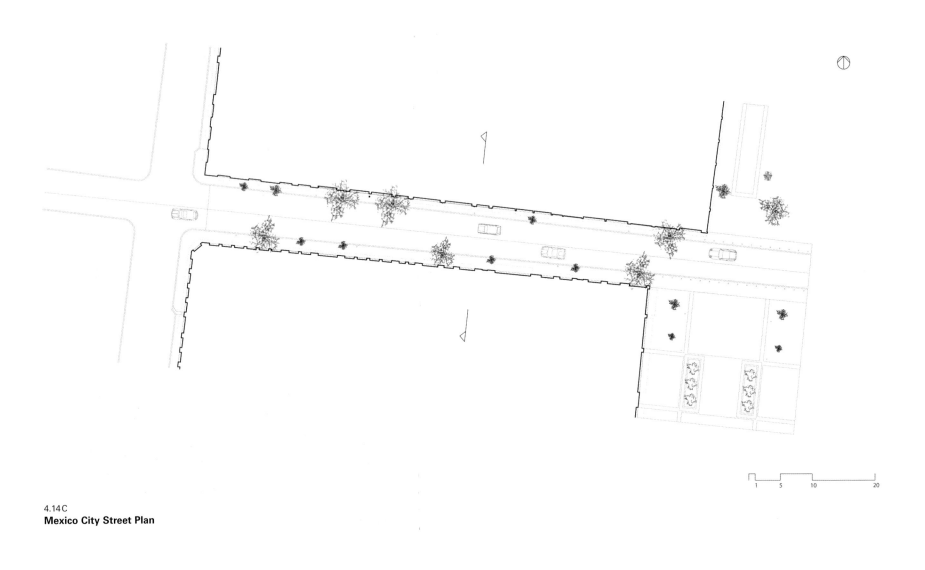

4.14 C
Mexico City Street Plan

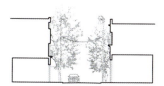

4.14 D
Mexico City Street Section

4.14 E
Mexico City Photo

4.15A
Montevideo City Plan

4.15B
Montevideo City Section

Montevideo, Uruguay   Lat. 34°50'00" S – Long. 56°10'02" W

Founded in 1726 by the Spanish in response to Portuguese settlement of the area, Montevideo became an important trading port with military value in the late 18th and early 19th century. The city wraps around the Bay of Montevideo, along the North shore of the Rio de la Plata on the Southern coast of Uruguay. The city's topography is flat, with the exception of two hills, the Cerro de Montevideo West of the Bay of Montevideo and the Cerro de la Victoria to the North East of the colonial centre of the city. The historical city has a colonial grid street pattern, with shifts in the gridded additions around local geographic features and late baroque boulevards and avenues. The city has a range of architectural styles, from various 19th and 20th

0 100 250 500 · 1000m

0 100 250 500 · 1000m

century European styles to contemporary international buildings, with the majority of the buildings low to mid level blocks, with some higher towers in the commercial centre, particularly along the Avenue Libertador Brigadier General Juan Antonio Lavalleja, as well as luxury high rise development along the waterfront to the South. Montevideo has a horizontal spatial character, with streets that form enclosed volumes around medium scaled streets, while the broad late baroque diagonals add monumental elements to the urban fabric. Like most cities, the 20th century concern with the automobile has had an impact, with some consequent neglect of the street's social uses, however Montevideo's cultural growth of the last three decades has seen a new focus on the physical aspects of the city. The streets of Montevideo have strong urban properties and an open spatial quality that supports an active public realm.[15]

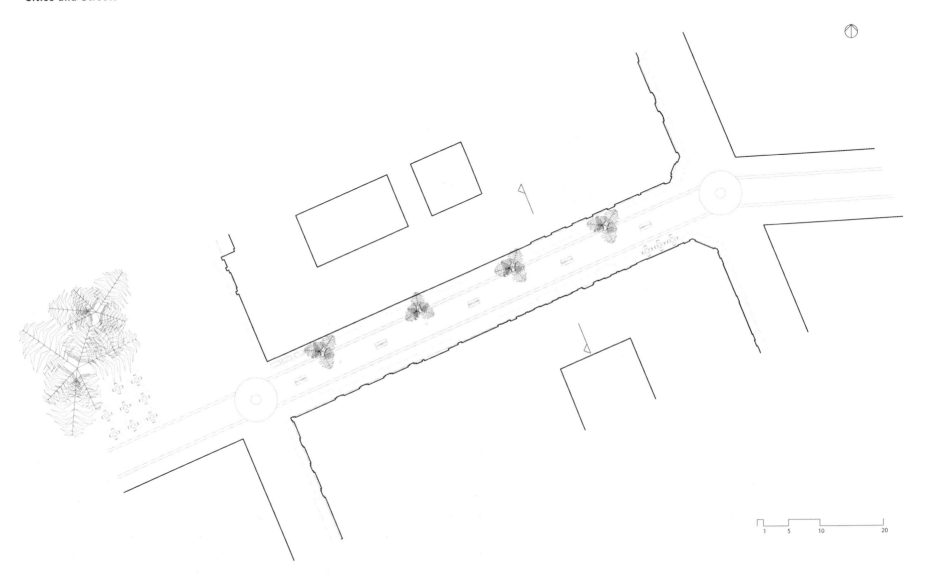

4.15 C
Montevideo Street Plan

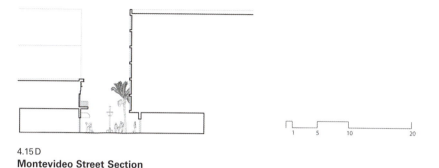

4.15 D
Montevideo Street Section

4.15 E
Montevideo Photo

Sarandi, Montevideo

Sarandi is a pedestrian street that is oriented East to West in the centre of the colonial grid, running between the Plaza Independencia and the Rambla Montevideo along the waterfront. The street is formed by 4–6 storey buildings, dating from the 19th century eclecticism to post WWII modernism, with chiefly retail uses on the ground floor. The street has a paved surface that varies in width along its length, (from approximately 15.8 meters/52 feet at the Eastern end, reducing to as small as 7.8 meters/25 feet 7 inches), before widening again after the Plaza Constitucion. There are no spaces between the buildings, which maintains the enclosure of the street. The difference in the heights of the buildings creates an active top edge to the street wall. The ground floors are on the same level as the pavement, with some recessed underneath the upper floors to form entry spaces and most of the spaces connect directly to the street. The facades have awnings, balconies, advertising signs and architectural details to animating this edge of the street space. The street contains lighting fixtures, trees, both public and private seating and is used by vendors to sell handicrafts and other small items. All of these features produce an active public place.

4.16A
Montreal City Plan

4.16B
Montreal City Section

Montreal, Canada   Lat. 45°30'31"N – Long. 75°35'16"E

Montreal was founded in 1642 by Paul de Chomedey not far from previous Huron settlements at the edge of the St. Lawrence River in South Eastern Canada. The city is situated on Montreal Island and spreads from the edge of the river and around Mount Royal, producing a generally downward slope from the North West to the South East. The city centre is comprised of mid level blocks interspersed with high rise towers, surrounding the centre are streets of low rise terraced housing. The industrial section of the city is in the South West and the port is to the East of the business district. The original city form was characterised by dense 2–3

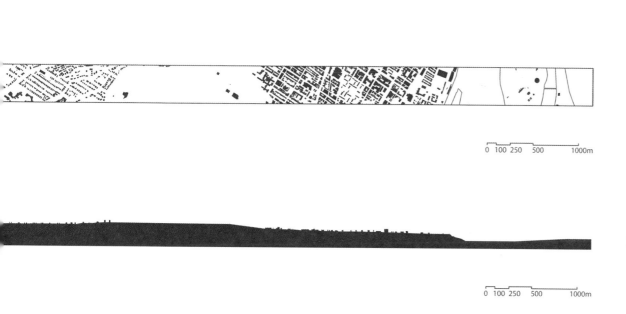

storey streets, with landmark public buildings of finer architectural quality. The post WWII city has seen the introduction of peripheral motorways, a revision of the road network to increase the efficiency of traffic circulation and the many taller buildings that ignore the context of the street. This has lead to many streets that are dominated by the car, instances of unengaged ground floors, where the interior is disconnected from the street and some streets with poor spatial definition. For the most part Montreal's streets maintain enclosure, with the density and scale required to contain the street to form coherent public places. Also worth noting is a unique feature of Montreal's urbanism, a network of underground retail walkways linking many downtown buildings that while lacking spatial richness, do have some of the vitality of a street. Like many cities, Montreal has been revising its public realm for the last three decades to support social activity and has been successful in revitalising many areas of the city.[16]

Rue St. Denis, Montreal

Rue St. Denis runs South East to North West, from near the waterfront out to the Western edge of the island, becoming mostly residential once it passes the expressway West of the city centre. The street is a broad street and a major East-West route for vehicular traffic and has a wide roadway (19.2 meters/63 feet) and sidewalks on both sides that vary in width (from 7 meters/23 feet to 3 meters/9 feet 10 inches), which creates a horizontal volume. The base of the street wall is treated in numerous ways, with many of the commercial properties annexing portions of the sidewalk as service areas and still others who have built permanent additions which project into the space of the sidewalk. Most of the ground floors are occupied by retail use and restaurants, with residential units above. Some of the ground floor units are lower than the sidewalk, with small light wells in front, which vary in depth from just a few steps to half a level below the sidewalk. Many of the residential units are accessed from a single flight of steps directly from the sidewalk, even in instances when the residential level is raised a full storey above the sidewalk. This creates a distinctive streetscape and creates spatial pockets along the sidewalk around which pedestrian traffic flows. The street wall is constant without gaps and slight variations in the height of the top edge and activated with balconies, awnings and signs projecting into the space, generating a consistent volume that is also dynamic and open. The spatial differentiation created by the diversity of the street wall base and the integration of the interior spaces with the street, coupled with the numerous visually engaging physical features and abundant social interaction, result in a physically and experientially rich street.

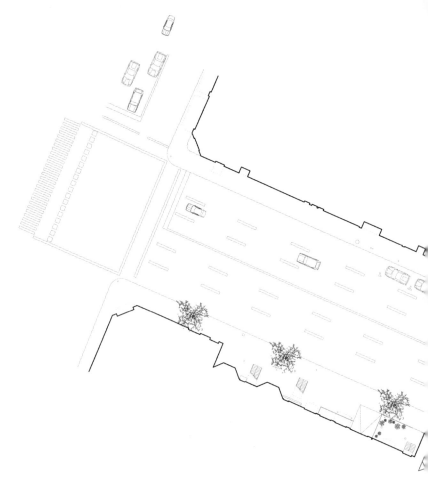

4.16C
Montreal Street Plan

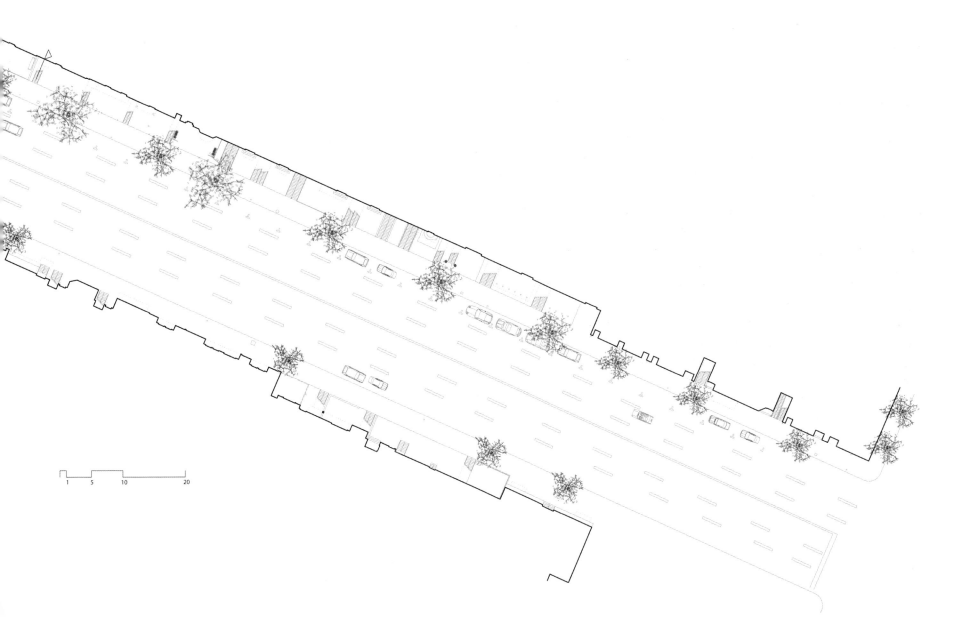

1 5 10   20

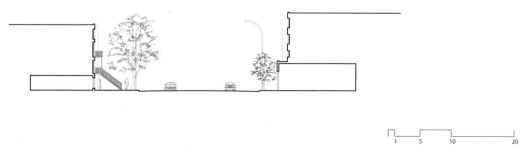

4.16 D
Montreal Street Section

4.16 E
Montreal Photo

4.17 A
Mumbai City Plan

4.17 B
Mumbai City Section

Mumbai, India   Lat. 19°00'51"N – Long. 72°50'52"E

The site of Mumbai has been occupied by humans since prehistoric times and
has been a centre of trade since at least 1000 BCE. The city is located on Bombay
Island on the Western coast of India in the Arabian Sea. The city is on a peninsula
in the South West of the island, created by joining seven smaller islands through
land reclamation and drainage efforts. The historic city occupies the Southernmost
point of the peninsula and the city has spread North to encompass a vast area (239
square miles/619 square meters). The city has a population of over twenty million

0 100 250 500   1000m

0 100 250 500   1000m

people and is the centre of the Indian economy, being the home of the industrial, commercial, financial, entertainment and technology industries. The city is built on flat plain, bordered by low hills to the East and West. The city is linear in form, with a street pattern that is a complex mix of organic patterns, areas of rectilinear streets, diagonal thoroughfares, the railway lines and the Eastern Freeway, with an additional layer of illegal settlements, whose circulation is comprised of tight unplanned networks. Mumbai is an extremely dense city, with mainly medium rise urban fabric of 5–8 storeys, with a range of street widths, from the very tight to broad roadways with many lanes of traffic. While there may be no overriding order

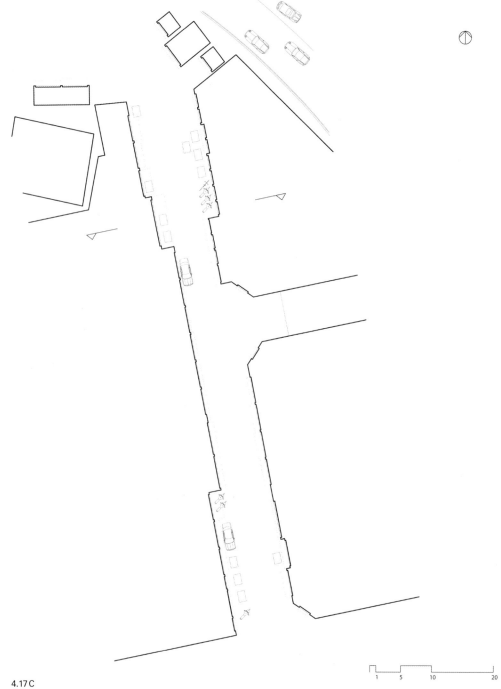

4.17 C
Mumbai Street Plan

to the urban form, and often physically chaotic, the streets of Mumbai are filled with every conceivable activity and use, giving the space of the city a vibrant, stimulating quality.[17]

Nagdevi Path, Mumbai

Nagdevi Path runs North-South and is located North of one of Mumbai's main railway stations, the Chhatrapati Shivaji Terminus, and just West of the elevated JJ flyover. The street wall varies in height from 3-5 storeys, which changes in plan, with additions and recesses that modify the width of the circulation space (ranging from 6 meters/19 feet 8 inches to 11 meters/36 feet). The resulting street has a strong sense of enclosure, with a vertical orientation. There are no pavements bordering the circulation space, with vehicles and pedestrians sharing the space. The ground-floor spaces accommodate commercial activity and open directly onto the street space, with numerous product displays that form an additional layer of space between the interior spaces and the open centre of the street, which integrates the ground floor into the space of the street. In addition to these horizontal spatial overlaps, the face of the street wall is modulated by numerous balconies, overhangs, signs and architectural features, resulting in vertical spatial stratifications. The combination of this horizontal and vertical interplay is an intricate spatial border that blurs the edge of the public space, creating a visually complex container for the activity of the street. While the street is not "pretty" and is often chaotic, it is a "living" space, with room for social exchange, economic activity and circulation, the essential requirements of a street.

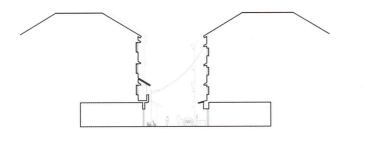
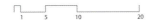

4.17 D
Mumbai Street Section

4.17 E
Mumbai Photo

4.18A
Newcastle upon Tyne City Plan

4.18B
Newcastle upon Tyne City Section

Newcastle upon Tyne, England   Lat. 54°58'23"N – Long. 1°36'50"W

The city of Newcastle upon Tyne dates back to the Roman fort and bridge from the 3rd century and continued to be a strategically important fortified town through the middle ages. Located on the North shore of the River Tyne in the Northeast of England, Newcastle has been an important commercial and industrial centre since the 14th century. Occupying the banks of the river, the historic commercial streets slope down to the river to the former docks and industrialised waterfront. The numerous bridges crossing the river to Gateshead on the South bank have a strong

0   100 250   500   1000m

0   100 250   500   1000m

spatial and visual impact, accentuating the steep slopes of the river. The medieval street pattern has survived and the city centre is mainly low rise, with buildings ranging from 2 to 6 storeys and very few high-rise towers. The city has a national motorway cutting through it just East of the central business district and has an elevated railway viaduct that runs East-West between the heart of the city and the river. The city is noted for the early 19th-century streets of buildings in the neoclassical style, which have a finely considered street volume and carefully designed street wall. The spatial character of the city is very unique, with low contained streets that dip down to the river topped by the lines of the raised bridges and the railway viaduct.[18]

Grey Street, Newcastle upon Tyne

Grey Street is located in the historic core of the city, running North-South from the Grey's Monument to Mosley Street continuing as Dean Street to the river's edge. The street curves to the Southeast as it slopes down to the river and is lined with 4–5-storey Georgian buildings. The Northern end of the street has been pedestrianised, followed by a section of shared surface between Hood Street and Market Street. South of this the street has a typical arrangement of a roadway with pavements on both sides. The volume of the street is broad and open, with the wide roadway (15 meters/49 feet) and large pavements (4.2 meters/13 feet 9 inches) combining to produce a height to width ratio of 1:1.74. The ground-floor spaces open directly onto the pavement, except when the slope requires a small flight of stairs and there is a strong visual connection between the interior spaces and the street. The classical facades are articulated into a base, piano nobile and attic and the pattern of regular openings, columns and pilasters establish a rhythm on the street. The streetscape is accented with historic light fixtures and substantial paving materials, and is well maintained, generating a high quality and refined public realm. The street has a human scale, is ordered and balanced, with subtle dynamism created by the curving space.

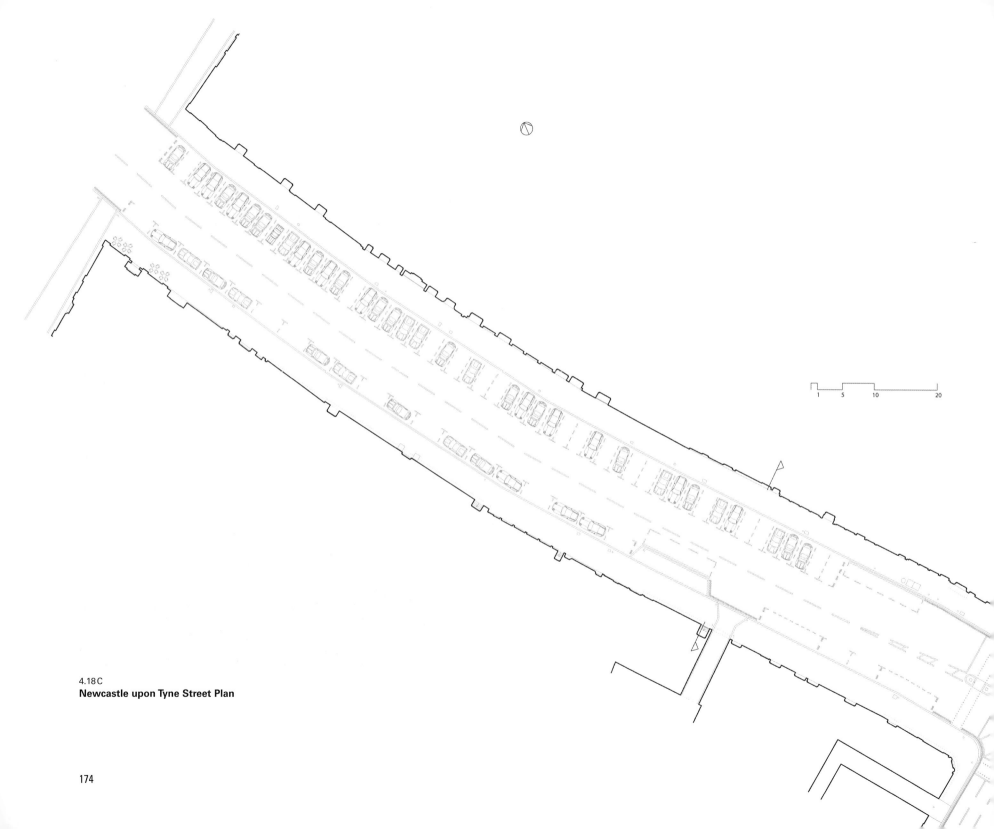

4.18 C
Newcastle upon Tyne Street Plan

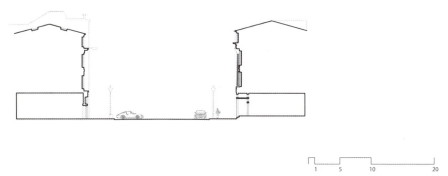

4.18 D
Newcastle upon Tyne Street Section

4.18 E
Newcastle upon Tyne Photo

4.19A
New York City Plan

4.19B
New York City Section

New York City, United States   Lat. 40°42'51" N – Long. 74°00'21" W

New York City was founded as a Dutch trading post in 1626 and grew in economic and cultural significance to be the dominant city of the United States and one of the most important cities in the world. Situated on Manhattan, Staten Island, the Western edge of Long Island and the Southern tip of the mainland, the city is located at the mouth of the Hudson River on the East coast of the United States, and its landscape was formed by glacial activity in the last ice age. The city is organised with a gridded street pattern that shifts to align with topographical features and

0 100 250 500   1000m

0 100 250 500   1000m

historical roads, particularly at its edges in Brooklyn, Queens, Staten Island and the Bronx. The earliest part of the city at the base of Manhattan has an irregular street network, with gridded sections North of City Hall. The streets are aligned to the waterfronts on the perimeters, while the centre section is aligned to the North-South axis of Broadway. North of Fourteenth Street New York's famous orthogonal grid spreads in a uniform fashion until the North eastern tip of Manhattan, with only Broadway's sinuous path cutting across it. The city is increasingly vertical in form in Manhattan, with mainly 4–5-storey fabric in the dense areas which are immediately adjacent and 2–3-storey streets at the edges. The density of New York

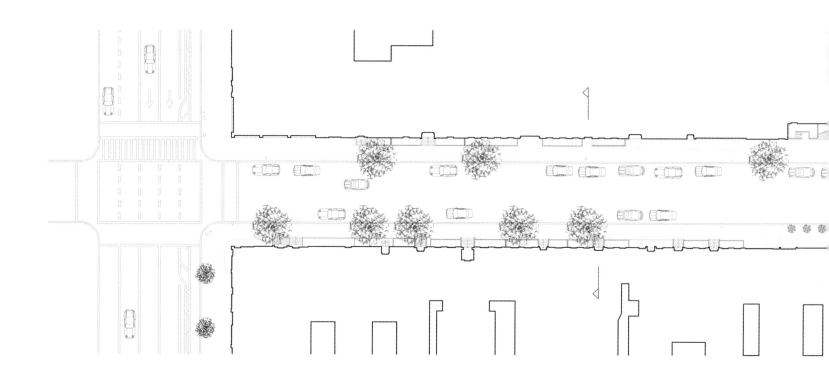

4.19 C
New York Street Plan

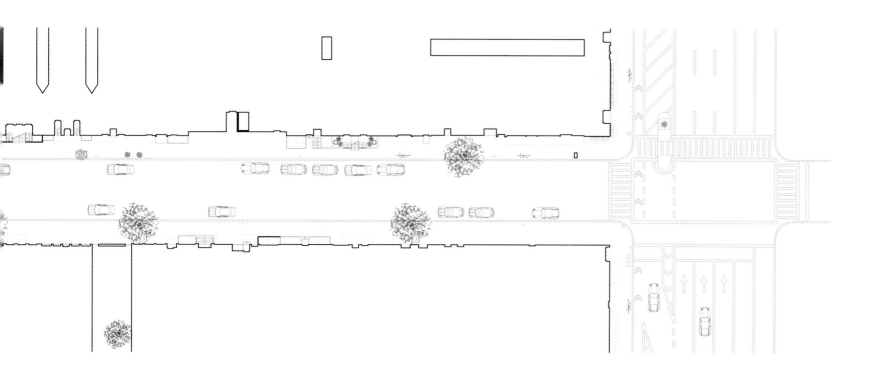

generally results in street walls that are consistent and built to the property line at the pavement edge, the exception being high-rise buildings that are set back in exchange for greater height and the outer boroughs where density is reduced. While the spatial identity of the city is vertical, the streets of New York cover an incredible range of spatial characters, but in every instance they are public spaces in which a great deal of the social life of the city takes place.[19]

East Third Street, New York City

East Third Street runs East-West from the Bowery to Avenue D just North of Houston Street and is formed by 4–6-storey apartment buildings. The street is mainly residential with some commercial use on the ground floor. The roadway is small (9.2 meters/30 feet) with moderately sized sidewalks on either side (3.5 meters/11 feet 6 inches) creating a volume that is nearly square. The base of the street wall has numerous conditions; as there are interiors which open directly onto the street, while others have light wells between the sidewalk and the street wall, with a ground floor that is raised half a storey above the street, or in some instances there are small yards that are enclosed with low fences. This transition zone activates the street, as interior activity occupies the street, where tables are set up for eating or people sit on the steps and watch the life of the street. The street has trees and light poles at the pavements edge and vehicular traffic is buffered by parking lanes on both sides of the roadway. The facades are typically clad in brick and have regular fenestration patterns, with a mix of architecturally detailed and plain openings and frequently have steel fire escapes that extend into the street space, that combine to articulate the street wall. The various horizontal and vertical layers overlap to create a rich interlocking spatial enclosure.

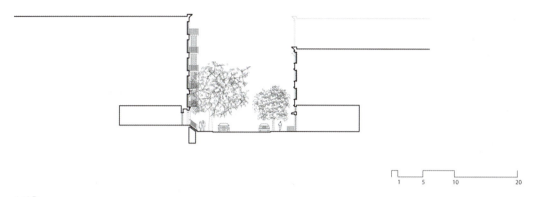

4.19 D
New York Street Section

4.19 E
New York Photo

4.20 A
Paris City Plan

0 100 250 500   1000m

4.20 B
Paris City Section

0 100 250 500   1000m

Paris, France   Lat. 48°51′12″ N – Long. 2°20′55″ E

The site of present day Paris has been inhabited by people since the 8th century BCE and the first permanent settlement was established in the 3rd century BCE, which has evolved into the economic, political and cultural centre of France; consequently the city had immense cultural influence particularly in Europe and the Western hemisphere. The city is located in the Seine river valley in the Northwest of France, encircled by low hills that mark its outer perimeter. The original city occupied the Île de la Cité and the city has grown out from this centre, and has a circular form. As the centre of the political turmoil and the industrialisation of France, by the early 19th century Paris was a dense mixture of medieval streets, renaissance-inspired squares, baroque avenues, industrial districts and railway lines. Under Napoleon III, from 1852 to 1870, Baron Haussmann transformed Paris into the model of modern urban planning, setting the template for city building around the world until modernist planning ideas became popular after WWII. Haussmann utilised a range of techniques, aesthetic, mechanical, engineering, and graphic to accomplish construction projects on a vast scale. The building programme modernised the sewage and water systems, introduced standards for roadways and street walls, erected four new bridges across the river and created a network of wide streets to improve circulation. It is these streets cutting diagonally through the organic pattern of the historic city, with their generous scale and consistent neoclassical facades lined with trees connecting monumental public places, that give Paris its specific spatial identity. Paris is fundamentally a horizontal city, with the broad open streets contained by 6–7-storey buildings with wide pavements producing spacious volumes.[20]

Rue Saint-Honoré, Paris

The Rue Saint-Honoré is situated in the centre of Paris, running Southeast to Northwest from the Rue de Rivoli in the Southeast continuing as the Rue du Fauburg Saint-Honoré after the Rue Royale at the Northwestern end. The street runs parallel to the river and is part of Paris's historic street pattern. The street is formed by a 5–8-storey street wall, the majority of which dates from the 19th century in the neoclassical style. The narrow roadway (9.48 meters/31 feet) is flanked by tight pavements (2.2 meters/7 feet 2 inches) resulting in a vertical volume. The base of the street wall is very open, with frequent large openings and entryways that connect directly to the pavement, producing a rhythm along the street and filling the street with people and movement. Most of the ground floor is occupied by retail uses and the shop windows displaying goods add visual interest to the exterior space. The street furniture is limited to traffic signs and small bollards, while there are no trees on the pavement and the lighting fixtures are mounted on the buildings. The street wall is highly articulated by architectural details, balconies, signs and awnings, activating the vertical edge of the space and establishing a human scale for the street.

4.20 C
Paris Street Plan

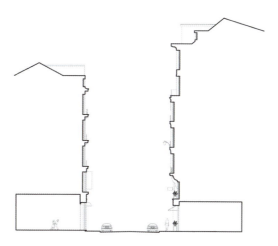

4.20 D
Paris Street Section

4.20 E
Paris Photo

185

4.21A
Pittsburgh City Plan

4.21B
Pittsburgh City Section

Pittsburgh, United States   Lat. 40°26'26" N – Long. 79°59'45" W

Pittsburgh was established as a military outpost, first by the French and later by the British, to control the strategically important point on the waterways of the then Western edge of the North American colonies and developed into a major industrial centre in the 19th century. The city is located where the Allegheny and Monongahela rivers join to form the Ohio River in South-western Pennsylvania, with central business district occupying the triangular point of land formed by the converging rivers. The city has a very steep topography as the land slopes away from the rivers and the street pattern is a mix of gridded sections and irregular networks that respond to the topographical conditions. The downtown commercial district has many high-rise towers and the city reduces in height as it spreads away from the core, first with mid-level blocks and then 2–3-storey residential streets. The impact of post-WWII planning practices and the loss of heavy industry beginning in the 1970's have resulted in changes to the urban structure and spatial character of the city. The city has three expressways intersecting it, resulting in the erosion of connectivity and spatial definition and the focus on improving vehicular circulation has turned many streets into roads, where vehicles dominate the space and little other activity occurs. Over the last 3 decades the city of Pittsburgh has made numerous efforts to address the problems caused by this approach to urban development, working with communities and business to build parks, improve streetscapes and develop economic activity to generate liveable urban environments.[21]

Filbert Street, Pittsburgh

Oriented North-South, Filbert Street is a residential street in East Pittsburgh that is two blocks long, running between Walnut Street and Ellsworth Avenue. The street is lined with detached 2-storey buildings that have narrow front yards. The roadway is small (6.6 meters/21 feet 7 inches) with thin sidewalks (from 1.24 meters/4 feet to 1.75 meters/5 feet 8 inches) on either side. The sidewalks have trees and electric poles with light fixtures in the amenity zone and the individual buildings have a variety of connections to the space of the street. Most have a raised ground floor above the sidewalk, with an exterior porch at the top of a set of stairs. Some of the buildings have sloping or terraced front yards, lifting them a full storey higher than the sidewalk and roadway. The street wall is not continuous, with gaps between the buildings, but these gaps are not large, maintaining the enclosure. The street has a small scale and the numerous changes in level and horizontal divisions of the transition between the sidewalk and the buildings combined with the landscape elements generates variation in the roof line, creating an active spatial envelope.

4.21 C
Pittsburgh Street Plan

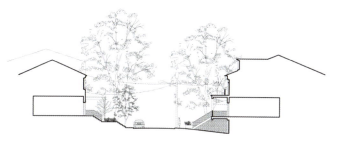

4.21 D
Pittsburgh Street Section

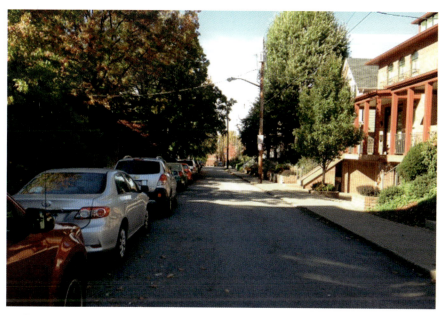

4.21 E
Pittsburgh Photo

4.22 A
Rio de Janeiro City Plan

4.22 B
Rio de Janeiro City Section

Rio de Janeiro, Brazil   Lat. 22°54′10″ S – Long. 43°12′27″ W

The city of Rio de Janeiro was founded by the Portuguese in 1565 to counter French efforts to colonise the area, developing into a major port for shipping first sugar, followed by gold and precious stones. The city became the capital of the Southern portion of the Portuguese colonies and in the early 19th century became the capital of the Portuguese empire, when the king of Portugal fled to escape Napoleon's invasion. The city is located on Guanabara Bay on the Atlantic coast as it curves West in Southern Brazil at the foot of the Brazilian highlands. The city centre is on a flat point of land North of the inlet to the bay, with the major industrial and residential extension to the city spreading North and West, while another residential and leisure district to the South along the coastal beaches is separated from the commercial centre by a line of mountains. The presence of these mountains, the backdrop of those to the North, the lush vegetation and the coastal beaches give Rio de Janeiro a remarkable scenic quality, providing the city with a powerful identity. The commercial centre retains the street pattern of the colonial city with mid-level streets of 8–10 storeys, and numerous very tall towers. As the city spreads North and West, the height reduces to a combination of 2–3-storey buildings and multi-storey residential blocks, interspersed with many very dense 1–2-storey neighbourhoods of unofficial settlements. The city is organised with a grid on the flat portions that shift slightly in response to topography, while the streets become curvilinear when negotiating the hills. Two expressways traverse Rio de Janeiro, one along the coast, serving the port, and the other entering from the Northwest of the city centre, cutting through the mountains and connecting the Southern zone to the city. Rio de Janeiro's streets range from the busy high-rise commercial through the small-scale 19th-century to wide roadways with a jumble of modernist concrete blocks, without a consistent spatial character across the whole city, but the streets typically have a continuous street wall that frames the public space of the street.[22]

Rua da Carioca, Rio de Janeiro

Running East-West the Rua da Carioca is located in the central business district of the city, just West of the most vertical part of Rio de Janeiro. The street is formed by 2–6-storey buildings, predominantly from the 19th or early 20th century, with a roadway that is not wide (10 meters/32 feet 9 inches) but the pavements are ample (3.4 meters/11 feet), creating a space of nearly 17 meters/55 feet 9 inches between the street walls, producing a horizontal spatial definition. Most of the ground floor is occupied with retail shops which open directly onto the pavement and have

4.22 C
Rio de Janeiro Street Plan

large openings spaced regularly along the street creating a permeable boundary between the interior and the exterior spaces of the street. The pavements are paved in a decorative pattern and there are street trees and light poles placed in the amenity zone. The mature deciduous trees lean into the space and their canopies shade the street. Many shop fronts have awnings and above the ground floor there are frequently balconies with decorative metal railings in front of large openings, all of which activate the street wall. The clear spatial definition of the street combined with the integration of interior and exterior space and the animated street wall result in a visual engaging public room.

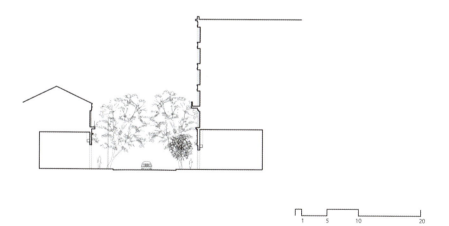

4.22 D
Rio de Janeiro Street Section

4.22 E
Rio de Janeiro Photo

4.23 A
Rome City Plan

4.23 B
Rome City Section

Rome, Italy   Lat. 41°53′41″ N – Long. 12°29′02″ E

While impossible to summarise any city in a short paragraph, Rome presents a
uniquely difficult challenge, both due to its age and the complexity caused by the
multiple layers of habitation. The site of Rome has been occupied from at least 1000
BCE, with the Roman city believed to date from the early 6th century BCE. The city
is located in the middle portion of the Italian peninsula amongst the famous seven
hills next to the Tiber River, approximately 15 miles (24 km) from the coast of the
Tyrrhenian Sea. Ancient Rome was a dense vertical city, with large public spaces
and monumental structures set out with aesthetic and ceremonial purpose. Much
of the ancient city was subsumed by the medieval city, with numerous ancient

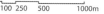

100 250 500   1000m

100 250 500   1000m

buildings being used as sources of building materials and much of the existing street pattern dates from this period. In the 16th century, Sixtus V constructed numerous wide streets and public infrastructure, dramatically altering the public space of the city with baroque urban design and giving Rome its current structure. The city's spatial definition is the result of the layering of these historic patterns, with some ancient public spaces, such as the Piazza Navona, site of an ancient circus or the Pantheon embedded in the tight medieval street pattern of 4–6-storey buildings, cut by baroque vistas connecting piazzas and peppered with architectural monuments. The streets of Rome are active public spaces and the centre of the economic and social life of the city.[23]

Via di Santa Maria dell'Anima, Rome

The Via di Santa Maria dell'Anima is located in the medieval centre of Rome, just West of the Piazza Navona, oriented North-South and framed by a 4–5-storey street wall. The paved space between the buildings is a continuous cobblestone surface used by pedestrians, restaurants and cafés as well as vehicles and bicycles. This area varies from approximately 7 meters/23 feet to as much as 10meters/32 feet 9 inches. This creates a tight vertical street space, compressing the activity of the street into constant negotiation between those who use the street. The inclusion of the seating areas for customers in front of the restaurants and cafés squeezes the shared space still further, but also adds the attraction of people and their social interaction to the street. The street wall is continuous and massive, with punched openings of various scales, in some cases retail or food establishments on the ground-floor spaces open onto the street, while many buildings have a large scale opening to a central court and the habitable level is half a storey above the pavement. The strong sense of vertical enclosure also produces a linear space with a plane of sky that caps the street. The street has many conditions that could be considered problems: it is cramped, somewhat dark, the street wall is heavy, there is a constant stream of people and vehicles moving through and around each other, but the street is alive and its choreography has an urban charm.

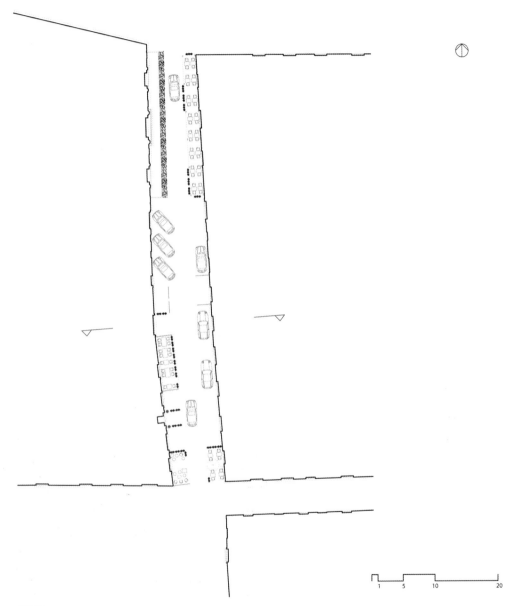

4.23C
Rome Street Plan

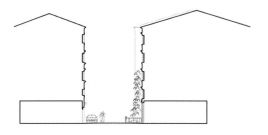

4.23 D
Rome Street Section

4.23 E
Rome Photo

4.24 A
San Francisco City Plan

0 100 250 500   1000m

4.24 B
San Francisco City Section

0 100 250 500   1000m

San Francisco, United States   Lat. 37°46'29" N – Long. 122°25'09" W

The first European inhabitation of the area of what is now San Francisco was a
fort and mission built by the Spanish at the mouth of San Francisco Bay in 1775,
followed by a small settlement to the East in the 1830's. During the Mexican-
American war the U.S. claimed California and the Spanish town of Yerba Buena
was renamed San Francisco in 1847, and after the gold rush the city grew rapidly,
becoming the centre of finance and commerce for the West coast of the United
States in the late 19th century. Spreading from San Francisco Bay in the East and
West to the Pacific Ocean the city covers the head of the San Francisco peninsula

overlooking the bay. The city sits on flat land at the water's edge and rises up steep hilly topography forming its famous precipitous streets. Except when the topography absolutely prohibits it the street pattern is laid out in a grid, with the diagonal of Market Street cutting North East to South West. One major exception is the alignment of the South of Market district perpendicular to Market Street. The downtown financial district is vertical in nature, due to the numerous tall buildings set in a fabric of densely packed mid-rise streets. Outside of this core, much of the city is made up of 3–4-storey street walls that enclose medium-width roadways with socially active street spaces. San Francisco's spatial character is shaped by the topography and the streets of terraced housing that form corridors of space opening onto the sky and the water, stressing the vertical even in the lower sections of the city.[24]

Polk Street, San Francisco

Oriented North-South just west of the city centre, Polk Street runs from Beach Street next to the bay until it terminates at Market Street, some thirty-nine city blocks. The Southern end of the street has a wide roadway and mid-level buildings including San Francisco City Hall and the Supreme Court of California on Civic Center Plaza. As the street continues North it reduces in scale and slopes uphill becoming mainly a 2–3-storey street wall, with retail on the ground floor and residential above. On this upper portion of Polk Street the roadway is wide (14meters/46 feet) and has moderately wide sidewalks (3.7 meters/12 feet) on both sides, making the space of the street wider than it is high. The sidewalks have younger trees, light poles and parking meters in the amenity zone next to the curb. The base of the street wall opens directly onto the sidewalk, with shop windows and entryways, some of which are recessed and there are frequently awnings and overhangs. Above the base there are bays that project out over the sidewalk into the space of the street, creating a rhythm on the upper-street wall. Upper Polk Street is an important circulation route, but it is a neighbourhood commercial street that supports the social life of its residents.

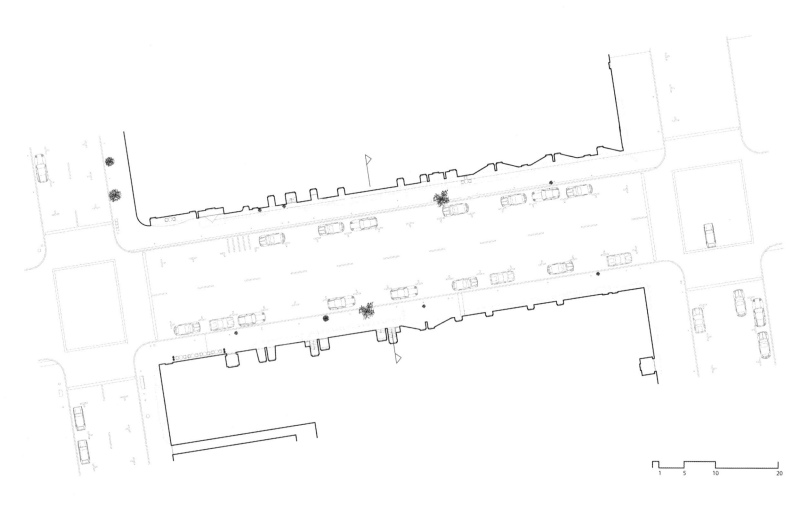

4.24 C
San Francisco Street Plan

4.24 D
San Francisco Street Section

4.24 E
San Francisco Photo

4.25 A
San Miguel de Allende City Plan

0 100 250 500 1000m

0 100 250 500 1000m

4.25 B
San Miguel de Allende City Section

San Miguel de Allende, Mexico　　　　　Lat. 20°55'00" N – Long. 100°45'00" W

Founded as a Spanish mission in 1542, San Miguel de Allende prospered in the
mid 18th century due to silver mining in the region. The city is located in the
mountainous region of central Mexico, 170 miles Northwest of Mexico City on a
flat plain and has two small rivers that join to the Northwest of the centre, with
the streets sloping away from the river in the heart of the colonial city. The city is
an example of Spanish colonial settlements throughout South America and has
maintained its historic architecture and spatial qualities. The city fabric is formed by

1–2-storey masonry buildings painted in bright colours, punctuated by the towers and domes of various churches dating from the 18th century. The street pattern is rectilinear in the historic core, while beyond this as it spreads more irregular patterns occur. The heart of the city is marked with a raised tree-filled central square, framed by the main church and grand arcaded mansions. The city has a low, compact and delicate spatial definition, with streets that enclose and a simple but visually engaging streetscape.[25]

San Francisco, San Miguel de Allende

The street is oriented East-West and is one of the major East-West axes of the colonial plan, running from the Eastern edge of the historic town to form the North side of the central square and then linking to the main thoroughfare leading West out of the city. San Francisco is formed by a 1–2-storey street wall with a roadway that is paved with regular stone pavers and is not very wide (9.4 meters/31 feet) but broad in relation to the low buildings that contain it and slopes from the East to the West. There are narrow flagstone pavements (1.85 meters/6 feet) with thin stone curbs and there is no street furniture on the pavements. The base of the street wall negotiates the slope with one to two steps and the ground floor spaces open directly onto the pavement. There is a mix of retail, commercial and residential uses on the street and the street wall is punctured by regular entryways and windows. The facades have large expanses of bare surface, but there is metalwork and architectural detailing accenting many openings and the street lighting is mounted to them as well. The volume of the street is horizontal and small in scale, and combined with the painted surfaces and subtle but strong street wall a plain and intimate space is formed.

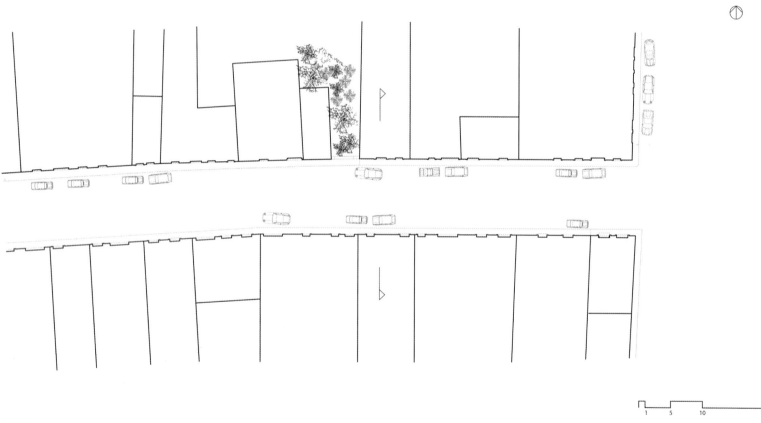

4.25 C
San Miguel de Allende Street Plan

4.25 D
San Miguel de Allende Street Section

4.25 E
San Miguel de Allende Photo

0 100 250 500 1000m

4.26A
St. Petersburg City Plan

0 100 250 500 1000m

4.26B
St. Petersburg City Section

St. Petersburg, Russia   Lat. 59°53'39" N – Long. 30°15'51" E

St. Petersburg was founded by Peter the Great of Russia in 1703, in an attempt to more directly engage the rest of Europe by moving the capital of Russia to the new city in 1712. The city is situated in the estuary of the Neva River where it joins the Gulf of Finland in the Northwest of Russia. St. Petersburg is built on the islands in the estuary and portions of the mainland that wrap around the gulf North and South of the river. The flat topography is intersected by numerous tributaries and canals, interlacing the city with water. The city was built using baroque urban principles then in fashion throughout Europe, so there are numerous broad avenues and long vistas which radiate out from the Admiralty, at the centre of the original city plan. The street pattern in the centre is regular and there are parks and public spaces laid out in geometric figures and there is a monumental architectural character to much of the city. The city has a large scale but it is not vertical, with mainly 4–5-storey buildings that enclose large streets with wide pavements.[26]

Maliya Sadovaya Ulitsa, St. Petersburg

Maliya Sadovaya Ulitsa is a pedestrian street running North-South between Italyanskaya Ulitsa and Nevsky Prospect in the North-Eastern part of the historic city. The street wall is formed by 4–5-storey buildings of a grand scale, with ornate architectural detailing. The ground plane between the buildings is wide (22.3 meters/73 feet) and is divided up into three sections by two rows of light fixtures and planters that define an area in the middle used for seating and outdoor activities, flanked by two broad walkways against the buildings. The street wall has regular punched openings in the mass of the wall and the base is opened frequently with shop windows and entries to the ground-floor spaces. The quality of the architecture, the variation in colour and the details of the facade create a visually engaging boundary to the street. The street is open, with a large volume of horizontal space, layered by the lines of light fixtures and provides a grand but comfortable urban place.

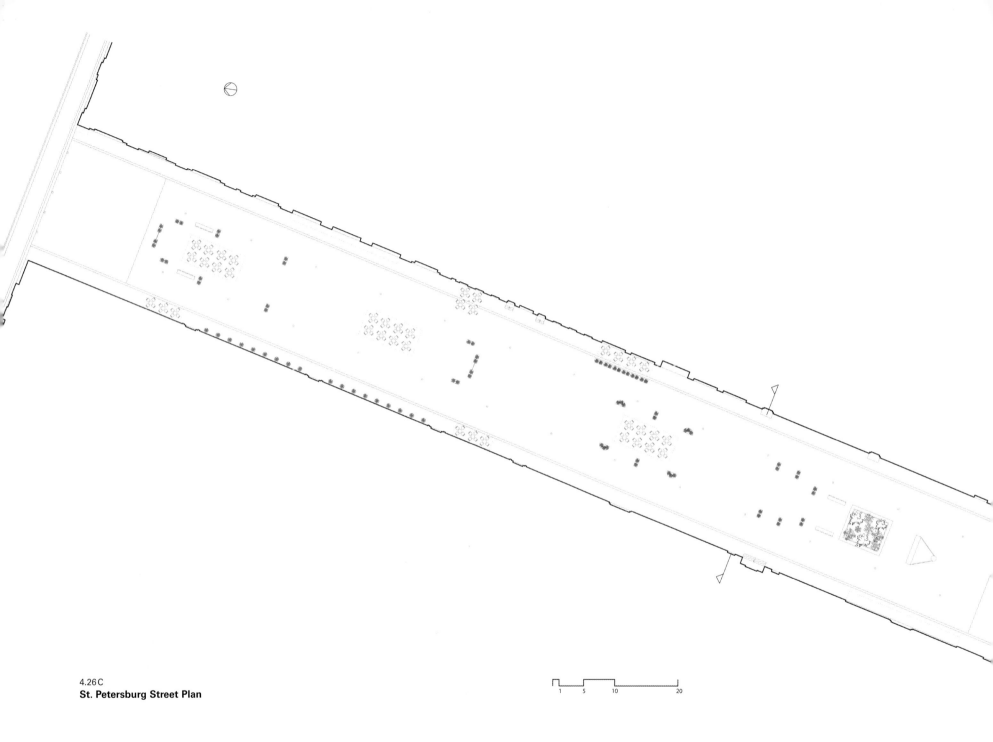

4.26 C
St. Petersburg Street Plan

1 5 10 20

4.26 D
St. Petersburg Street Section

4.26 E
St. Petersburg Photo

4.27 A
Shanghai City Plan

0 100 250 500   1000m

4.27 B
Shanghai City Section

0 100 250 500   1000m

Shanghai, China   Lat. 31°13′19″N – Long. 121°27′29″E

Shanghai originally developed as a small fishing village surrounded by agricultural
land, with serious trade beginning in the 11th century and due to its deep port
became the hub of Western trade in Asia in the middle of the 19th century and
developed into an important commercial and industrial centre. The city is located
on the East coast of the East China Sea at the mouth of the Yangtze River, on the flat
plain of the river delta that is laced with a system of canals, rivers and streams, the
largest of which is the Huangpu River. The original Chinese city was located on the

West bank of the Huangpu River and has an organic street pattern, while the former International Settlement just to the North has a grid plan. On the East bank of the river is Pudong, a formerly industrial area that has been developed as a commercial and financial district, with curvilinear streets radiating out from a traffic circle at the base of the diagonal Lujiazui East Road. Outside of this central core is a mixture of sections of gridded street, irregular roads, canals, rivers and streams. The central business district has numerous high-rise towers particularly near the river. Beyond this the city is characterised by an older lower residential fabric, studded with the multi-level residential development of recent years. Another unique feature of Shanghai is the many industrial sites embedded in the city, with housing for employees clustered around them. Shanghai has exploded with growth over the last 30 years and is one of the most energetic contemporary cityscapes. The spatial quality of the city is dense, vertical and dynamic, combining dramatic skyscrapers and streets filled with activity.[27]

Wuchang Road, Shanghai

The street runs from Wusong Road at the Eastern end West for two blocks to Sichuan North Road, in the Hongkou district, just North of the Wusong River. The roadway is narrow (8 meters/26 feet) with small pavements (1.75 meters/5 feet 9 inches) on either side. A continuous line of 2-storey buildings frame the street and the ground floor is occupied by retail units. The roadway is used by vendors, pedestrians and vehicles, creating an informal space of commercial and social activity. The street wall is animated by signs, awnings, canopies, equipment, wires and fenestration. The spatial enclosure is reinforced by a consistent edge at the top of the street wall, but dormers in the sloped roof create a roofscape that activates the top edge of the street space. The ground floor is connected directly to the street with large openings and entryways in a regular rhythm along the street, producing a permeable base to the street. The street has a small scale, full of commercial activity and circulating people, resulting in a vibrant public space.

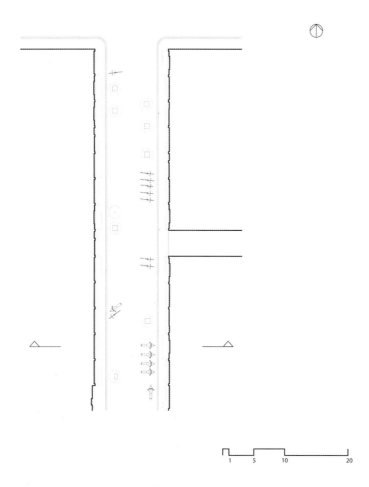

4.27 C
Shanghai Street Plan

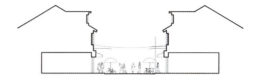

4.27 D
Shanghai Street Section

4.27 E
Shanghai Photo

4.28 A
Singapore City Plan

4.28 B
Singapore City Section

Singapore, Republic of Singapore   Lat. 1°17'22" N – Long. 103°51'00"E

Although Singapore Island has been occupied by fishermen and traders for centuries, the modern city began to take form after Sir Thomas Raffles established a trading post for the East India Company in 1819 and has developed into an important commercial centre and one of the largest ports in Asia. The city is situated on the Southern tip of Singapore Island and a group of small islands at the base of the Malay Peninsula. The downtown core and port are located on a flat coastal plain and the city and its suburbs spread over much of the island except

0 100 250 500 1000m

0 100 250 500 1000m

for some hilly portions away from the South coast. The historic city has a grid plan and the gridded organisation continues to the East close to the coast, but the street pattern becomes irregular as the city spreads north and is shaped by numerous high traffic roads that wind through the topography. The city has grown dramatically since the1970's and much of the original urban fabric has been replaced by multi-storey contemporary buildings, with some examples of British colonial architecture remaining. There is an expressway that cuts between the city centre and the port, connecting the airport to the city and the Malaysian mainland. The city's transformation from a low-rise colonial port has followed post-war planning principles, with roads designed to maximise vehicular circulation, single-use zoning and architectural objects situated in green space connected by roads. Many of the streets have undefined spatial enclosure, with empty spaces between large buildings surrounded by lawns with ground floors unconnected to the street. The downtown area has remnants of the colonial streets, with continuous street walls that contain readable volumes of space, but the city's spatial character is disjointed, with wide streets that cater to vehicles and not the social life of the city.[28]

South Bridge Road, Singapore

South Bridge Road runs Northeast to Southwest from the Singapore River to Maxwell Street, becoming Neil Road as it travels to the Southwest and connects the Eastern section of the downtown core to the original commercial centre. At the head of the bridge the street begins with low-rise buildings on the East side and a point tower on the West. As the street continues the East side stays low and the West is formed by 4–5-storey buildings until the street reaches Hong Lim Park. Facing the park is a large tower that occupies the complete block and the street widens dramatically. Once the street passes Pickering Street, the West side increases in scale dramatically, with two tall multi-storey buildings with retail at their bases, while the East side remains 2–3 storeys, with a mix of colonial and contemporary buildings. After Cross Street the West side reduces to 2–3 storeys to match the East side. There is a moderately wide roadway between the street walls (12.475 meters/41 feet), with a narrow pavement on the East side (2.3 meters/7 feet 6 inches) and a wider pavement on the West side (5.15 meters/16 feet 10 inches). Like much of South Bridge Road, on the portion of the street being examined, the ground floor on the East side is occupied mainly by retail stores and consequently the base of the street wall has large openings for the shop-front displays, some of which are recessed. These interior spaces are typically level with the pavement, but there are instances where the interior floor is raised slightly above the pavement. On the Western side of the street, the larger-scale building has an arcade facing the pavement with retail stores on the ground floor at the level of the pavement,

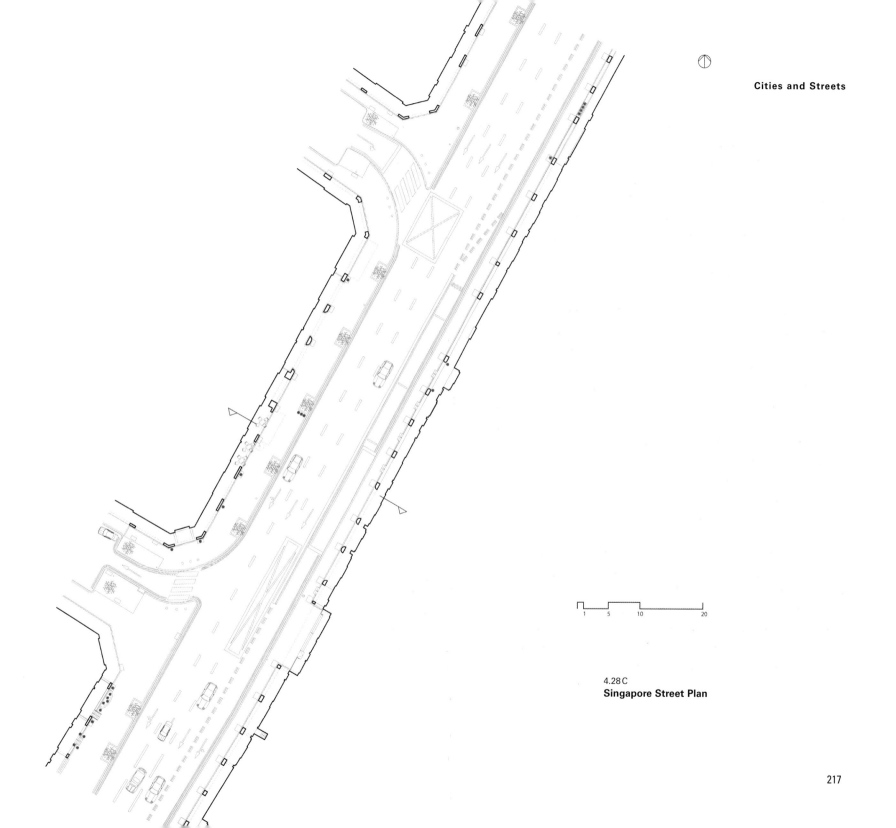

4.28 C
Singapore Street Plan

again this is the pattern for most of the high rise buildings on the street, while the mid-level buildings do not have arcades and have retail units connected directly to the pavement. The pavement on the West side has planting beds, street trees and light poles; and due to the broader pavement is more spacious, while the much tighter East side has no street furniture or landscaping. The street wall on the East side is articulated by architectural detail and signage, with wall-mounted lighting to illuminate the pavement. The conditions at the base of the street wall do support pedestrian use of the street and give the pavement a human scale and the space of the street is well defined, but the breadth of the roadway and the large scale of the Western side produces a street in which vehicles appear to dominate, somewhat inhibiting the social role of the street.

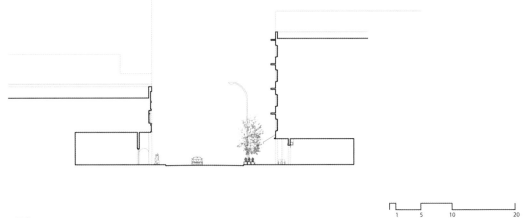

4.28 D
Singapore Street Section

4.28E
Singapore Photo

4.29A
Tokyo City Plan

0 100 250 500   1000m

0 100 250 500   1000m

4.29B
Tokyo City Section

Tokyo, Japan   Lat. 35°36′53″N – Long. 139°34′52″E

The site of Tokyo has been occupied by a fishing village named Edo since the 15th century, but became a city when the Japanese military ruler, Tokugawa Ieyasu, moved his government there in 1603. Over the next two centuries the city became the mercantile centre of Japan and its most populous city. The city was renamed Tokyo when the emperor moved the imperial court there in 1868. The city is located on the East coast of Honshu Island, the largest island in the Japanese archipelago, on Tokyo Bay. Historic Edo was built around a fortified castle in the flat plain West of the Sumida River and much of the city occupies reclaimed land in the river's estuary. Commercial activity was focused to the South and East of the castle, with the residential and government areas occupying the hilly terrain to the West. The castle became the imperial palace and is the centre of a radial organisational network, within which are sections of gridded streets aligned to the main arteries. However, the city is not concentric as the road network would suggest, but is in fact a polycentric city, with numerous distinct urban centres, which support large populations, with distinct economic, cultural and social characters. The city was traditionally comprised of 2–3-storey buildings, but since the 1970's it has become more vertical, with both the construction of more skyscrapers and a mid-level urban fabric due to the pressure of density and population growth. Central Tokyo is now generally 10–20 storeys, with numerous high-rise tower clusters at important nodes. The spatial character of the city is dense and vertical, as even when streets are wide they are enclosed by high street walls.[29]

Kabukicho 1-11-1, Tokyo

Running North-South in the Shinjuku district, the retail and entertainment heart of Tokyo and one of its satellite centres, to the West of the historic core, the street is a small-scale retail lane. The street is framed by 3–5-storey buildings, with a very dynamic street wall, due to the proliferation of advertising and variety of facade treatments. There is a narrow central paved area (6.4 meters/21 feet) with road markings defining thin strips next to the buildings (1.5 meters/5 feet) used to park bicycles and for temporary signs. The ground floor is typically directly connected to the exterior space of the street, with large openings into the retail units, but raised one step above the pavement. There are entryways to upper floors and some ground-floor facades are recessed, creating a pocket of space between the interior and the central circulation space of the street. The street has a vertical orientation and this space is condensed by the abundance of advertising at various scales, from small signs, whole surfaces covered in images to two-storey light boxes that project into the space. The strong sense of enclosure, the visual intensity of the street wall and the busy retail nature of the street result in an active and stimulating public environment.

4.29 C
Tokyo Street Plan

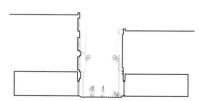

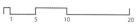

4.29 D
Tokyo Street Section

4.29 E
Tokyo Photo

4.30 A
Vancouver City Plan

4.30 B
Vancouver City Section

Vancouver, Canada   Lat. 49°14′58″ N – Long. 123°07′09″ W

Although the site of Vancouver has been inhabited for centuries by Native Americans and there were numerous European settlements nearby, the city was not founded until the 1870's, when a sawmill and logging activity helped create the permanent town of Granville. The arrival of the trans-continental railway, the Canadian Pacific, established Vancouver as the major trading centre of Western Canada and the city developed into a major port. The city is located in Southwestern Canada, on the

Burrard peninsula between Burrard Inlet to the North and the estuary of the Fraser River to the South. The topography of the city slopes upward from the Northwestern shore of the peninsula to the East and there are occasional low hills. The city is characterised by compact vertical urban core with the steep Southern slopes of the North Shore Mountains as a backdrop, giving the city a unique formal identity. The city is organised with a grid street plan in the commercial downtown area, that is rotated to align with the Northwest to Southeast orientation of the waterfront, while the grid for the rest of the city is laid out North-South and East-West, with the major diagonal of Kingsway cutting across the grid from the Southeast to the centre of the city in the Northwest. There is also a motorway along the Eastern edge of the city. Vancouver has an open, vertical spatial quality in the downtown area, with high-rise towers on wide streets in the dense core, which dissipates rapidly to a much lower city of 2–3-storey buildings with broad roadways between them. The city is a dynamic urban environment, which is attempting to address urban problems in a considered fashion, with a recent emphasis on pedestrians and sustainability. This has resulted in a city that has strong cultural and social amenities and liveable neighbourhoods.[30]

Robson Street, Vancouver

Oriented Southeast-Northwest in the heart of downtown Vancouver, Robson Street runs from Beatty Street in front of the BC Place Stadium to Lagoon Drive at the edge of Stanley Park in the Northwest. The Southwest end is comprised of large commercial office development, with a low-rise shopping district in the West End area and becoming residential as it moves Northwest towards Stanley Park. The ground floor of much of the street is retail, with commercial or residential space above, except in the residential area at the Northwest end. The portion of the street illustrated is from the shopping area, which has 2–3-storey buildings framing a wide roadway (13.7 meters/45 feet) bordered by very broad sidewalks (7.6 meters/25 feet). The street wall is varied with setbacks, canopies, louvered balconies and projecting bay windows and the ground floor connects directly to the exterior space of the street with large openings and shop windows. The sidewalks have street trees and light poles placed at regular intervals in the amenity zone and there are overhead wires, all of which frame the space of the roadway and define vertical volumes of space in front of the buildings, while the canopies and awnings that project over the sidewalks divide this space horizontally, giving an intimate scale to the street. The provision of space for pedestrians, the visually stimulating street wall, the layered space and the attention to detail creates an active social street.

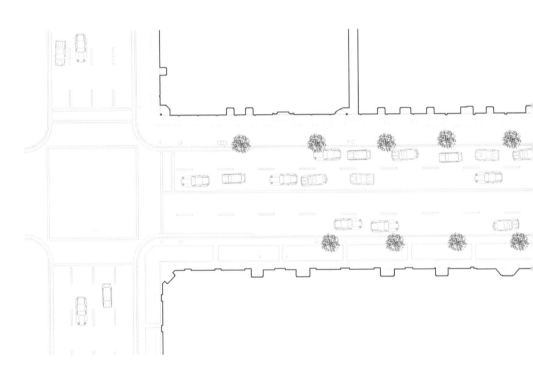

4.30 C
Vancouver Street Plan

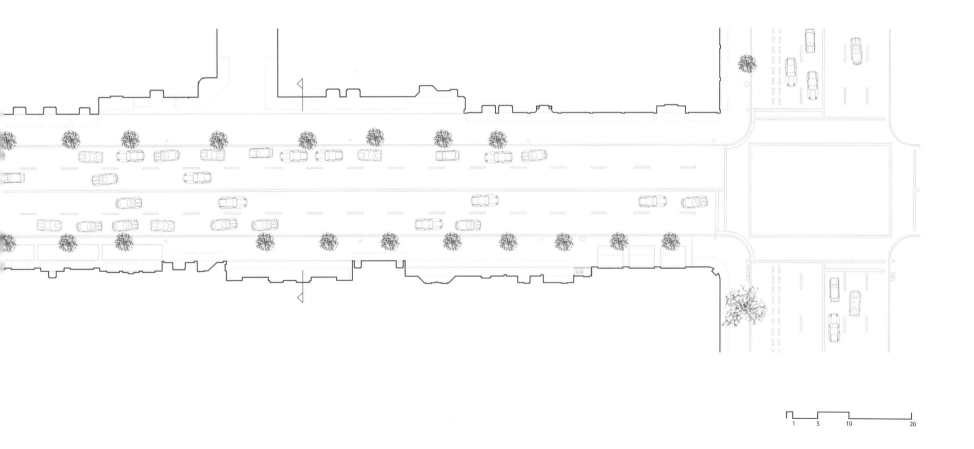

4.30 D
Vancouver Street Section

4.30 E
Vancouver Photo

Notes

In each case the basic background facts were provided by the Encyclopædia Britannica Online, with additional information from plans, sections, maps and the author's direct experience and general knowledge.

1. "Amsterdam." *Encyclopædia Britannica. Encyclopædia Britannica Online.* Encyclopædia Britannica, Inc., 2013. Web. 6 Oct. 2013. <http://original.search.eb.com/eb/article-9109380>.

2. "Bangkok." *Encyclopædia Britannica. Encyclopædia Britannica Online.* Encyclopædia Britannica, Inc., 2013. Web. 6 Oct. 2013. <http://original.search.eb.com/eb/article-24907>

3. "Beijing." *Encyclopædia Britannica. Encyclopædia Britannica Online.* Encyclopædia Britannica, Inc., 2013. Web. 6 Oct. 2013. <http://original.search.eb.com/eb/article-60542>.

4. "Boston." *Encyclopædia Britannica. Encyclopædia Britannica Online.* Encyclopædia Britannica, Inc., 2013. Web. 6 Oct. 2013. <http://original.search.eb.com/eb/article-9639>.

5. "Buenos Aires." *Encyclopædia Britannica. Encyclopædia Britannica Online.* Encyclopædia Britannica, Inc., 2013. Web. 6 Oct. 2013. <http://original.search.eb.com/eb/article-9106099>.

6. "Cape Town." *Encyclopædia Britannica. Encyclopædia Britannica Online.* Encyclopædia Britannica, Inc., 2013. Web. 7 Oct. 2013. <http://original.search.eb.com/eb/article-9106120>.

7. "Chicago." *Encyclopædia Britannica. Encyclopædia Britannica Online.* Encyclopædia Britannica, Inc., 2013. Web. 7 Oct. 2013. <http://original.search.eb.com/eb/article-61249>.

8. "Copenhagen." *Encyclopædia Britannica. Encyclopædia Britannica Online.* Encyclopædia Britannica, Inc., 2013. Web. 8 Oct. 2013. <http://original.search.eb.com/eb/article-9026183>.

9. "Fès." *Encyclopædia Britannica. Encyclopædia Britannica Online.* Encyclopædia Britannica, Inc., 2013. Web. 8 Oct. 2013. <http://original.search.eb.com/eb/article-9034128>.

10. "Genoa." *Encyclopædia Britannica. Encyclopædia Britannica Online.* Encyclopædia Britannica, Inc., 2013. Web. 8 Oct. 2013. <http://original.search.eb.com/eb/article-9036417>.

11. "Glasgow." *Encyclopædia Britannica. Encyclopædia Britannica Online.*

Encyclopædia Britannica, Inc., 2013. Web. 8 Oct. 2013.
<http://original.search.eb.com/eb/article-9036983>.

12. "Lagos." *Encyclopædia Britannica. Encyclopædia Britannica Online.*
Encyclopædia Britannica, Inc., 2013. Web. 8 Oct. 2013.
<http://original.search.eb.com/eb/article-9046836>.

13. "London." *Encyclopædia Britannica. Encyclopædia Britannica Online.*
Encyclopædia Britannica, Inc., 2013. Web. 8 Oct. 2013.
<http://original.search.eb.com/eb/article-9108472>.

14. "Mexico City." *Encyclopædia Britannica. Encyclopædia Britannica Online.*
Encyclopædia Britannica, Inc., 2013. Web. 10 Oct. 2013.
<http://original.search.eb.com/eb/article-9108721>.

15. "Montevideo." *Encyclopædia Britannica. Encyclopædia Britannica Online.*
Encyclopædia Britannica, Inc., 2013. Web. 10 Oct. 2013.
<http://original.search.eb.com/eb/article-9053528>.

16. "Montreal." *Encyclopædia Britannica. Encyclopædia Britannica Online.*
Encyclopædia Britannica, Inc., 2013. Web. 10 Oct. 2013.
<http://original.search.eb.com/eb/article-9108740>.

17. "Mumbai." *Encyclopædia Britannica. Encyclopædia Britannica Online.*
Encyclopædia Britannica, Inc., 2013. Web. 10 Oct. 2013.
<http://original.search.eb.com/eb/article-9106091>.

18. "Newcastle upon Tyne." *Encyclopædia Britannica. Encyclopædia Britannica Online.*
Encyclopædia Britannica, Inc., 2013. Web. 10 Oct. 2013.
<http://original.search.eb.com/eb/article-9055575>.

19. "New York City." *Encyclopædia Britannica. Encyclopædia Britannica Online.*
Encyclopædia Britannica, Inc., 2013. Web. 10 Oct. 2013.
<http://original.search.eb.com/eb/article-9108761>.

20. "Paris." *Encyclopædia Britannica. Encyclopædia Britannica Online.*
Encyclopædia Britannica, Inc., 2013. Web. 11 Oct. 2013.
<http://original.search.eb.com/eb/article-9108530>.

21. "Pittsburgh." *Encyclopædia Britannica. Encyclopædia Britannica Online.*
Encyclopædia Britannica, Inc., 2013. Web. 11 Oct. 2013.
<http://original.search.eb.com/eb/article-9060233>.

22. "Rio de Janeiro." *Encyclopædia Britannica. Encyclopædia Britannica Online.*
Encyclopædia Britannica, Inc., 2013. Web. 11 Oct. 2013.
<http://original.search.eb.com/eb/article-9109485>.

23. "Rome." *Encyclopædia Britannica. Encyclopædia Britannica Online.*

Encyclopædia Britannica, Inc., 2013. Web. 11 Oct. 2013.
<http://original.search.eb.com/eb/article-9109501>.

24. "San Francisco." *Encyclopædia Britannica. Encyclopædia Britannica Online.*
Encyclopædia Britannica, Inc., 2013. Web. 11 Oct. 2013.
<http://original.search.eb.com/eb/article-9109513>.

25. "San Miguel de Allende." *Encyclopædia Britannica. Encyclopædia Britannica Online.*
Encyclopædia Britannica, Inc., 2013. Web. 11 Oct. 2013.
<http://original.search.eb.com/eb/article-9065371>.

26. "Saint Petersburg." *Encyclopædia Britannica. Encyclopædia Britannica Online.*
Encyclopædia Britannica, Inc., 2013. Web. 12 Oct. 2013.
<http://original.search.eb.com/eb/article-9109512>

27. "Shanghai." *Encyclopædia Britannica. Encyclopædia Britannica Online.*
Encyclopædia Britannica, Inc., 2013. Web. 12 Oct. 2013.
<http://original.search.eb.com/eb/article-9109537>.

28. "Singapore." *Encyclopædia Britannica. Encyclopædia Britannica Online.*
Encyclopædia Britannica, Inc., 2013. Web. 12 Oct. 2013.
<http://original.search.eb.com/eb/article-9067912>. & <http://original.search.eb.com/eb/article-9111151>.

29. "Tokyo." *Encyclopædia Britannica. Encyclopædia Britannica Online.*
Encyclopædia Britannica, Inc., 2013. Web. 12 Oct. 2013.
<http://original.search.eb.com/eb/article-9072783>.

30. "Vancouver." *Encyclopædia Britannica. Encyclopædia Britannica Online.*
Encyclopædia Britannica, Inc., 2013. Web. 12 Oct. 2013.
<http://original.search.eb.com/eb/article-9074787>.

Chapter Five
Analysing Streets: The Methodology

Streets are a complex combination of factors; social, cultural, economic, programmatic and physical: and it is abundantly clear that understanding the physical attributes of a street cannot produce a complete picture of the place. However, it is also beyond question that the physical properties of a street have significant impacts on the experience, perception and identity of a specific street and that developing a clear grasp of the physical and spatial characteristics contributes to building a comprehensive understanding of a street.

Observation and documentation are critical, but a structured investigation is invaluable, providing clarity and depth, while also allowing comparisons to be drawn. Through the isolation of individual aspects in sectional diagrams, with a step-by-step analysis, basic components are identified and the fundamental conditions established. Combining the information from the various diagrams permits the relationships between the elements to be examined. Drawing the diagrams catalogues what the elements are, how they interact, the spaces they form and the qualities that result. This detailed investigation in section generates a framework for exploring the spatial consequences of specific arrangements and generates valuable in-depth knowledge.

In the study of the physical and spatial qualities of streets, visual analysis gives clear and direct access to the issues being discussed. The sectional diagrams focus on specific features, while also communicating the organisation of the constituent parts. Drawings can only approximate the experiential and perceptual richness of three-dimensional spaces; however, the visual examination of environmental configurations improves understanding, as spatial faculties are used to process the information and assess relationships; mentally processing visual material requires the engagement of perceptual faculties and judgement, which strengthens the transfer and reception of this information. Drawings allow multiple interrelated layers of data to be understood simultaneously, revealing connections and patterns. While these sectional diagrams are reductive and abstract, requiring a familiarity with the conventions of the device; to the trained practitioner they are an efficient means of describing volumetric and material characteristics.

Comparative analysis is a powerful tool for revealing information about both individual circumstances and broader issues. This type of analysis reveals common elements, highlighting fundamental components and their organisation. Differences, large and small, illustrate the distinctive qualities of specific configurations, with variations between broadly similar arrangements as fascinating as cases of very disparate conditions. When information is evaluated through comparison, basic relationships are questioned and reassessed, stretching and extending understanding. Structured comparative analysis also permits select sets of data to be interpolated into general concepts, expanding the body of knowledge for the individual and the discipline. Examining existing models through comparison can provide useful guidance and develop a reference resource, which, used in conjunction with firsthand experience, can generate valuable instrumental knowledge.

Orientation

While it is a very simple and elementary piece of information and to some degree ignored, the orientation of the space of the street is a significant basic characteristic. Drawing a simple rectangle that delineates the broad volume of the street to identify whether the space is horizontal or vertical is the first step in the investigation.

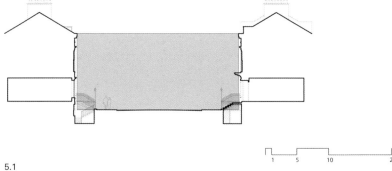

5.1
Orientation

Proportion / Height to Width Ratio

Determining the proportion of the space is also vital. The relationship between the height of the street walls and the width between them is one of the keys to establishing the nature of the enclosure on a street. The two primary dimensions, height (H) and width (W), are measured and expressed as a ratio; this ratio is recognised as an indication of the level and type of spatial definition.

5.2
Proportion / Height to Width Ratio

Scale of Parts

Using the human body as a unit of measure to determine the size of the street in the two major dimensions sets up a foundation for examining the scale of the street; this is extended by using the same measure on other components. Understanding the relationship between the human body and the overall frame of the street and its parts helps to reveal how the street is scaled and gives some indication of the possible effects of scale on the perception and experience of the street.

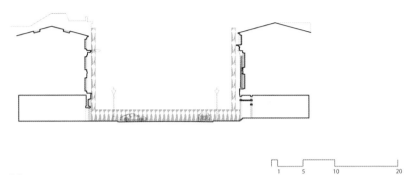

5.3
Scale

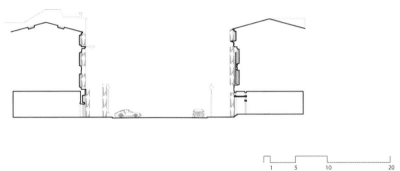

5.4
Scale of Parts

Horizontal Layers

Examining the street to identify these layers graphically exposes the horizontal structure of the space, one of the two primary components of the spatial organisation. This indicates the boundaries and thresholds between distinct zones and subtle differentiations and overlaps. The definition of these layers highlights a key spatial characteristic of the street.

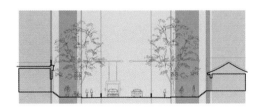

5.5
Horizontal Layers

Vertical Layers

Analysing the street to determine the number and position of vertical layers diagrammatically illustrates the other primary component that structures the street space. These lines demarcate the stratification of the space between the street walls and interact with the horizontal edges to describe volumes within the street.

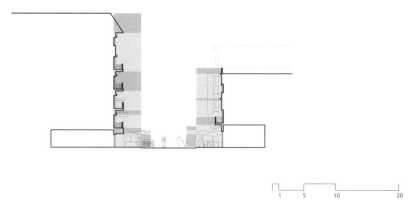

5.6
Vertical Layers

Public/Private Character

The habitable space of the street should be divided into zones positioned on a spectrum from private to public. The combination and nature of these zones strongly influences the social function of the street. Defining the distinct zones and determining the position of each zone on this spectrum is important in understanding the social aspects of the street. The terms used for differentiating these zones are: Private (PR), Semi-Private (SPR), Semi-Public (SP) and Public (P). Private space is controlled/owned space which requires permission to enter. Semi-Private space is related to a private space and accessible by a limited group via Private spaces. Semi-Public space is connected to Public space, but has socially discernible boundaries and can be occupied on a casual basis. Public space is shared space which is open to all users.

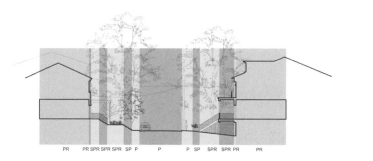

5.7
Public/Private Character

Spatial Definition

The space of the street can have a variety of spatial definitions or none at all; from the open or closed, stacked or layered, horizontal or vertical to a lack of containment generating no legible space. Examining the volumes of space on the street to identify the presence and quality of spatial definition is critical to evaluating the attributes and nature of the enclosure on the street. Clear definition with readable enclosure is an important contributor to spatial identity; poor definition weakens the perception of specificity, which is often experienced as unattractive or uncomfortable.

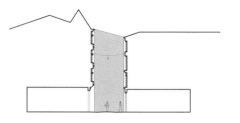

5.8
Spatial Definition – Simple

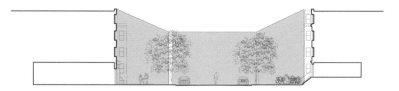

5.9
Spatial Definition – Layered

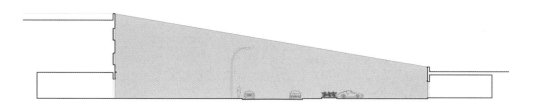

5.10
Poor Spatial Definition

Enclosure and Exposure

Mapping the quantity, location and sequence of enclosed space and the relationship to those places which are exposed, establishes the instances of architecturally defined territory and protection, which can vary from strong to weak. This analysis overlaps with both the examination of public to private and street edge character, but is specifically identifying containment created with physical components. This is distinguished from territorial definition created by landscape elements or street furniture.

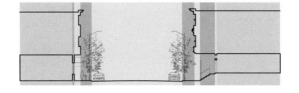

5.11
Enclosure and Exposure

Base of the Street Wall

The base of the street wall plays a critical role in structuring the sidewalk/pavement area of the street and ultimately having a major impact on the street. Consequently a review of this portion of the street is required. Determining if the configuration is hard or soft, abrupt and direct or layered and modulated establishes the character of the street edge. Soft street edges invite social gathering and blur the distinction between interior and exterior spaces. Hard edges result in direct connections and can lead to interaction and the linkage of inside and outside.

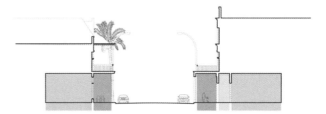

5.12
Base of the Street Wall – Soft

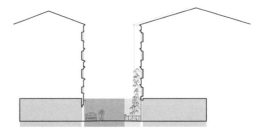

5.13
Base of the Street Wall – Hard

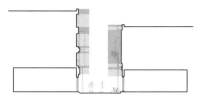

5.14
Facade Articulation

Facade Articulation

The level of detail on the street wall influences the optical quality of the perimeter of the street space. Highly detailed facades create dynamic surfaces and lead to increased visual stimulation, engaging those using the street. Facades with significant changes in depth generate dramatic shadows and spatial variation, again producing an active street wall. Detail also provides scale to the edge of the street room, indicating effort and craft. Simple, flat facades stress the planar and produce tight boundaries, with strong borders. Smooth faces draw the eye rapidly across the surface, minimising differentiation. Unadorned facades can also frame a street in a compelling fashion and the street wall for each street must be assessed in relation to the other elements of the street.

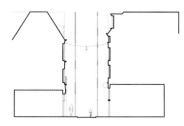

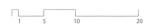

5.15
Transparency and Opacity

Transparency and Opacity

A significant characteristic of the street wall is the relationship between transparency and opacity, as the positions of windows and openings, or a wholly transparent facade affect the perception and experience of a street. Regular patterns of openings can indicate interior organisation, give scale and produce visual rhythm. Large openings create connections between the interiors and the street. Transparent facades produce complex networks of reflection and interpenetrating layers, producing rich optical effects that change in response to variations in light and environment.

Volumetric Interaction

Drawing a border around the individual volumes of space formed by the elements of the street allows the interpenetration and overlapping to be observed. This analysis reveals the interplay of horizontal and vertical subdivisions and illustrates the volumetric structure. The description of distinct pieces of space and the interaction between them communicates the level of spatial complexity on the street. Dense arrays create animation, while simple networks form stable spaces.

To demonstrate the use of the diagrammatic methodology, two streets have been selected from those included in Chapter Four for analysis.

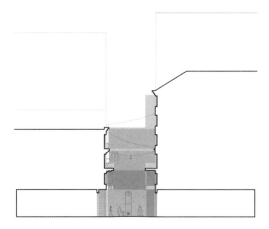

5.16
Volumetric Interaction

1   5   10   20

Visual analysis of East Third Street, New York City

Orientation

East Third Street in Manhattan is perceived as strongly vertical in orientation, but when examined with a rectangle drawn between the street walls it becomes clear that the volume of the street is only slightly vertical. The perception of the street as vertical is shaped by other factors which become clear after further investigation.

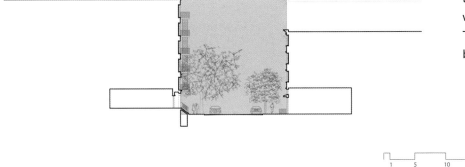

5.17
Orientation – East Third Street

Proportion

The street is 18 meters/59 feet (H) at the top of the highest street wall and 16.6 meters/54 feet 5 inches (W) wide from edge to edge. This results in a Height to Width ratio of 1:0.92, which provides strong enclosure and clear spatial definition. Using the lower North side street wall (13.05 meters/42 feet 9 inches) in a height to width ratio calculation produces a Height to Width ratio of 1:1.27, still providing adequate definition.

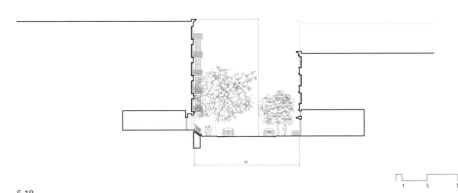

5.18
Proportion / Height to Width Ratio – East Third Street

Scale

The analysis of the scale of the street illustrates that the overall framework of the street has a moderate scale, with the sidewalks and street walls close enough to allow visual recognition and vocal exchange. This is not an intimate space, but it is not too large for communication. The examination also reveals that the North side of the street is smaller in scale, with a lower street wall and smaller openings. The South side has a larger scale entry and openings that do not change scale on the upper floors. The study of separate elements on the street shows that the openings in both street walls are close to the dimension of the human body, that there are details that divide the surface and that the sidewalks are not wide.

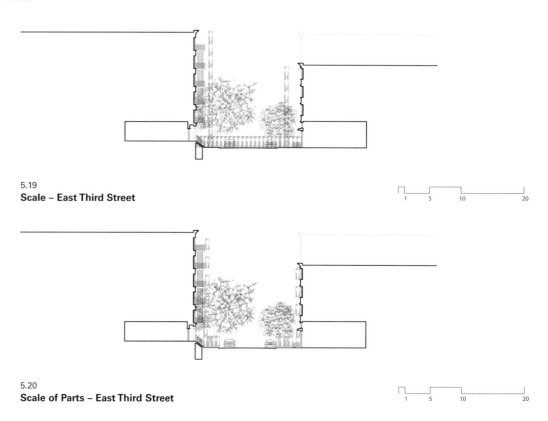

5.19
Scale – East Third Street

5.20
Scale of Parts – East Third Street

Horizontal Layers

Diagramming the horizontal layers on the street illustrates the typical overall organisation of the street, with sidewalks divided into the zones as detailed in Chapter 3 (transition, circulation, amenity and curbside), what also becomes clear is that the modest size of the space results in these zones being tight, satisfying the needs of the street without excess. The investigation also shows the difference between the two transition zones, with the South side having a greater number of layers between the interior and the exterior and the way these divisions frame the various spaces of the street.

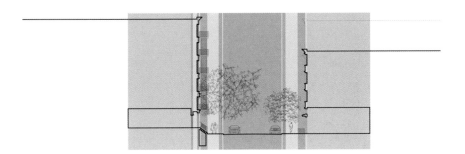

5.21
Horizontal Layers – East Third Street

Vertical Layers

Examining the vertical layers of the street exposes the distinct nature of the transition zones on both sides of the street. The horizontal dimensions are very similar, but the vertical variation creates the distinguishing features. The ground floor of North side of the street is on the same level as the sidewalk, connecting directly to the street, with a small fenced-in area adjacent to the entry. The entry on the South side is raised half a storey and has a small vestibule reached by a set of stairs. This change in level inserts a raised pocket of space overlooking the street to mediate between the more private space of the interior and public space of the sidewalk. The steps also provide an opportunity for informal seating adjacent to the street and social interaction. Across the street the transition zone directly interacts with the pavement and social exchange takes place in the standing position. Above the base of the street wall the vertical layers are stacked regularly and delineated by the window openings and the fire escapes. The canopies of street trees also produce a vertical layer, which encloses the space of the sidewalk.

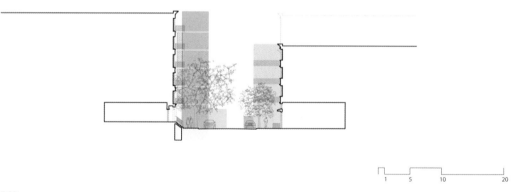

5.22
Vertical Layers – East Third Street

Public/Private Character

Determining the gradation of the street from public to private further distinguishes the two sides of the street, emphasising the more modulated quality of the South side. There are more thresholds controlling the transition from the public space of the street to the private spaces of the interior on the South side, with the Semi-Public stair and porch, the Semi-Private entry vestibule, entry threshold and shared access corridor. The North side has a Semi-Private buffer yard and a Semi-Private entry threshold before the Semi-Private corridor or retail unit is accessed. While there are instances where this is occupied by retail uses, this is not always the case and this rapid passage from public space to semi-private interior can be abrupt.

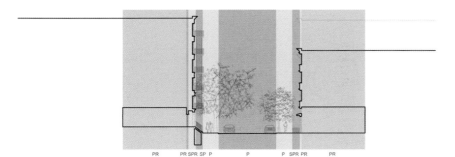

PR   PR SPR SP P   P   P SPR PR   PR

1   5   10   20

5.23
Public/Private Character – East Third Street

Spatial Definition

The analysis of the spatial definition on the street reveals three distinct enclosures, with the street trees creating a central vertical space with two tall spaces between the trees and the street walls. The layering of these three vertical spaces generates the perception of tall enclosure on the street. Also highlighted is the interaction between the trees and the facades, with the underside of the stacked fire escapes on the South side lowering the top edge of the sidewalk space, while the relative flatness of the facade on the North side extends the definition to the cornice.

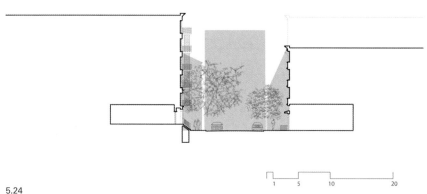

5.24
Spatial Definition Layered – East Third Street

Enclosure and Exposure

The examination of the street to identify the range from enclosure to exposure again illustrates the more direct and open connection between the exterior and interior on the North side and the mediated nature of the South side. The North side has a small overhang at the entry enclosing a thin piece of space and the frame of the entry. The South side has multiple enclosures and the level change reduces the sense of exposure.

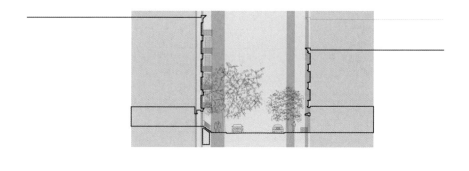

5.25
Enclosure and Exposure – East Third Street

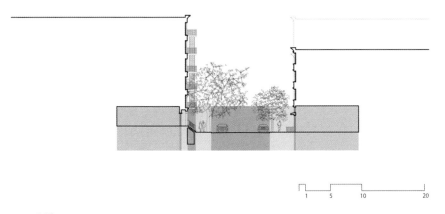

Base of the Street Wall

The investigation of the street edge of East Third Street indicates that the street has a moderately hard edge. The North side has a small fenced yard and the South side is conditioned by the set of stairs, while these features do modulate the edge, they do so in a limited fashion. The street edge on the South side has a stronger buffer than the North side, with the steps projecting into the street generating spatial variation. The small fenced area on the North side generates a minimal inflection, emphasising the direct nature at this edge.

5.26
Base of the Street Wall – Soft or Hard – East Third Street

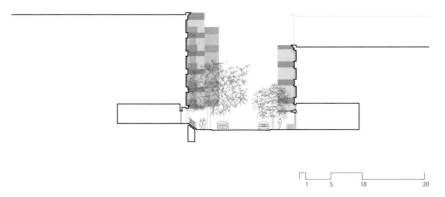

Facade Articulation

The facades that frame the street are not highly articulated. The diagram shows a great deal of vertical division, but little variation in depth and limited architectural detail. Again the North side is the more humble boundary, with only simple window openings and modest cornice. The South side is more differentiated, with stone accents around the openings. The South side is divided into smaller plots, increasing the number of buildings that form the street wall, which also leads to a larger number of fire escapes. While this variation of the facade is intermittent, it does impact the periphery, with the tracery of lines creating a play of light and shadow that animate the edge of the street space.

5.27
Facade Articulation – East Third Street

Transparency and Opacity

This investigation reveals that the majority of the street wall is solid, with punched openings that occur at regular intervals in relation to the floor levels. The mass of the opaque walls contain the space and do not bounce light or expand space with reflective surfaces. The scale of the openings let light and view into the interior and do not expose the activity inside to the street. This limits the interaction between the outside and the inside.

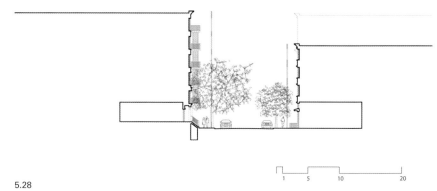

5.28
Transparency and Opacity – East Third Street

Volumetric Interaction

The volumetric analysis shows that the orientation of the spaces on the street is predominantly vertical, with the horizontal volumes occurring in the section at the ground level. These horizontal areas happen in the circulation zones on the street, relating to the interior spaces and the roadway. The vertical spaces are predominantly visual, above the ground floor, creating the tall, stacked perception of the street. The interaction between the two types of volume takes place on the sidewalk, where the horizontal interior volumes overlap with the vertical slice of space in the centre of the sidewalk, creating a series of interpenetrating volumes that articulate pockets of space.

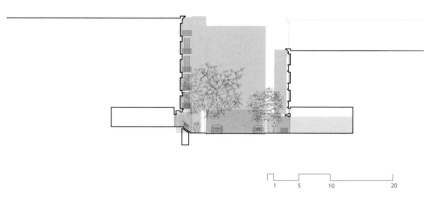

5.29
Volumetric Interaction – East Third Street

Visual analysis of South Bridge Road, Singapore

Orientation

Examining the street graphically with a rectangle around the perimeter indicates that the street has a neutral orientation, being only slightly taller than it is wide, although the visual cues emphasise the vertical appearance of the street. The registration of the actual periphery is an important step, as it highlights the perceptual impact of other elements.

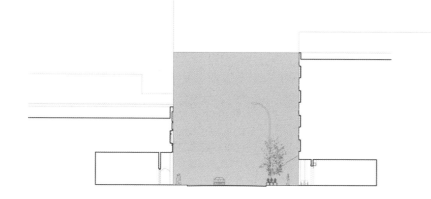

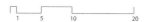

5.30
Orientation – South Bridge Road

Proportion

The street is 20.5 meters/67 feet 3 inches (H) at the top of the higher street wall on the West side and 19.94 meters/65 feet 5 inches (W) wide between the street walls. This results in a Height to Width ratio of 1:0.97, which is nearly 1:1 and results in clear spatial definition. Evaluating the height to width ratio based on the lower wall (12.05 meters/39 feet 6 inches) results in a ratio of 1:1.65, falling in the range which is considered as an acceptable level of definition.

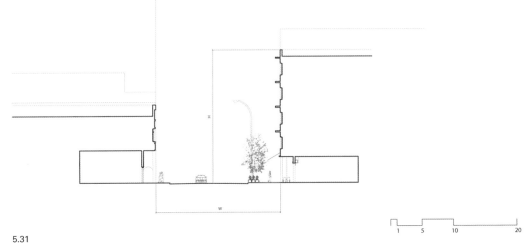

1   5   10   20

5.31
Proportion / Height to Width Ratio – South Bridge Road

Scale and Scale of Parts

The investigation into the overall scale of the street demonstrates the significance of basic dimensions, as the framework of the space is large and the variation of specific elements illustrates how size affects perception. The width of the roadway allows basic visual connections, but limits verbal communication. The East side of the street has small plot sizes and 2–5-storey buildings, with proportions that allow the higher portions of the facade to relate to the human scale, while the West side is 4–5-storey buildings on wider plots and the street wall is consistently taller than the East side. The wide roadway and the high West street wall give the street a large sense of scale, outweighing the smaller scale character of the East side. Examining the scale of specific components illustrates the more intimate scale of the Eastern street wall, as both the overall dimension and the size and articulation of the elements is relatively small. The base of the Western street wall has a human scale, and the facade is divided at regular intervals with canopies and window openings that roughly correspond to the human body; however, the height of the street wall and the geometric detail give a large-scale reading.

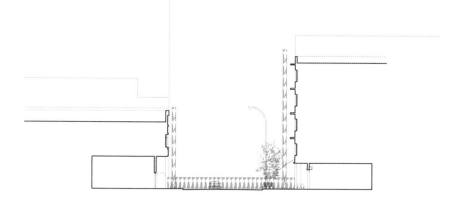

1　　5　　10　　20

5.32
Scale – South Bridge Road

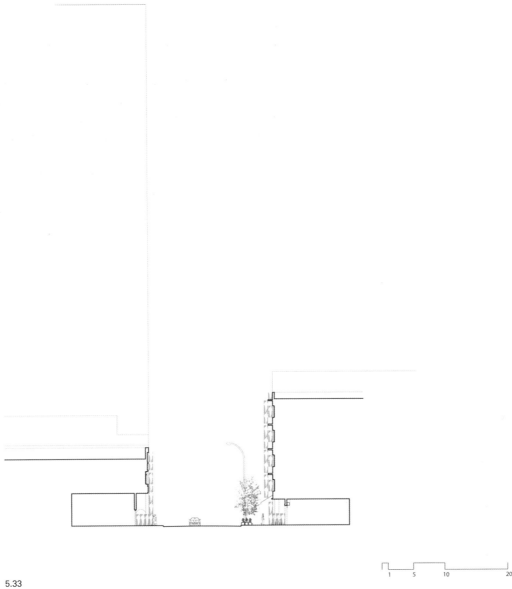

5.33
Scale of Parts – South Bridge Road

Horizontal Layers

Examining the horizontal divisions of the street shows how different the two sides of the street are structured, as the East side has a simple open pavement, with a recessed arcade, while the West side has a series of layers created by landscaping, street furniture and an articulated transition zone. The minimal nature of the Eastern edge still provides spatial modulation through the recess of the entry and the shop windows, creating a shaded area off the pavement, for coming and going, window shopping and casual social exchange. The more elaborate layering on the other side of the roadway introduces a layer of amenity to buffer the pavement from vehicular traffic and creates a layer of space in front of the recessed ground floor with an awning. These additional elements can increase the activity on and adjacent to the pavement, potentially improving the social use of the street.

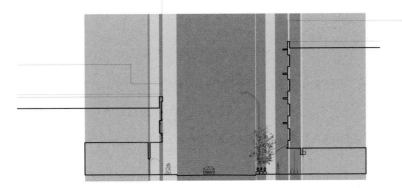

1 5 10 20

5.34
Horizontal Layers – South Bridge Road

Vertical Layers

Diagramming the vertical layers of the street again illustrates the difference between the two edges of the space of the street. The smaller East side has fewer vertical divisions, which get progressively smaller towards the top of the street wall. The Western street wall has more vertical layers at the base, with a regular pattern above this and has the added layers of space created by the addition of street trees and infrastructure. The vertical structure that results draws the space down to the pavement on the East side and raises the West side, emphasising verticality and increasing the scale.

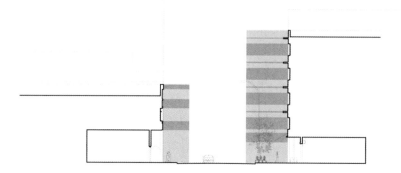

5.35
Vertical Layers – South Bridge Road

Public/Private Character

Analysing the public to private sequences on South Bridge Road reveals a straight-forward progression. Both sides mediate the transition from the public space of the pavement with a zone of intermediate space, on one side with a Semi-Private space with seating to service customers and an awning, on the other with the Semi-Public space of a shaded overhang. The threshold between this area and the pavement is marked by the brief compression of columns that frame these spaces connecting the interiors to the public pavement. The West side has two distinct pieces of public space, the circulation zone and the amenity zone with landscape elements providing opportunities for informal seating or standing.

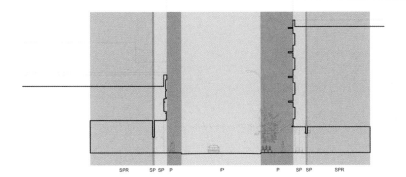

SPR   SP SP P   P   P   SP SP   SPR

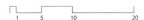

1   5   10   20

5.36
Public/Private Character – South Bridge Road

Spatial Definition

The spatial definition of the street is open, with the East side expanding across the roadway to the top of the tree and continuing to the face of the building. The delineation of space on the West side is more complex, with two spaces described by the overhang of the awning and the canopy of the tree and the street wall. Analysing the spatial definition of this street illustrates the impact of a consistent street wall, height to width ratio and the moderating effect of street trees, as the wide roadway is contained by the enclosure of the facades and narrowed by the vertical of the trees.

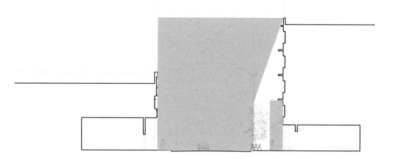

5.37
Spatial Definition Open Layered – South Bridge Road

Enclosure and Exposure

As discussed in the investigation of the horizontal layers and the public to private sequence, there are enclosed areas between the interior spaces and the pavement on both sides of the street, while on the West side this enclosure is amplified by the overhang of the awning and the canopy of the street trees. These pockets of space buffer the interior from the movement of the street, offering containment out of the fully exposed space of the pavement.

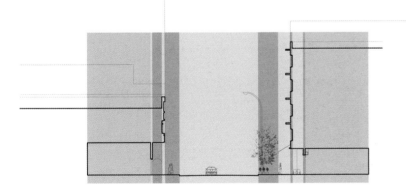

1   5   10   20

5.38
Enclosure and Exposure – South Bridge Road

Base of the Street Wall

The street edge on South Bridge Road can be defined as moderately soft due to the recesses discussed above, while the consistent alignment of the facade with the property line provides a clear definition of this edge. The West side has a softer edge as the awning adds another slice of space to the interface between the interior and exterior. These layers of space help blur the boundary between the inside and the outside, allowing activity from the interior to extend out towards the pavement and support social interaction by providing opportunities for pedestrians to stop.

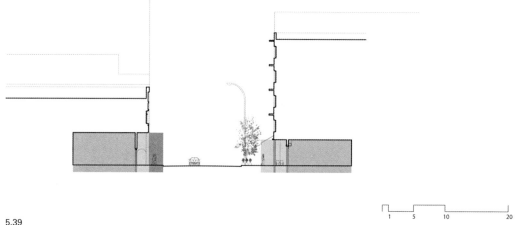

5.39
Base of the Street Wall – Soft or Hard – South Bridge Road

Facade Articulation

Analysing the facades that frame the street exposes the simplicity of the East side and the regularity of the West side. The plane of the East side facade has elements of relief, stringcourses and mouldings. These decorative features are modest, but they do provide visual accents and give the facade a human scale. The facade on the West side has regular window openings and smooth surfaces, with some depth added by deep overhanging horizontal brows above the windows. This unadorned facade produces a flat boundary on the Western side of the street.

1   5   10   20

5.40
Facade Articulation – South Bridge Road

Transparency and Opacity

Examining the street walls to assess the amount of transparency in the facade establishes that the majority of both facades are solid, with very few openings in the Eastern street wall and openings on every floor of the Western street wall. At the base of the building on the East side there are large shop windows, creating a visual connection between the interior and the exterior, while the small window on the second floor serves the interior space adding no visual stimulation to the street. The openings in the ground floor of the Western facade give access and view to the seating area out front and the pavement from inside, linking the exterior spaces of the street to the interior of the building. Again, the windows on the upper floors are limited to providing light and view to the interior and do not have a strong impact on the street.

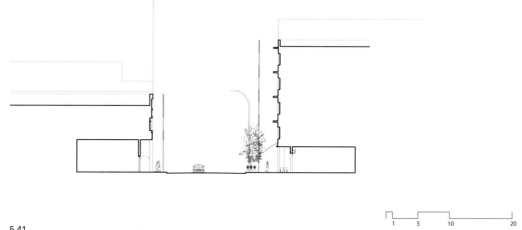

5.41
Transparency and Opacity – South Bridge Road

Volumetric Interaction

Analysing the volumes on the street reveals that the larger sections of space are stacked horizontally in relation to divisions created by the top edges of the two street walls, with smaller horizontal volumes formed by the ground floors, recessed entries and the underside of the tree canopy. The vertical volumes are defined by the tree, the awning and the facade on the West side, while the recess is a vertically oriented space on the Eastern side of the street. The perceivable interaction occurs at the pavement level, but there is some overlapping revealed by the diagram along the face of the Western facade.

5.42
Volumetric Interaction – South Bridge Road

Comparing East Third Street, New York City with South Bridge Road, Singapore

The benefit of comparing two streets comes from the way that the differences and similarities develop expanded and more specific information about each and the possibility of defining wider principles for use in other investigations. Many of the comparisons of individual diagrams do not reveal momentous differences or critical information; however, the simple act of assessing both diagrams in relation to each other expands understanding. Comparison requires fine judgement and the consideration of each set of data with two sets of criteria, which can consolidate knowledge.

Orientation

Reviewing the diagrams for both streets shows a similarity in the orientation of the two spaces, as the measured perimeter for both is nearly neutral, but the perceptual orientation is vertical. Drawing the boundary to establish the actual orientation of the space highlights the importance that the combination of spatial components has on the perception of street space. Comparing the two perimeters shows that South Bridge Road is a larger volume.

Proportion / Height to Width Ratio

South Bridge Road has a Height to Width ratio of 1:0.97 and East Third Street has a Height to Width ratio of 1:0.92. The nearly equal Height to Width ratio on both streets establishes a strong sense of enclosure, even though on both streets one of the street walls is larger; the lower wall is high enough to maintain the definition of the space. The comparison of the height and width dimensions shows that South Bridge Road is a larger street, with a broader roadway and a larger volume of space enclosed on the street. The higher street wall on South Bridge Road is taller (20.5 meters/67 feet 3 inches) than its counterpart on East Third Street (18 meters/59 feet), while the lower wall (13.05 meters/42 feet 9 inches) on East Third Street is larger than the smaller wall (12.05 meters/39 feet 6 inches) on South Bridge Road. This affects the perception of the two streets which will be discussed further below.

Scale and Scale of parts

Using the human body as a unit of measure to assess the scale of both streets shows that East Third Street is smaller in scale, as well as in overall dimensions. The distance from pavement to pavement on South Bridge Road is greater, making visual connections across the roadway less direct and generating a larger area of open sky at the top of the street space; when this is combined with the higher street wall on the West side is increased the sense of scale. East Third Street has high street walls, with the windows on the top of the South side being too far away for strong visual and verbal communication, but the majority of the street wall allows this, reinforcing the smaller scale of the street.

Analysing of the scale of the components on the streets also emphasises the larger scale of the South Bridge Road, as the scale of the Western side dominates the scale reading of the street and when examined next to East Third Street is shown to have consistently larger elements. The height of the base accessed from the pavement on both sides of South Bridge Road is greater than on East Third Street, even on the South side which is raised half a level. The floor to floor height on South Bridge Road is larger than on East Third Street, which also amplifies the scale of the street. The detailed study of the street walls reveals that the openings on the South side of East Third Street are larger than those on the West side of South Bridge Road, but this increase in dimension does not diminish the sense of scale, because the openings are still close to the scale of the human body, but also are articulated individually with detail which enhances the scale reading.

The scope of the present discussion does not allow extensive coverage of the general principles of scale illustrated by the comparison of these two streets; however, it is useful to point out a few examples. As discussed above, dimension alone does not determine scale; it is the combination of elements and the relationships they establish which expresses scale. Distance and enclosure play an important part in defining scale, being able to see faces and close containment generate a sense of intimacy, so while East Third Street may not be as intimate as small neighbourhood streets, it is perceived as a local street, a street where people come into contact on a more regular basis. This obviously has something to do with the function and uses of the street, but it is also the result of the scale.

Horizontal layers

The study of the horizontal divisions on these streets illustrates the general similarities, with both streets having one side which has more divisions and that each street is organised with a roadway bordered by strips of sidewalk/pavement. The closer examination shows that the structure of East Third Street is tighter, with the layers more closely packed and that both sides of this street have a greater number of horizontal breaks. The investigation also shows that the two sides of East Third Street are similar in basic structure, that while there are differences they are not as marked as those on South Bridge Road. The inclusion of an amenity zone and landscape features on the West side of South Bridge Road emphasises its similarity to the sidewalk zones on East Third Street, further differentiating it from the East side. The lack of horizontal layers on the East side of South Bridge Road underlines the minimal spatial differentiation of this space, accentuating the open and exposed quality of the pavement. This area is much smaller than the opposite side of the street and very close in dimension to the circulation zones on East Third Street, but is perceived as larger. Increased horizontal layers provide greater containment, sequential transition and opportunities for casual occupation. This expands the possibility for social exchange, less separation and undifferentiated space minimises visual activity and encourages movement, diminishing social interaction.

Vertical layers

Comparing the vertical layers on the two streets demonstrates how different the two streets are, with East Third Street being more consistent on both sides, each having regularised divisions above the base, while the two street walls on South Bridge Road are very different. East Third Street stacks in even bands, but South Bridge Road has even layers only on the West side, with progressively smaller divisions on the East. The vertical structure of South Bridge Road is characterised first by the overall difference in height and the variation in layers which in both cases is more significant than the difference on East Third Street. Further study illustrates the difference between the street wall on the East side of South Bridge

Road from the other street walls. As with the horizontal layers, there are far fewer divisions and they have a distinct pattern, diminishing in dimension as they move up the facade, whereas on the other three facades the layers have a regularity above the ground floor. With less vertical division and a more singular pattern this elevation has individuality, while the regularity of other facades causes them to recede. The reduction in layers also diminishes the scale of the street wall, even though the ground-floor opening is the largest of all four facades. The investigation also illustrates the direct connection of the ground floors on South Bridge Road, while the relationship to the sidewalk varies on East Third Street. Vertical structure is both a function of the number and dimensions of the layers, but also the pattern of these layers and the interaction within and between the sets of these vertical layers.

Public/Private character
The gradation from Public to Private on the two streets has some similarities, with the threshold between the public areas and the private mediated in all cases. The size and configuration of this transition is different however. On South Bridge Road this transition is managed with a distinct piece of enclosure, as both boundaries have recessed volumes under the line of the facade, creating a shaded and protected area to buffer the private zone of the ground floor. This has the added benefit of providing a place for social interaction to take place, as people circulate in and out of the buildings, but also as people stopping in these spaces can lead to more people using the street. East Third Street uses more exposed versions of transition, as the South side has unenclosed stairs and a small vestibule linking public to private and the North side has a small fenced area designating the edge between these zones. The change in elevation on the Southern side does stretch the separation, making it less direct than the opposite side of the street, but both of these transitions are smaller and more exposed. In dense urban situations the manner in which movement from public to private is structured has a critical significance; a mediated sequence provides sense of protection and can actually encourage connections, while direct linkages can cause unwanted contact, possibly leading to less interaction.

Spatial definition

The spatial definition on both streets is clear and vertical, with the height and continuity of the street walls containing the room of the street. East Third Street has more consistent definition, as both sides of the street have similar street wall heights and street trees to describe space against the face of the buildings. South Bridge Road has a varied frame of enclosure, as the East side has a lower street wall, but the street trees on the West side introduce another vertical element to reduce the width of the open space, which reinforces the vertical spatial definition. East Third Street is more contained, with the narrower space squeezed by the lines of trees bordering the roadway, while South Bridge Road is more open, due to the increased width, the larger plane of sky overhead and the presence of only one line of trees to reduce the width of the space. Clear consistent street walls that contain space lead to spatial definition, which can be enhanced with the addition of vertical lines of trees.

Enclosure and exposure

The analysis of the enclosure on the two streets reveals that South Bridge Road has stronger formal enclosure, as both bases have recessed areas at the ground floor, while East Third Street has more layers of informal enclosure, as the trees that line the sidewalk create pockets of enclosure. As discussed previously, the mediation provided by the enclosure of the recessed entries on South Bridge Road enhances the transition between the interior and exterior. This is extended on the West side of the street by the additional enclosure of an awning. The South side of East Third Street has more enclosure than the North, with an entry vestibule at the top of a set of stairs, with both the enclosure and the change in level minimising the sense of exposure. The transition on the North side of East Third Street is the most exposed, with only a small overhang over the entry to moderate the connection to the public space. The amount of enclosure on the sidewalk/pavement varies between the streets, as East Third Street has narrower sidewalks, a line of trees and spaces created by projections into the sidewalk space. South Bridge Road has consistent edge at the base of the street wall, with any variation being a recess and not a projection so there are no areas to stop off the main circulation zone of the pavement except for the complete removal into the recess. Also the East side has no trees, leaving the pavement area very exposed. The pavement on the West side has various layers, with trees and planting areas creating small moments of enclosure on the pavement. Defined areas of enclosure, either highly structured instances with permanent elements or more informal moments created by trees or projections into the street space, contribute to social interaction by providing pieces of discrete territory which can be occupied.

Base of the street wall

The comparison of the Street Wall diagrams shows that South Bridge Road has a softer spatial edge at the base of the street wall than East Third Street, but some modulation of the base of East Third Street is produced by the access stairs on the South side and the small yards on the North side. The West side of South Bridge Road is the most differentiated, as there are more slices of space than on the East side of the street and they are larger in scale than the South side of East Third Street. The North side of East Third Street has the most abrupt edge, with a direct connection at the same level as the sidewalk. Layers of space and variation in levels help manage the transition between the exterior and interior and can also help to connect them, providing opportunities for social exchange on the sidewalk/ pavement and allowing the internal activities to extend into the street.

Facade articulation

Using the diagrams to investigate the articulation of the facades on South Bridge Road and East Third Street establishes that none of them are highly articulated. Both streets have simple facades, with some detail to create variations of light and dark, but neither has significant architectural expression or elaborate decorative elements. The East elevation of South Bridge Road has some architectural detail, with projections and recesses and some modest decoration. The South side of East Third Street has carved stone features around the windows and there are more building plots, so there is more variation in detail and vertical elements between buildings and additional fire escapes. The lack of strong articulation on South Bridge Road establishes a plain edge to the street space, while the projecting fire escapes on East Third Street create a play of light and shadow and add a network of intricate lines, generating visual stimulation at the edge of the space. Active facades, with depth and detail, whether this is produced by architectural expression, human habitation or building services, blur the perimeter of the space, while some of these do not add beauty, they often add a lively, fluctuating quality to a street which can enhance the experience of the street.

Transparency and opacity

Both streets have predominantly solid street walls, with regular small-scale openings above the ground-floor level. The base of South Bridge Road has large openings to serve the retail uses that occupy this part of the street, with the openings on the East side being both higher and wider than those across the street. This level of the interior space of South Bridge Road engages the exterior directly, both visually and physically, above this the openings provide light, ventilation and view, but do not display activity to the street. The street walls on East Third Street have this type of opening at all levels, protecting the interior residential spaces from the public space of the street. The regular patterns of openings on both streets indicate the stacking of occupied space in the buildings and create a rhythm on the facades and the solid surfaces delineate a clear boundary to the space of each street.

Volumetric interaction

Comparing the diagrams highlights that most of the volumetric interaction occurs at the base of the street walls, where the interior volumes project into the sidewalk/pavement space, overlapping the vertical slices created by the street trees and the frame of the building edge. The diagrams show that South Bridge Road has two main stacked horizontal volumes, while East Third Street has one vertical volume that overlaps a horizontal volume created by the underside of the tree canopies. Examining the diagrams further reveals the increased scale and less complex structure of South Bridge Road, with the wider roadway and less varied Eastern facade producing fewer but larger volumes. The elements on East Third Street describe more volumes on both sides of the street and these volumes are smaller. While neither street has elaborate volumetric interplay, there are distinct spaces formed, which illustrate spatial interaction that exists on the streets and which plays a role in how the space of the street is perceived. Diagramming the volumes that exist on a street establishes another layer of essential spatial information, uncovering important relationships that shape the experience and perception of a street.

All analysis excludes information to focus on selected aspects. Diagrams abstract phenomena, necessarily reducing the complexity and depth. The process undertaken above has limitations; however, it does provide a systematic way to examine streets carefully and provides a framework for speculating about the physical features and spatial conditions on streets. The analysis presented of streets and cities is a starting point, with the interpretations of the analysis open to the interests and expertise of the individual researcher. The disciplined use of this methodology, combined with real-world experience and the wide range of exploratory techniques, such as planimetric analysis, photographic documentation, drawing, digital modelling, etc., can greatly expand the understanding of streets.

Uses for the methodology

The impetus for this book and the development of the methodology has been to provide a tool for design and research. A tool for making explicit information and knowledge that is implicit to experienced practitioners. A tool designed to ensure that ideas, because they are familiar and part of tacit knowledge, are not taken for granted and ignored or most problematically uncommunicated in discussions regarding the city and streets. The basic approach is based on the use of comparative analysis: the macro-scale investigation employs a large-scale city section in combination with a plan to examine the organisation and vertical structure of a city, and extends the understandings achieved by comparing the results with the investigation into a different city; the micro-scale exploration uses a diagrammatic analysis to catalogue physical and spatial aspects of an individual street for evaluation in relation to another street. This methodology can be applied in numerous situations, wherever circumstances require an in-depth understanding of the physical and spatial characteristics of urban environments. The scope of the current investigation prohibits a full discussion regarding the application of these analytic strategies, surely the subject of another book; however, it is useful to give some examples of its applications. Below are summaries of possible benefits in relation to certain areas of urban design, which give some indication of how the information and techniques might be used by researchers and designers. Much of the information gathered with the technique is similar for each application; it is the framework of the enquiry that shapes the relevance of the information gathered.

Urban regeneration is a complex mix of economic projection, politics, administration, societal goals and practical design. Central to both the process and the challenges of this field are the different forms of urban analysis, a significant aspect of which is the study of physical properties. Systematically researching the current conditions at the city-wide level and the local scale of the street supplies fundamental knowledge about the circumstances and relationships in the existing urban form. Examining a city with large-scale sections and plans, to explore the organisation and interaction between the constituent parts, as well as the structures which connect them, can supply data and insight to inform judgements related to broad issues and specific instances, such as the appropriate location of a resource or the size and/or configuration of a development. How the streets in a district work or don't work, what is the scale of the public space, are the relationships within a network coherent? These and numerous other questions can be examined by carefully mapping the physical features of the site as a project develops. The techniques can also be used to investigate other areas of the city with comparable attributes and qualities to those pursued in the regeneration project. Again, questions related to the material and spatial characteristics of a successful example can be used to inform a range of aspects, from the approach and organisation to design and communication. The methodology is specifically designed to examine and compare precedents and working models. The disciplined investigation of projects which faced similar issues and physical arrangements generates detailed information and broad principles, to provide instructive guidance in the development of strategies for a specific project or potentially a regeneration policy.

Establishing a firm knowledge base of the physical properties of an individual element, a street or a neighbourhood is vital to urban conservation. The use of the methodology can expand historic research, by providing additional data and insights. Constructing large scale sections of historic urban forms or diagramming the spatial relationships of a street in an earlier state can generate key information. For example on a macro level, planimetric morphological studies can be enhanced, as mass and scale can be inferred through the addition of the vertical dimension, helping to develop a picture of the urban qualities and formal interactions which fostered the material fabric being preserved. While at smaller scale, understanding the historic streetscape and public spaces out of which an existing situation has developed is essential to the task of maintaining and/or restoring a specific environment. The diagrammatic technique described above can be used to examine either an arrangement of buildings or a specific structure, producing knowledge about a variety of significant spatial relationships and structures. The visual analysis of historic models or previous incarnations of a selected object or setting can identify critical spatial properties and relationships between the components which have defined the context for the subject of the research. The system can also be used to study historic precedents from other cities and streets, informing the process and designs, by helping to generate appropriate solutions and alternatives. Just as evaluating examples from similar time periods or with cultural resonance deepens the investigation, comparing and contrasting these with the existing situation creates an even more refined awareness of the particular condition. As well as extending historic research, the exploration of the current circumstances can also be enhanced using this method of sectional and visual evaluation. Alongside the cataloguing and documentation of the existing conditions, techniques for analysing these conditions are essential to building a comprehensive understanding. Drawing the diagrams to study the current configuration and constituent parts generates a base line from which judgements can proceed; this same process can be used to evaluate proposed solutions. Sectional analysis of proposals can test solutions in relation to precedents, historic site conditions and with the current configuration. These tests can help improve proposals through the highlighting of conflicts and the confirmation of correct relationships.

Understanding the complex network of physical, economic, social, and cultural issues surrounding the built environment requires a range of research strategies. This means of investigating urban form and locales gives urban designers another way to gather, assess and deploy information at various scales. As discussed before the examination of larger patterns and interactions of the physical aspects of a city are enhanced when vertical data is included. The combination of plans and sections facilitates spatialisation, strengthening the designer's grasp of three-dimensional relationships and allowing more informed judgements. One of the most valuable exercises for urban designers is the careful examination of existing circumstances, finding as much information as possible and analysing this to provide a comprehensive appreciation of the situation. The additional knowledge gained from the sectional exploration also extends knowledge from other sources, through the increased detail and relational possibilities. All of the above is true with the use of the analytic method to examine design precedents. Increasing the detail and depth of understanding of suitable completed designs through the close study fostered by visual analysis can assist in developing design solutions and identify possible problems. Investigating the similarities and differences of urban design projects that have confronted similar challenges or attempted to supply comparable public spaces is a valuable means of informing the design process, as adding more layers of information has obvious benefits. The techniques can also be used to test design proposals, both through the evaluation of the configuration and consequences of the design and in the assessment of the interactions with the existing conditions. By analysing the spatial and physical properties that will be created through the interaction of the design solution with the context, the design can be calibrated to meet criteria and establish coherent relationships to the surroundings.

The use of this methodology as a tool for increasing knowledge about spatial factors and the impact these have on the experience and perception of urban environments is not limited to the examples above; on the contrary these examples cover very few of the possibilities and the discussions were limited to a brief indication of potential types of knowledge revealed and benefits to be gained. The goal of these summaries is to supply suggestions that stimulate thinking and encourage the consideration of the underlying principles inherent in the approach, such that additional applications can be conceived and attempted. Architects, designers, researchers, anyone with an interest or need can develop ways to apply the basic technique. The purpose of the methodology is to provide a disciplined structure for very close looking; looking analytically at how physical configurations form space and the impact variations have on the qualities of this space.

Chapter Six
Conclusion

Cities are complex. They are an elaborate interaction of numerous factors, from the economic, to the political, physical, social and cultural, and each of these factors has multiple layers of considerations. To understand cities, the way people use them, and how they work, has developed into a vast field of enquiry, with a wide variety of approaches, each with specific analytic methods and a developed discipline. While there is little doubt that no single approach can provide all the answers and that all of them have limitations, the critical application of thinking from each extends the practice of urbanism. The expansion of knowledge from these different examinations has had profound impacts, establishing issues, concerns, theories, strategies and suggested solutions, with each particular body of thought providing unique information and lessons.

The last 60 years of urban thought has established that numerous factors play a part in the quality of an urban environment and it is clear that physical properties alone are not responsible for making a public place successful. However, it is equally true that these properties have a major effect, contributing significantly to quality spaces; damaging or limiting others. For designers the ultimate goal of building a comprehensive understanding and a varied intellectual approach is to improve judgement in relation to physical propositions. It is the configuration of the physical that is the activity of the practice of design and consequently understanding this aspect of the city is crucial to designers.

At the outset the intention of this book was to provide a clear means of examining cities. The premise was that a collection of visual information from a wide range of cities and a systematic framework for analysing this information would be useful for designers and urbanists. To this end a set of drawings have been supplied, which offer the opportunity to examine cities at a large scale and streets at a smaller scale. The drawings use the convention of the analytic plan and section, specifically because this type of drawing uses visual abstraction as a means of isolating information for emphasis and makes critical relationships more apparent. The use of precise scale drawings facilitates disciplined evaluation, supplying a robust framework for investigations. A diagrammatic methodology for exploring these drawings has been demonstrated, and it is proposed that the use of this methodology makes explicit information and relationships critical to the comprehensive understanding of cities and streets. The drawings, investigative techniques and discussions contribute to the developing field of urban design through the extension of analytic processes and by expanding the tools and information available for use in research and during the design process.

The examination of the history of urban design, some current influential thinking and the exploration of how the physical approach has developed establishes the context for the concerns and methodologies presented in the book. How physical features define space and the contribution these make to the identification of place highlights the importance of physical analysis. The history of the plan as a means for investigation and design underlines the value of this critical tool, which is enhanced when used in conjunction with a careful methodology and the vertical data provided by the section.

The intellectual device of the section, particularly in relation to urban structures, has a developing tradition, typically used to communicate conceptual ideas, while as an analytical tool in a more limited fashion. There is an obvious benefit to expanding the use of the section as inferred information can be quantified and considered. By using large-scale city sections to explore specific cities, which exemplify a variety of urban forms, the spatial impacts of organisational structures can be identified and vertical relationships can be examined. The value of this enhanced three-dimensional reading, provided by a sectional analysis at the macro scale is significant, with important consequences for the study of the urban environment. This is especially true when sections and plans are combined to compare cities, with the individual vertical order of each city revealed and similarities discovered that make spatial connections between different configurations.

The challenges and deficiencies of urban environments caused by the explosive growth of urban centres through industrialisation in the 19th century were met with efforts to radically alter the organisation, space and form of cities. From some perspectives these alternatives can be seen as attempts to actually eradicate the city, by proposing to manage the provision of cities without those characteristics which were perceived as negative: overcrowding, bad sanitation, poor light, sensory overload, deprivation and "immoral" social interaction. The primary instruments of these alternatives were circulatory systems, organisation, space and the insertion of various landscape elements to configure the built environment. These alternatives were wildly successful in achieving certain goals; it is hard to argue that garden city suburbs do not have desirable qualities or that residential high rises have not improved sanitation and provided more space. It is also true that these models have certain negative impacts of their own, most notably social and ecological.

Particularly as the world becomes both more industrialised and more urban, the essential problems of the built environment centre on how it is organised and the form it takes. When buildings are placed together to form a group the space between them, its organisation and configuration has profound consequences, perceptual, experiential, social, economic, cultural, ecological and political. The historical models for shaping this space, commonly referred to as the "street", have been increasingly identified as superior at meeting critical social needs, and extensive resources for the design and regulation of streets have been developed. The primary components of streets and the roles they play in the spatial, functional and social operation of the street can be identified and the addition of vertical information and sectional analysis broadens and deepens insight into how these components work, providing clear benefits to designers.

The presentation of analytic drawings and descriptions from a range of cities and streets supplies a precise data set, which can be used to investigate specific urban conditions or general principles. The range of cities and the ordinariness of the streets provide a flexible resource with wide applications, which can be used to examine recognisable circumstances and to explore unfamiliar situations. While very good streets have a great deal to teach and are important precedents, there are a great many more unexceptional, modest streets which can supply a wealth of valuable information. Building a strong understanding of how many cities and streets work, what components form them and what spaces and relationships result is critical and the drawings provided are a powerful tool for developing this knowledge.

Graphic techniques for the investigation of streets and cities provide specific benefits, especially for designers, and the methodologies presented have numerous applications. At the macro scale the careful reading of vertical and horizontal information exposes significant structural conditions and noteworthy correlations. In the case of the street, the isolated study of particular issues reveals linkages and recurring arrangements and incrementally builds a detailed picture of a situation. Visual information is necessarily relational, with multiple pieces of information presented simultaneously, which is especially appropriate to the examination of urban environments. Practitioners focused on various aspects of urbanism will find a use for the techniques, with relevant facts and insights revealed within the specific context, expanding both research and the design process.

The complexity of urban constructs can be approached from a variety of analytical and theoretical positions and while ignoring any one of these is counter-productive, for designers the physical properties of cities hold a particular interest, being the means of achieving the object of their practice: the improvement of cities for people. Rigorous analysis of the physical characteristics of multiple existing urban environments with orthographic drawings and diagrams produces an extensive catalogue of useful data and also allows two distinct conditions to be compared. This type of evaluation reveals another collection of operable information, as well as supplying a means of testing design proposals. Investigating appropriate examples through comparison delivers specific lessons, highlights general principles and can develop models for use in the design process.

Ground-floor spaces should be designed to connect directly to the exterior space of the street. Designers should conceive of the street as a room, with the distinction between interior and exterior a question of modulation, where the goal is visual and physical integration and interaction. Understanding that these two types of space are complementary transforms the relationship, requiring spatial and experiential coherence. Design solutions which pursue architecturally structured connections between the external and internal spaces of the street and which use this place of transition to supply opportunities for people to vital sensory experiences, social exchanges and physical support will lead to "attractive" streets, streets which people will use and identify with. Key to this is eradicating the simplistic conception of these spaces as separate, they are different and "separated" by a building envelope, but they are necessarily linked and when linked intelligently and effectively they create vibrant urban spaces.

The active street is essential to urban environments, providing experiential richness, a social resource and practical benefits. The permeable, engaged and materially varied edge is an extremely effective means of achieving activity and use. The public room of the street is enhanced when ground-floor activity is part of this civic space. Most importantly removing the distinction between urban interior and exterior brings the architectural concept of continuous, flowing space to bear on urban conditions. In urban environments, the key architectural challenge is structuring this critical interface and techniques for analysing existing models and synthesising solutions are crucial tools for designers.

The goal of this book has been to make explicit expert knowledge about how streets work, founded on the belief that this knowledge is also essential to comprehending the identity of a place and the city it is situated in. Years of research, teaching and constructive dialogues have reinforced the basic insight; the complexity of streets and cities can be analysed with plans, sections and diagrams to build a detailed spatial understanding and this can improve the design of urban spaces. Based on this a rudimentary methodology has been synthesised, from a wide variety of sources and from personal experience and perceptions. The proposed techniques have a particular focus and consequently have distinct limitations; however, the benefits are equally clear, providing a restricted, but valuable contribution.

Seeing and drawing are the primary tools of the architect and the designer and the complexity of urban phenomena makes this more difficult. Trying to communicate how a small aspect of this complexity could be understood led to the examination of tacit knowledge, which resulted in an exploration of urbanism and the development of a clear and transparent means of examining the material facts of streets and cities at multiple scales. Vertical information is critical, visual analysis is powerful, and the demonstration of these ideas and the drawings included provide a starting point for designers; which will hopefully lead to individuals developing their own version of this tool.

Index

Page numbers in *italic* indicate figures.

advocacy groups 47–9

aesthetic qualities 2, 4, 30

Alberti, Leon Battista 2

amenities zone of sidewalks 57, 75, *76*, 77, 255

American Association of State Highway and Transportation Officials 50, 51

American Society of Landscape Architects 50

Amsterdam *98*, 99; Oude Hoogstraat 99, *100*, *101*

analysis of streets *see* street analysis

Appleyard, Donald 18, 45

Argentina *see* Buenos Aires

autocratic government 4–5, 30

automobiles *see* vehicular traffic problems

Averlino, Antonio 9

Bangkok 102–3, *102*; Thanon Khao San 103, *104*, *105*

Barcelona 10; Paseo de Garcia 67

baroque city planning 2, 4–5, 10, 15

baroque city type 30; Paris 37–9, *38*, 42

base of street walls 85–8; analysis 238, *238*, 247, *247*, 258, *258*, 267; *see also* ground-floor spaces

Bath Street, Glasgow 71, *74*, 76, 83, 86 7, 143, *144*, *145*

Beaux Arts city planning 10

Beijing 106–10, *106–7*; Gulou East Street *108–9*, 110, *111*

Boston 5, 55, 112–13, *112*; Newbury Street 113, *114*, *115*

Boulevard Saint-Michele, Paris 67

boundaries: curbs 77–8, 79; interior and exterior spaces 69–70, 85–6; *see also* street walls

Brazil *see* Rio de Janeiro

Buenos Aires 116–17, *116–17*; Calle Florida *118*, 119, *119*

Calle De Mesones, Mexico City 155, *156*, *157*

Calle Florida, Buenos Aires *118*, 119, *119*

Canada *see* Montreal; Vancouver

Cape Town 120–1, *120*; Long Street 121, *122*, *123*

Carmona, Matthew 4

Center for Livable Communities 50

centralised government 4–5, 30

Charlotte Street, London 151, *152*, *153*

Chicago 124–5, *124*; city section 39–42, *40*; South State Street 71, *73*, 77, 125, *126–7*, *128*, *129*

China *see* Beijing; Shanghai

circulation zone of sidewalks 57, 75, 76–7, *76*, 255

Cité Industrialle 11

Cité Radieuse 11

City Beautiful movement 5, 10

city sections 12–14, 19–20, 25–8; Chicago 39–42, *40*; city types 29–31; Fès, Morocco 33–4, *33*; Genoa 31–3, *31*, 42; Glasgow *34–5*, 35–6, 42; New Urbanist transects 13–14, 27–8; Paris 37–9, *38*, 42; valley section diagrams 26–7

city types 29–31

colonial occupation 30

community, sense of 17, 44–6

comparative analysis 19–20, 233; Allan B. Jacobs' research 64–5; East Third Street and South Bridge Road 262–9

Complete Streets *see* National Complete Streets Coalition (NCSC)

Computer Village, Lagos *148*, 149, *149*

Congress for New Urbanism *see* New Urbanism

Copenhagen 46, 130–1, *130*; Vimmelskaftet 132–3, *132*, *133*

curb extensions 78

curbside zone of sidewalks 57, 75, *76*, 77–8

Denmark *see* Copenhagen
density 7–8; and New Urbanism 28, 50
Department for Transport, United Kingdom 52–4
diagrammatic methodology *see* methodology
digital modelling 9
drainage *see* storm water management
Duany, Andreas 13, 14, 27–8, 49

East Third Street, New York City *178–9*, 180, *181*; comparison
    with South Bridge Road 262–9; visual analysis 241–8,
    241–8
ecological issues 8, 13
ecological system of human habitation 26–7
enclosure 82, 89; analysis 238, *238*, 246, *246*, 257, *257*,
    266–7; and height to width ratios 71, 91, 234, 241, 262;
    and scale 90–1, 263; and spatial definition 83–5, 237, 246,
    256, 266
enduring sociability 55
energy consumption 8
enlightenment 30
environment 5, 8, 13; and human habitation 12, 26–7, 28
exposure analysis 238, *238*, 246, *246*, 257, *257*, 266–7
exterior and interior spaces 58, 67–70, 85–6

facades 15, 88–9; facade articulation analysis 239, *239*, 247,
    247, 259, *259*, 267–8; permeability 58, 65–6, 67–8, 86;
    transparency and opacity analysis 239, *239*, 248, *248*, 260,
    260, 268; *see also* street walls
Fès, Morocco 134–5, *134*; city section 33–4, *33*; Rue Talaa
    Kebria 71, *74*, 76, 135, *136*, *137*
Filarete (Antonio Averlino) 9
Filbert Street, Pittsburgh 187, *188*, *189*
Flauhault, Charles 27
fleeting sociability 55
Florence 4, 14
France: Versailles 4, 10, 15; *see also* Paris

garden cities 5, 11
Garnier, Tony 11
Geddes, Patrick 12, 13, 25–7
Gehl, Jan 46, 68, 75, 91
General Urban zone 28
Genoa 14, 15, 138–9, *138*; city section 31–3, *31*, 42; Via San
    Bernardo 139, *140*, *141*
geometric plans 4, 9, 10, 11, 15, 35–6
Glasgow 142–3, *142*; Bath Street 71, *74*, 76, 83, 86–7, 143, *144*,
    145; city section *34–5*, 35–6, 42
government: and advocacy groups 47–9; centralised 4–5,
    30; guidance on streets 18, 51–4; and professional
    expertise 49–51
Greenbook 51
Grey Street, Newcastle upon Tyne 173, *174*, *175*
grid city type 30; Chicago 39–42, *40*
ground-floor spaces 66, 67–70; *see also* base of street walls
Gulou East Street, Beijing *108–9*, 110, *111*

Haussmann, Georges-Eugène 5, 10, 15, 37
health, public 6–7
height to width ratios 64, 65, 71, 91; analysis 234, *234*, 241,
    241, 250, *250*, 262
historic analysis 7
horizontal layers 90; analysis 235, *235*, 243, *243*, 253, *253*, 264
Howard, Ebenezer 2, 5, 11
human scaled streets 90–1

immersive environments 28
Imola 9
India 56; *see also* Mumbai
industrialised cities 5, 6
Institute of Transport Engineers (ITE) 50–1
interior and exterior spaces 58, 67–70, 85–6
Islamic culture 30, 33–4
Italy: renaissance city planning 2, 4, 9, 11, 14–15; *see also*
    Genoa; Rome

ITE *see* Institute of Transport Engineers (ITE)

Jacobs, Allan B. 18, 59–66, 67, 71, 75, 91
Jacobs, Jane 3, 7, 17, 45, 66–7, 75
Japan *see* Tokyo

Kabukicho 1-11-1, Tokyo 221, *222*, *223*
Krier, Leon 7

labyrinth city type 30; Fès, Morocco 33–4, *33*
Lagos 146–7, *146–7*; Computer Village *148*, 149, *149*
landscape elements 57, 58, 75, 77, 80–2
late baroque city planning 2, 5, 10, 15
Le Corbusier 3, 11, 16
L'Enfant, Pierre 11
Leonardo da Vinci 9
LGC *see* Local Government Commission (LGC)
lighting, street 52, 77, 80–1
living conditions, improving 3, 5–7, 10, 17, 69
Local Government Commission (LGC) 50
London 4, 8, 150–1, *150*; Charlotte Street 151, *152*, *153*
Long Street, Cape Town 121, *122*, *123*

McHarg, Ian 8, 13
Maliya Sadovaya Ulitsa, St. Petersburg 207, *208*, *209*
Manual for Streets (United Kingdom) 52–4
Masdar, Abu Dhabi 8
materials: curbs 77–8, 79; roadway surfaces 72–5;
    sidewalks 79
mechanistic model 6, 17
medieval urban form 5, 30
Mehta, Vikas 54–9, 67–8, 75, 76–7
methodology 19–21, 232–73; aspects used in analysis 234–40,
    234–40; comparison of East Third Street and South Bridge
    Road 262–9; East Third Street visual analysis 241–8, *241–8*;
    South Bridge Road visual analysis 249–61, *249–61*; uses
    for 20–1, 269–73

Index

Mexico *see* Mexico City; San Miguel de Allende, Mexico

Mexico City 154–5, *154*; Calle De Mesones 155, *156*, *157*

modernist town planning 2–3, 4, 5–7, 11, 16–18, 69

Montevideo 158–61, *158–9*; Sarandi *160*, 161, *161*

Montreal 162–4, *162–3*; Rue St. Denis 164, *164–5*, *166*, *167*

Morocco *see* Fès, Morocco

Mumbai 168–71, *168–9*; Nagdevi Path *170*, 171, *171*

Nagdevi Path, Mumbai *170*, 171, *171*

National Complete Streets Coalition (NCSC) 47–8

nature 5, 13

NCSC *see* National Complete Streets Coalition (NCSC)

Netherlands *see* Amsterdam

Newbury Street, Boston 113, *114*, *115*

Newcastle upon Tyne 172–3, *172*; Grey Street 173, *174*, *175*

Newington, Australia 8

New Urbanism 8, 11; advocacy 48–9; streets 18, 49, 50, 51; transects 13–14, 19, 27–8, 49

New York City 176–80, *176–7*; *Street Design Manual* 52; *see also* East Third Street, New York City

Nigeria *see* Lagos

Norman Foster and Partners 8

Olmstead, Frederick Law 5

organic city type 29–30; Genoa 31–3, *31*, 42

orientation analysis 234, *234*, 241, *241*, 249, *249*, 262

Oude Hoogstraat, Amsterdam 99, *100*, *101*

overcrowding 3, 6–7, 10, 17

parametric urbanism 9

Paris 4, 5, 10, 15, 182–3, *182*; Boulevard Saint-Michele 67; city section 37–9, *38*, 42; Rue Saint-Honoré 183, *184*, *185*

parking 53–4, 72

parks 5

Paseo de Garcia, Barcelona 67

passive sociability 55

pavements *see* sidewalks

paving materials 79

pedestrians 8, 72; walkable streets 48, 50, 51, 53; *see also* sidewalks

permeability of facades 58, 65–6, 67–8, 86; *see also* transparency and opacity analysis

perspective drawings 11

physical tradition of urban design 1–9

Pittsburgh 186–7, *186*; Filbert Street 187, *188*, *189*

place-making tradition of urban design 4

planned city, 18th-century 30; Glasgow *34–5*, 35–6, 42

plans 9–12, 19–20; *see also* geometric plans

plant association 27

planting 78, 79; *see also* trees, street

Polk Street, San Francisco 71, *72*, 77, 85, 199, *200*, *201*

postmodern criticism 16

private character see public/private character analysis

professional expertise 49–51

progressive thinking 2–3, 5–6, 10–11, 16, 69; *see also* modernist town planning

proportion analysis 234, *234*, 241, *241*, 250, *250*, 262; *see also* height to width ratios

public health 6–7

public/private character analysis 236, *236*, 245, *245*, 255, *255*, 265

public spaces 7–8, 17; streets as 44–6, 63

regional culture 8

renaissance city planning 2, 4, 9, 11, 14–15

Rio de Janeiro 190–1, *190*; Rua da Carioca 191–3, *192*, *193*

roadways 71–5, *72*, *73*, *74*

Robson Street, Vancouver 225–6, *226–7*, *228*

Rogers, Richard 8

Rome 2, 4, 10, 11, 15, 194–5, *194*; Via di Santa Maria dell'Anima 195, *196*, *197*

roofscape 89–90

Rossi, Aldo 7

Rowe, Colin 11

Rua da Carioca, Rio de Janeiro 191–3, *192*, *193*

Rudofsky, Bernard 18, 45

Rue Saint-Honoré, Paris 183, *184*, *185*

Rue St. Denis, Montreal 164, *164–5*, *166*, *167*

Rue Talaa Kebria, Fès 71, *74*, 76, 135, *136*, *137*

Rural Preserve zone 28

Rural Reserve zone 28

Russia *see* St. Petersburg

St. Petersburg 206–7, *206*; Maliya Sadovaya Ulitsa 207, *208*, *209*

San Francisco 198–9, *198*; Polk Street 71, *72*, 77, 85, 199, *200*, *201*

San Francisco, San Miguel de Allende, Mexico 203, *204*, *205*

sanitation problems 3, 6–7, 10, 17, 35

San Miguel de Allende, Mexico 202–3, *202*; San Francisco 203, *204*, *205*

Sarandi, Montevideo *160*, 161, *161*

scale 90–1; analysis 235, *235*, 242, *242*, 251, *251*, *252*, 263

Seaside, Florida 11

seating, street 56, 57, 81

sections *see* city sections

Semi-Private space 236, *236*, 245, 255

Semi-Public space 236, *236*, 245, 255

sensory stimulation, of streets 58

Sforzinda 9

Shanghai 210–11, *210*; Wuchang Road 211, *212*, *213*

shop windows 67

sidewalks 57, 75–80, *76*, 255

Singapore 214–15, *214–15*; *see also* South Bridge Road, Singapore

Sitte, Camillo 2, 5, 16

Sixtus V 2, 10

slum clearance schemes 7

Smart Growth America 47–8

social cohesion 3, 8

social interaction 7–8, 17; streets 45–6, 54–9, 63, 76–7, 86

social usage tradition of urban design 3–4

South Africa *see* Cape Town

South Bridge Road, Singapore 216–18, *217, 218, 219*; comparison with East Third Street 262–9; visual analysis 249–61, *249–61*

South State Street, Chicago 71, *73*, 77, 125, *126–7, 128, 129*

Spain *see* Barcelona

spatial continuity 66–70

spatial definition 83–5, *83, 84*; analysis 237, *237*, 246, *246*, 256, *256*, 266

Stipo 67

storm water management 78, 79

street analysis 19–21, 232–73; aspects used in analysis 234–40, *234–40*; comparison of East Third Street and South Bridge Road 262–9; East Third Street visual analysis 241–8, *241–8*; South Bridge Road visual analysis 249–61, *249–61*; uses for 20–1, 269–73

street culture 56

Street Design Manual (New York City) 52

street furniture 57, 58, 75, 77, 80–2

street patterns 61; *see also* geometric plans

streets 14–18, 44–92; advocacy groups 47–9; comparative analysis 20; Jacobs' research 59–66, 67; Mehta's research 54–9, 67–8, 76–7; professional expertise 49–51; roadways 71–5, *72, 73, 74*; scale 90–1; sidewalks 57, 75–80, *76*, 255; spatial continuity 66–70; spatial definition 83–5, *83, 84*; street furniture and landscape elements 57, 58, 75, 77, 80–2; *see also* street analysis; street walls

streetscape 79, 80–2, 88

street walls 82–90, *83, 84*; base of street wall analysis 238, *238*, 247, *247*, 258, *258*, 267; facade articulation analysis 239, *239*, 247, *247*, 259, *259*, 267–8; transparency and opacity analysis 239, *239*, 248, *248*, 260, *260*, 268; *see also* facades; ground-floor spaces

Stubben, Joseph 16

Sub-Urban zone 28

sustainable urban design 8

Thailand *see* Bangkok

Thanon Khao San, Bangkok 103, *104, 105*

Tokyo 220–1, *220*; Kabukicho 1-11-1 221, *222, 223*

traffic *see* transportation infrastructure; vehicular traffic problems

transects 12–14, 26–9; New Urbanism 13–14, 19, 27–8, 49

transition zone of sidewalks 57, 75, 76, *76*

transparency and opacity analysis 239, *239*, 248, *248*, 260, *260*, 268; *see also* permeability of facades

transportation infrastructure 6, 7, 8, 11, 50–1; *see also* vehicular traffic problems

trees, street 63–4, 75, 77, 80, 88

United Kingdom: *Manual for Streets* 52–4; *see also* Glasgow; London; Newcastle upon Tyne

United States 11; advocacy groups 47–9; City Beautiful movement 5, 10; professional organisations 50–1; *see also* Boston; Chicago; New York City; Pittsburgh; San Francisco

Urban Centre zone 28

Urban Core zone 28

urban design: physical tradition 1–9; plans 9–12, 19–20; *see also* city sections; methodology; streets

urban renewal schemes 3, 7

urban sprawl 8, 13

Uruguay *see* Montevideo

valley section diagrams 26–7

Vancouver 224–5, *224*; Robson Street 225–6, *226–7, 228*

vehicular traffic problems 3, 7, 18, 45–6, 48, 53, 71–2

Versailles 4, 10, 15

vertical layers 90; analysis 236, *236*, 244, *244*, 254, *254*, 264–5

vertical structure 25, 27, 82–3; *see also* sections

Via di Santa Maria dell'Anima, Rome 195, *196, 197*

Via San Bernardo, Genoa 139, *140, 141*

Ville Contemporaine 11

Vimmelskaftet, Copenhagen 132–3, *132, 133*

visual analysis 233; East Third Street, New York City 241–8, *241–8*; South Bridge Road, Singapore 249–61, *249–61*

visual stimulation 58, 67–8, 87–8

volumetric interaction analysis 240, *240*, 248, *248*, 261, *261*, 268–9

walkable streets 48, 50, 51, 53

Washington D.C. 11

Whyte, William 76–7

widths: roadways 71; sidewalks 57, 77; streets 91; *see also* height to width ratios

Wuchang Road, Shanghai 211, *212, 213*

zero carbon cities 8

zones: in New Urbanist transects 28; public/private character 236, *236*, 245, *245*, 255, 265; of sidewalks 57, 75–8, *76*, 255

zoning, single-use 3, 6, 11, 48